Moving into the Mainstr

Moving into the Mainstream

LEA provision for bilingual pupils

Jill Bourne

NFER-NELSON

Published by The NFER-NELSON Publishing Company Ltd.,
Darville House, 2 Oxford Road East,
Windsor, Berkshire SL4 1DF, England.

First Published 1989, Reprinted 1990
© 1989 National Foundation for Educational Research

British Library Cataloguing in Publication Data
Bourne, Jill
    Moving into the mainstream : LEA provision for
    bilingual pupils – (NFER research library).
    1. England. Education. Implications of
    bilingualism.
    I. Title   II. Series
    370.19'34

ISBN 0-7005-1235-7
ISBN 0-7005-1236-5 pbk

Printed by Antony Rowe Ltd, Chippenham, Wiltshire
ISBN 0 7005 1235 7 (Hardback)
Code 8323 02 4

ISBN 0 7005 1236 5 (Paperback)
Code 8324 02 4

Contents

Acknowledgements

Chapter 1   Introduction   1

The Background   1
  'Bilinguals' and 'bilingualism'   1
  Background to provision   3
  The policy context   7
'Bilingual education'   11
  Specific provision or reorganized mainstream?   16
The Bilingual Pupils' Project   17
  Response to the questionnaire survey   20
LEA language surveys   23
  The language background of pupils   24
  Bilingual pupils in 37 English LEAs   25
  The 'naming' of languages   28

Chapter 2   Extra Staff and Special Funding   33

  Provision of staffing   33
  Funding provision for bilingual pupils   37
  'Section 11'   40
    Section 11 uptake   45
    Section 11 language provision   46
    Community languages and Section 11   49
    Section 11 advisory teachers   50
  Section 11 – the case studies   50
    Section 11 job descriptions and Section 11 abuse 54
    Section 11 reviews   55
    Monitoring and consultation   58
  Summary   60

Chapter 3   English Language Support   61

  The background   61
    Definitions of mainstream English and bilingual support
    teaching   65
  Staffing and organization   66

English language support staff in schools 66
The organization of English language support 67
English language centres 72
Team or school-based support structures 74
Changes in provision and practice 76
Changes in provision 76
Changes in practice over the past five years 79
Future changes expected in provision and practice 81
Resources and in-service training 83
Summary 87

Chapter 4   English Language Support: The Whole School Studies 88

Multicultural education/antiracist/equal opportunities policies 88
Staffing and deployment 89
Overall staffing levels 89
Deployment of English language support teachers 91
'Withdrawal' 95
Developing mainstream responsibility 99
Staff organization 101
Qualifications and roles 104
Qualifications 104
Roles of English language support teachers 106
Creating whole school change 108

Chapter 5   Community Languages, Bilingual Support, Linguistic Diversity 111

Language development in multilingual classrooms 112
Bilingual support and community languages teaching 114
Community languages in English schools 116
Languages taught and supported within schools 119
Supply and training of teachers 122
In-service and curriculum development 124
Line management 126
Team or school-based structures 128
Support for community languages outside the curriculum 129
After-school classes provided by LEAs 129
Voluntary community-based classes 131
Resource centres and in-service for voluntary tutors 136
Summary 138

Chapter 6   Community Languages – Policy and Provision 140

Changes in policy and provision in LEAs 140

Examples of provision in schools 144
  Community languages teaching 145
  The role of bilingual support teachers 148
Organization of provision in six LEAs 152
Future plans for community languages in LEAs 162

Chapter 7   Welsh Language Education 165

Policy 165
  The development of Welsh medium education 168
Local authority provision 169
  Welsh language surveys 170
  Primary schools 171
  Secondary schools 172
Finance 173
Organization of provision in schools 174
  Provision for speakers of languages other than English
  and Welsh 175
The in-depth study 178

Chapter 8   Conclusion 185

Implicit policy on bilingualism 185
National policy or politics of neglect? 188
Drawing on the Welsh experience 192
More specific analyses of provision 195
In conclusion 199

Appendix 203
References 205

The National Foundation for Educational Research

The National Foundation for Educational Research in England and Wales was founded in 1946 and is Britian's leading educational research institution. It is an independent body undertaking research and development projects on issues of current interest in all sectors of the public educational system. Its membership includes all the local education authorities in England and Wales, the main teachers' associations, and a large number of other major organizations with educational interests.

Its approach is scientific, apolitical and non-partisan. By means of research projects and extensive field surveys it has provided objective evidence on important educational issues for the use of teachers, administrators, parents and the research community. The expert and experienced staff that has been built up over the years enables the Foundation to make use of a wide range of modern research techniques; in addition to its own work, it undertakes a large number of specially sponsored projects at the request of government departments and other agencies.

The major part of the research programme relates to the maintained educational sector – primary, secondary and further education. A further significant element has to do specifically with local education authorities and training institutions. The current programme includes work on the education of pupils with special needs, monitoring of pupil performance, staff development, national evaluation and major curriculum programmes, test development and information technology in schools. The Foundation is also the national agency for a number of international research and information exchange networks.

The NFER-NELSON Publishing Company are the main publishers of the Foundation's research reports. These reports are now available in the NFER *Research Library*, a collection which provides the educational community with up-to-date research into a wide variety of subject areas. In addition, the Foundation and NFER-NELSON work closely together to provide a wide range of open and closed educational tests and a test advisory service. NFER-NELSON also publish *Educational Research*, the termly journal of the Foundation.

Acknowledgements

First, many thanks must go to the advisers, officers and heads in the seven LEAs studied by the Project, who gave so generously of their time and experience; and to the teachers, instructors, and pupils in the schools we visited, who shared their classes with us. I am also grateful to all those LEAs who responded to our survey.

Particular thanks and acknowledgements are due to Ann Brumfit, who as research officer made an important contribution to the direction of the Project, and on whose fieldwork most of the information on three of the LEAs depends. I should also like to acknowledge the fieldwork and insights of Ann Davies, Niru Desai, Jaswant Grewal, Minhaj Khan, Perminder Sandhu, Yasmin Sheikh, Fauzia Siddiki and Nalini Wood.

I am grateful to Peter Bourne, Chris Brumfit, Ann Kispal, Morag MacDonald MacNeil, Eurwen Price, Kuldip Singh Rai, Ben Rampton and Euan Reid, who all provided valuable comments on the first draft of the book; to the members of the Project steering group; to Tom Gorman, Project Director; to Neil Rubra, for computing and statistics; to Daphne Parsons, who provided impeccable administrative backing; to Hilary Hosier for preparing the manuscript; and finally to my family, who always helped.

1 Introduction

The aim of this book is to provide information on policy and provision in England and Wales in the mid-1980s to those concerned with the education of bilingual pupils, including local education authority (LEA) officers, inspectors, advisers, teachers, community associations, parents, teacher trainers and policy makers. It is based on the findings of a two-year nine-months project, sponsored and carried out by the National Foundation for Educational Research (NFER), into 'Educational Provision for Bilingual Pupils'.

The project was set up in 1985 to examine whether provision for bilingual pupils had been redefined, and in what ways it had been reorganized, since the last NFER surveys by Townsend (1971) and Townsend and Brittan (1972).

The findings have been brought together to present a picture of LEA provision nationally. It is not a study of bilingual pupils, but a study of provision, and changes in provision, *as perceived within LEAs*. As such, it is a study of largely monolingual institutions, and of the way they have defined and responded to what they see as the 'needs' of bilingual pupils.

It is hoped that this picture of provision will provide a historical record of LEA responses to bilingualism in the 1980s, and a baseline against which the impact on educational provision for bilingual pupils of the 1988 Education Bill can be evaluated in future research.

The Background

'Bilinguals' and 'bilingualism'

Following current educational usage in England, in this report any pupil is defined as 'bilingual' who uses more than one language in his/her daily life, outside the formal modern language learning classroom. 'Bilingualism' stands for the alternate use of two languages in the same individual. The definition is not intended to suggest equal proficiency ('balanced bilingualism') nor any judgement of range or quality of linguistic skills.

This definition of bilingualism has obviously very limited use. However, there are generally as yet neither the staff with the linguistic skills available in LEAs to make more detailed assessments practicable, nor any agreed method of assessing relative proficiencies in two or more languages. On the one hand, then, the definition is trivial. On the other hand, the fact that everyone is potentially bilingual warns us of the danger of assuming that 'bilinguals' have very different (or special) educational needs from the rest of the community; needs that can be defined for them as a homogeneous 'special' group.

Bilingual pupils come from a variety of ethnic groups, each, in turn, composed of different sub-groups. They have different educational and socioeconomic backgrounds and different experiences of racism. Some are individuals who have newly arrived in this country; others are members of communities that are well established as part of English society.

Many 'bilingual' pupils may in fact be multilingual, with access to three or more languages and dialects, and a range of skills in those languages. They may be equally at home in English and other languages – or be making the first tentative steps in using English for their own purposes; or they may be operating fluently in English, while at the same time wishing to develop their ethnic community language further.

Even when focusing just on linguistic needs, it is impossible to isolate needs shared by all bilingual pupils which are not also shared by monolingual pupils. These include the need to develop language use in a range of domains for conceptual development; to have access to and awareness of varieties of language in our society, including forms of public 'standard' English; and a greater understanding about how languages are used in their written and spoken forms.

As Baker (1988:2) points out:

> Given the great number of dimensions of skill in each language and the great range of different contexts where a language may or may not be used, it becomes apparent that a simple categorization of who is or who is not bilingual is almost impossible.

From this standpoint it is clear that it is not enough to define pupils as 'bilinguals' in order to decide on appropriate provision for their education.

Redefining the issue as 'educational provision for pupils from minority ethnic group backgrounds using at least one language other than English' does not clarify the position greatly; but it does introduce a useful focus on social context (cultures) and intentions (including the desire to belong to a particular group or groups), which is missing from the exclusive linguistic focus in 'bilingual'. For ethnicity is something which is chosen as well as 'other-defined' (Giles and Byrne: 1982). The concept of ethnicity introduces the question of attitudes, group conflicts of interest, and societal constructions and categorizations. In addition, the term 'minority' reveals the highly political nature of provision, since minorities are created and maintained, through such instruments as immigration control as well as education, for example.

It is important, however, not only to examine closely the definition of 'bilingual' to understand its use, but also to look at the way it is used in educational discourse in England and Wales.

Background to provision

As part of Britain, England has always been a multilingual society. Census data on Welsh within Wales shows that currently there are around 500,000 Welsh speakers in Wales (OPCS, Census, 1981). Today there are still about 80,000 speakers of Scottish Gaelic (Mackinnon, 1988). As the Linguistic Minorities Project (LMP, 1985: pp. 11-12) commented: 'There is in Britain local experience to draw on which illustrates some of the positive and negative effects of educational and social legislation on language'.

Educational interest in bilingualism in the education system based in England has had a very short history. In 1847 English education officials had described the Welsh language as 'a vast drawback to Wales' (Baker, 1985), and advised the quickest possible assimilation of Welsh speaking pupils into English. This position was often shared by Welsh parents, who saw their children's needs as needs to 'get on in the world' (ibid., p. 42); and Wales and its English medium education system was described as the 'breeding grounds from which the professional classes of England – teachers, doctors, lawyers and ministers – are recruited' (Board of Education Report, 1927, quoted by Baker, ibid., p. 42). Yet the eradication of the Welsh language was not total. Indeed, the effects of negative legislation on languages can often increase solidarity which is reflected in the increased use of minority languages in informal spheres. However, the last half century has seen an official reaction to policies of assimilation into English, both in Wales and in Scotland, which in the first half of the century would have been hard to predict.

The largely negative response of successive British administrations to the languages of minorities whose education it controlled in the last century was not limited to Wales and Scotland, but also to what was then British India. While, like the Welsh, many Indian families wanted their children to be educated in English in order 'to get on', this was a natural reaction when:

> It was the wish and admitted policy of the British Government to rend its language gradually and eventually the language of public business throughout the country (Lord William Bentinck, 1829, cited in Pattanayak, 1981).

By 1935, policy was still explicit. A Resolution of 7 March 1935 declared:

> the great object of the British Government ought to be the promotion of European literature and science among the natives of India; and that all the funds appropriated for the purpose of education would best be employed on English alone .... (ibid., p. 176).

In colonial Africa, on the other hand, successive British administrations appeared to favour the development of 'vernacular' language policies in education. Since the 1960s, these policies generally seem to have been reversed by the administrations of independent African states, in favour of policies which emphasise the teaching of a language of wider communication (in most cases, English). The emphasis on mother-tongue teaching policies by colonial authorities was widely interpreted as an attempt to deprive learners of the language skills necessary for success in the modern world (Gorman, 1974).

The crucial element in determining whether a particular policy is regarded as inimical to or as fostering the interests of the learners concerned is the degree to which they and their communities trust the policy makers to act altruistically, and the extent to which they have control over the formulation and implementation of policy. In a situation in which racialism is institutionalized any imposed policy is likely to be regarded as discriminatory.

Little attention was paid in the last half of the nineteenth century and the first half of the twentieth to the presence of children speaking Polish, Ukranian, Chinese, Yiddish, French, Italian and many other languages within English schools, sometimes located within strong local bilingual communities. Indeed, there appears to have been no discussion of the special linguistic needs of these children in the educational literature of the first half of this century.

It has only been since the 1960s that the language needs of pupils speaking languages other than English have become an issue in England. These needs were at first defined as essentially the need for special tuition in English for 'immigrant' pupils (Ellis, 1985; Reid, 1988). A special term was coined for this tuition, 'ESL', distinguishing a method of teaching English to those in an English speaking environment from foreign language teaching methods (Stern, 1983). The first languages of pupils appeared to have been largely ignored, if not considered a 'drawback'.

While it has become customary to describe developments in provision for bilingual pupils since the 1960s as a move from separate English teaching 'language centres' into providing language support within the 'mainstream' classroom, it should be stressed that the majority of bilingual pupils have always been in the mainstream. Even in the 'heyday' of the Language Centres, few pupils spent their entire school career in separate language classrooms. Townsend's (1971) survey of LEAs revealed great diversity in arrangements, with many LEAs expressing the view that in a mainstream class, 'immigrant infants...will pick up the language just as a child picks up his native language from an early age' (Townsend, 1971: p.38). Other LEAs expressed reluctance to 'draw attention to the immigrant community' by making special provision, or 'to make provision for immigrant pupils which was not equally available to non-immigrant pupils' (ibid.).

By pointing to this history I am trying to indicate briefly that bilinguals have always had a history of being 'mainstreamed', but that being assimilated into an unchanged monolingual system is not what proponents of 'mainstream provision' in the 1980s mean by the term. Nevertheless, with a short history of 'special' provision, it may be easier for schools to return to a tradition of ignoring diversity in language needs, rather than to begin exploring new teaching strategies, unless they are given careful support.

It was within a historical context of approaches within the education system to managing what was seen as a 'crisis' brought about by the need for schools to adapt to accommodate the entry of large numbers of 'immigrant' pupils that provision for bilingual pupils in the 1960s and early 1970s was first developed as a 'specialism'. The focus was on teaching English as quickly as possible, with the minimum of disruption to the on-going school routine. The preface to the last NFER survey of LEA provision (Townsend, ibid.) indicated the 'race relations' context that lay behind definitions of need and evaluations of provision:

> the problems are far from being purely educational: local authorities and schools face the reality that the solutions they propose will be judged within the wider social context in which racial discrimination is an inflammable issue. Thus it may be that proposals that appear educationally profitable and administratively convenient, are also politically indefensible (Wiseman, in Preface to Townsend, 1971, p. 5).

The close link between bilingual language policies, provision for the education of minority groups in society, and the political purposes defined by the majority which are reflected in educational provision, have always made the subject of bilingual provision a volatile one, which raises strong feelings. Within England, the issue of bilingual education is linked to the politics of race and race relations as well.

Reid (1988) has shown how from being defined as 'immigrant children' or 'non-English speakers', the subjects of 'ESL' provision have been redefined in the educational literature over recent years as 'bilingual pupils'. This definition is claimed to give positive recognition to pupils' skills in more than one language. However, it seems often to be used just in connection with provision for pupils who are considered to need support in schools; that is, it has come to replace 'ESL' as a descriptive term in much educational discussion. Unless it is accompanied by real change in educational treatment, it has been pointed out that this is merely a terminological change (Alladina, 1985a; Mukherjee, 1985), which may lead to the term 'bilingual' taking on the same deficit connotations as have come to cluster around 'ESL'.

It is also important to understand that for many White monolingual English speakers currently, to speak of bilingual pupils has come to be understood largely as referring to Black pupils of Asian origin. Thus one Welsh LEA replied to the 1987 NFER survey by saying that as a 'predominantly white authority', 'the bilingual/mother tongue factor is therefore not our prime concern', despite the fact that it is known to make substantial provision for Welsh. If 'bilingual' has come to be used in educational contexts as a euphemism for 'Black', it is necessary to appraise who the subjects of any bilingual provision are, and what its outcomes are in terms of wider educational achievements. Reeves (1983) has said that the covert use of racial terminology is capable of 'justifying racial discrimination by providing other non-racist criteria for differential treatment of a group distinguished by racial characteristics' (p. 4). Although much of the overt debate about bilingual education is presented in terms of culture and language, it is important to remember this underlying racially defined dynamic.

The mainstream context of provision for bilingual pupils remains one where racial harassment remains a constant threat (CRE, 1988a). Routine school streaming, setting and banding arrangements have been shown to have discriminatory effects on Black pupils (Eggleston, et al., 1986). The mainstream school has been repeatedly suggested to be a place of inexplicit, covert evaluation and stratification of pupils, a process within which certain groups underachieve disproportionately (Bourne, 1988). Incorporation of provision for bilingual pupils into the mainstream, then, is not without its dangers.

The recognition and monitoring of the place of any form of specific educational provision for specific groups within the wider social context must be vital in evaluating responses to bilingualism and multilingualism. However, any evaluation of provision will need to include an analysis of who it is in a multi-ethnic society who defines and decides on appropriate provision, and who delivers it, as well as in what ways and with what effects education for one group differs from education for another (Hall, 1983). To date, as this book will make clearer, there appears to have been little involvement of minority linguistic groups in defining and determining both the type of educational provision most appropriate for themselves, and the sorts of changes in mainstream provision necessary to accommodate diverse needs and interests.

In later chapters we will examine the staffing and deployment of extra provision for bilingual pupils, and offer a description of LEA provision on which it is hoped others may draw for more critical analysis. However, the book cannot offer data on the *effects* of local authority provision. For this, long-term research is needed. It is startling but significant that little research to date appears to have emphasized the monitoring of different structures and strategies.

The policy context

In the course of the project it became clear that the three most profound changes in policy for bilingual pupils in England in the 1980s have been:

(a)   The recognition of pupils' skills in languages other than English and of the desire of certain communities to maintain their languages; and the opening up of debate on whether and how most appropriately to develop bilingual skills within the school system.

(b)   An attempt to reappraise and redefine the mainstream curriculum, classroom organization, and teaching strategies in order to take account of language diversity in the pupil population as the classroom norm rather than exception; in order to give access to the curriculum for *all* pupils by providing for diverse language needs.

(c)   Most recently, an attempt to make any *specific* provision for bilingual needs negotiable with the linguistic minority groups concerned, and accountable to them in terms of the effectiveness of the delivery.

These changes in policy have been the result of a multiplicity of influences, much of the pressure coming from the grass roots rather than administration. Most readers will recognize them as ideals, more rarely observable in practice. They emerged as public documents in quite different areas, the first through the European Communities (EC); the second from a DES Committee of Inquiry, and the third through the Home Office. Each of these will be briefly discussed below.

An important influence on current discussion was the 1977 EC Directive on the Education of Children of Migrant Workers. The Directive provided an opportunity to widen educational debate on the place of pupils' languages other than English in the school system. However, as the Linguistic Minorities Project (LMP, 1985) point out, the Directive was particularly significant in focusing discussion not on typologies or systems of bilingual education and bilingual theory being developed across the world, but on a much narrower framework of education for migrants, immigrants and refugees; that is, not on an 'elite' model of bilingualism, such as that developed for 'prestige' groups (e.g. in business or diplomatic circles); but one which was premised on disadvantage.

As finally enacted, Article 3 of the Directive reads that Member states:

> shall, in accordance with their national circumstances and legal systems, and in co-operation with States of origin, take appropriate measures to promote, in co-ordination with normal education, teaching of the mother tongue and culture of the country of origin .....

In 1981 the DES issued Circular 5/81, laying out for LEAs information about the Directive, but offering no clear policy lead, other than that, however implemented, the Directive should be taken to apply to pupils from EC Member and non-member states equally.

In the UK the Directive had a mixed response. While some pressure groups were willing to use it to legitimate a demand for 'mother tongue' provision, others saw it, in the climate of increasing restrictions on immigration of the late 1970s, as a possible first step towards policies of 'repatriation', and were understandably unwilling for language teaching issues to be discussed within the framework of education for 'migrant workers'.

Within government and LEAs, most discussion centred around the impossibility of implementing EC directives within a decentralized education system, which was defended in a way that seems surprising in 1988 in the context of the development of a National Curriculum.

In 1984, HMI reporting on 'Mother tongue teaching' in four LEAs indicated that: 'There is evidence that such provision is increasing but it is by no means clear that there is total agreement that it should and, if it should, in what form and at what levels of education'.

An EC report (1984) on the implementation of the 1977 Directive showed that Britain was at that time making little effort to comply with the directive compared to other member states, with only 2.2 per cent of primary children from home backgrounds where languages other than English are spoken receiving 'mother tongue teaching' at school compared to 80 per cent of children in the Netherlands.

A second major influence on the development of policy in England in the 1980s was the Swann Committee of Inquiry into the education of 'ethnic minority children'. The report (GB. DES, 1985) marked a milestone in making explicit policy for bilingual pupils in schools. The major issue addressed was, the report states, a larger one than simply a question of what was best for 'second language learners'. It was that of: 'what organisations and strategies have the best potential for creating for all learners equal access to the starting points of their learning and understanding' (p. 392).

Furthermore, rather than seeing language education for ethnic minority group children in terms of supporting English and of meeting community demands for 'mother tongue' teaching, each isolated from the other and from whole school language policies, the report continued: 'ethnic minority children's language needs serve to highlight the need for positive action to be taken to enhance the quality of education for *all* children' (ibid., pp. 385-6).

Policy for bilingual children was, within Swann, clearly framed in a broader approach to multicultural education, and to the dual aims of broadening and reorganizing the mainstream to accommodate more of ethnic minority cultures, meeting minority demands, while at the same time working towards educating the whole society in order to alleviate racism and hostility. Swan recognized clearly that racism exists in contemporary society. Racism is seen not only in racial violence and personal prejudice, but also in established institutional practices and procedures, which, regardless of intent, work in effect to exclude, deprive and disadvantage certain groups.

The Swann response to language needs appears to have been aimed essentially at defusing racially marked ethnicity as a point of potential conflict within schools; in the UK context this became an exercise in 'race relations'. With social cohesion as the main theme, stress was laid on provision for bilingual pupils within a mainstream system responsive to linguistic diversity, but within a curriculum framework common to all pupils.

In this context of concern for the rights of disadvantaged minority groups, Swann made a number of recommendations for provision for bilingual pupils which appear to have influenced practice. On English language support, Swann came out firmly against *separate* provision ('withdrawal') of all kinds. The English language needs of bilinguals should be organized within the mainstream 'as part of a comprehensive language policy for all children' (para. 5.2). Furthermore, *all* teachers have the responsibility to cater for the linguistic needs of their pupils, of whatever language background, and the DES and LEAs should give them 'appropriate support and training' to be effective (para 5.5). The theme is equality of opportunity within a shared curriculum – delivered in a programme of whole school change.

However, within Swann, bilingual development got an ambivalent response. The Committee's concerns here focused on what it saw as the 'dangers' of any separate provision. They were 'opposed in principle to the withdrawal of ethnic minority pupils as an identifiable group' for any purpose (para 3.16).

Other languages, the report continued, should be 'valued' in the mainstream, and 'should enrich' the linguistic awareness of monolingual children, thus helping towards intercultural understanding.

Bilingual support to help pupils to make the transition from the home language into English as the language of the school curriculum was accepted, together with the inclusion of languages at 14+ as option subjects in the modern languages curriculum. However, the development of bi-literacy in the years before 14+, and full bilingual education itself, were not recommended within the state school sector by Swann. No continuity in educational response to bilingualism was formulated.

In later sections we will be looking at the ways these recommendations appear to have influenced, opened up and constrained the provision for bilingual pupils in different LEAs.

A third major influence on contemporary provision for bilingual pupils arose out of the decision by the Home Office to review the use of funding under Section 11 of the Local Government Act (1966) during the 1980s. This legislation, its administration and influence on provision for bilingual pupils in England and Wales will be examined fully in the next section. At this point, however, it is necessary only to make the point that the potential influence of the Home Office on the provision made for bilingual pupils cannot be underestimated, since this government department has administered the allocation of the largest source of funding for specific educational provision for minority groups since the 1960s. New criteria (Home Office, 1986) for grant allocation were established in 1986, in consultation with minority group representatives. These recognized the need for any specific provision to be negotiated within LEAs with the linguistic minority groups concerned, and to be made accountable to them in terms of the effectiveness of the delivery of service.

However, the recognition of the need to involve minority groups in the use of funding made specifically to meet their own needs was only part of the changes brought about in funding policy in 1986. Although allocation of Section 11 funding had always been at the discretion of the Home Secretary, prior to 1986 the deployment of Section 11 staff was largely left to local authorities and their education services. In the new criteria for funding embodied in the Home Office circular 72/86 (Home Office, 1986), funding became subject to far more centralized control and direction; however, this control and direction lay outside the education department. While HMI could advise on the most useful redeployment of teachers, the use of the Section 11 teaching force was accountable to the Home Office.

The power of funding directed from the centre to shape provision in the decentralized education system of the 1980s is clearly illustrated throughout this book. One effect is to enable central government to shape provision without having to make explicit its policy on minority education. In Chapter 2 we will examine the criteria for Section 11 funding in more detail, and the actual numbers and deployment of teachers funded by the Home Office, and therefore subject to the new criteria.

'Bilingual education'

Before moving on to look at local authority provision for the education of bilingual pupils, it may be useful to briefly step outside the LEAs' perspectives to examine the options. A number of sociolinguists and educationalists have attempted to draw up a typology for bilingual education. Swann (GB. DES, 1985: p. 399) lays out three main types of provision:

(a) *'Bilingual education'* – using two languages as the medium of instruction.

(b) *'Mother tongue maintenance'* – the development of pupils' fluency in their mother tongue as an integral part of a primary school's curriculum in order to extend their existing language skills by timetabling a set number of hours each week for mother tongue (or 'first language') teaching.

(c) *'Mother tongue teaching'* – the teaching of ethnic minority communities' languages as part of the modern languages curriculum in secondary school.

Swann's typology, however, is based entirely on identifying organisational strategies. It gives little indication of the *purposes* behind each strategy and, more seriously, gives no indication of the context of schooling in which the typology might be set; for example, how other ethnic groups (majority or minority) fit into or work alongside the organisational strategies. Furthermore, by defining the languages concerned as 'mother tongues', the role these languages might play in the education of all pupils is excluded by definition.

Fishman and Lovas' (1972) earlier typology offers four types of bilingual education based on aims, or purposes. Provision might be seen as designed to achieve:

(a)   *Transitional bilingualism* – early learning in the first language, with the second language introduced slowly, leading to second language education and eventually dominance of the second language in spheres outside home and family.

(b)   *Monoliterate bilingualism* – the maintenance and development of the first language, while developing the second language through programmes which value pupils' languages, but which develop literacy only in the second language.

(c)   *Partial bilingualism* – some formal bi-literate skills are developed but only in the 'Language Arts' area, where they are restricted to classes on the cultural 'heritage' of the linguistic group.

(d)   *Full bilingualism* – which aims to develop oracy and literacy in both languages across a number of curriculum areas.

It can easily be seen that the different forms of organization laid out by Swann, especially early years 'mother tongue maintenance', might have the aim either of leading to monolingualism in the second language or of leading to full bilingualism; therefore the purposes for which different strategies are adopted need careful examination, since they are likely to have such different effects and outcomes.

Skutnabb-Kangas (1981: p. 127) draws a number of typologies together to come up with an interesting model which not only conjoins aims to organizational strategies, but also changes the nature of the discussion. In her list, rather than being a marginal issue just referring to minority education, educational strategies for *all* children are examined, with the medium of instruction for all pupils open to discussion instead of taken for granted.

Skutnabb-Kangas' typology can be summarized as follows:

(a)   Programmes of monolingual education for majority and minority group children in the dominant language; acting on the assumption that the school is linguistically homogeneous in the majority language, whether it is or not.

(b)   Monolingual education in the second language of minority group children – or 'language shift' education – in which the minority are required to take on the majority language in their education with the support of 'ESL' programmes.

(c)   Monolingual education in the first language of minority group children, leading to segregation and disadvantage in the majority society where the majority education system remains unchanged and minority group education has low status in society.

(d)   'Language shelter' programmes in which pupils receive several years of schooling in the minority language while receiving instruction in the dominant societal language, leading to a gradual change in the balance of languages in later years, and full bilingualism.

(e)   'Immersion' programmes for majority group children in educational programmes in which the medium of education is a minority language. This could be alongside children in 'Language Shelter' programmes (d). (This conjunction of (d) and (e) happens in some Welsh Units where Welsh speaking children learn alongside children from English home backgrounds learning through Welsh, before going on to English medium secondary schools; see Chapter 7.)

(f)   'Transitional' bilingual programmes, in which first language support is given to pupils in order to help them gain access to the majority language programme as quickly as possible, after which bilingual support is stopped.

(g)   'Bilingual education', where children from minority and majority groups learn both languages and where both languages have equal status, leading to shared, societal bilingualism. (This form of education is possible in some areas of Wales.)

Of course, the social context in many parts of England, and to some extent in parts of Wales, is, like most societies in the modern world, multilingual rather than bilingual, with more than two languages in common use in the community. The new paradigm which is emerging in current policy on education in the UK does not fit comfortably into Skutnabb-Kangas' typology, although sceptics might suggest it is a covert form of her second form of provision ('language shift' education). However, since its aim appears to be to challenge the monolingual status quo, rather than being assimilationist in intent, it will be given a separate category.

This paradigm might be called 'multilingual education', where it is accepted that classrooms are linguistically diverse, where all children are encouraged to draw on their full range of linguistic resources in communication and learning in the classroom in an informal way and with the aid of multilingual personnel and resources, but within which flexible small group strategies can be developed to bring pupils together to develop literacy in languages other than English whenever this is both practically feasible and supported by pupils and parents. Support for English across the curriculum as the main medium of a common education is an integral part of such a comprehensive multilingual approach. This approach fits well with dominant ideas in educational theory, in which teacher intervention in language development is limited; and where the provision of an environment rich in opportunities for talk and literacy is central.

There is another step, less often stressed. From an equal opportunities perspective, the 'multilingual' paradigm would also require making any standards set by the teacher, the curriculum and the examination system accessible to pupils from very different linguistic backgrounds. This requires explicit examination of the criteria by which pupils' work is evaluated and progress monitored.

There are some concerned with the education of bilingual pupils who do not feel that the sort of provision outlined above as 'multilingual education', even if extended more widely and made more secure, would fully meet the educational needs of bilingual pupils and maintain minority ethnic group languages. It might lead simply to a 'celebration' of diversity. There is an argument that pupils need more intensive development of minority languages to achieve the most positive cognitive advantages from their bilingualism (Cummins and Swain, 1986), perhaps by bilingual education on the Welsh lines, with the establishment of bilingual schools, or bilingual units attached to schools. Interestingly, this position is rarely strongly argued in English educational forums. Again, this would appear to be because of the underlying connection between issues of 'bilingualism' and those of race relations within the debate in England. Proponents of full bilingual education in the present context would have to weigh up the educational advantages against the disadvantages of the possible resulting 'marginalization' of issues relating to bilinguals and bilingual education as a special system of minority education, leaving the mainstream education system unchanged and unresponsive.

The problem identified by Wiseman in 1971 (see p. 5 above) remains, that any form of provision, ideal in a context of equal opportunities, may be transformed so as to be both politically indefensible and educationally unprofitable in an intentionally or unintentionally racist context.

A CRE report (1988b) claims that minority ethnic group teachers already often feel marginalized within 'special services' for ethnic minority pupils, while being proportionately under-represented across the education service as a whole. In these circumstances, the establishment of bilingual education institutions without strong and vocal minority community support would be likely to be greeted with some suspicion, and might lead to a 'type 3' form of education in Skutnabb-Kangas' typology. As the section on provision for Welsh will indicate, the more formal bilingual structures set up in Wales have been organized so that Welsh is included within the curriculum for all pupils, and with the intention that bilingual schools would cater for pupils from non-Welsh speaking as well as Welsh speaking backgrounds.

The introduction of separate education structures without strong minority group backing would be neither feasible nor justifiable. The likelihood of pressures for bilingual education, along the lines of the Welsh system, cannot be ruled out in the future, however, as minority groups become more secure and more influential in society, while wishing to maintain their own linguistic identities.

In this report, '*community languages teaching*' is assumed to refer to a timetabled period in which the language and perhaps the literature of one of the local community languages is the focus of the study; with the aim of developing literacy as well as oracy in the language.

'*Bilingual support*' is taken to refer to the use by a teacher or instructor of both the languages spoken by bilingual pupils to support learning across the curriculum areas in mainstream schools and classrooms. It therefore differs from multilingual approaches (see Chapter 5) which merely allow space and encourage pupils to use other languages in class themselves, without requiring bilingual staffing.

A third form of provision for languages other than English is full '*bilingual education*'. This is taken to refer to an education in which two languages are used to deliver the curriculum, and for which separate arrangements would have to be made, either in setting up separate bilingual schools, bilingual 'units' attached to schools; or separate streams in each year group, so that pupils who chose to could have a curriculum delivered by bilingual teachers in the chosen languages. Such a school would probably require pupils either to be fluent bilinguals or to make a choice to be educated in a language other than English in the first years of schooling. Bilingual education in this form is found in Wales, and in some privately funded schools in England (e.g. the Lycée Français in London). However, such arrangements were not identified in this survey of LEA provision for bilingual pupils in England. Arrangements for bilingual education will be looked at, then, in the chapter on provision for bilinguals in Wales.

Specific provision or reorganized mainstream?

There is an immediate apparent tension in current policy and provision for bilingual pupils which is clearly marked in the title of this book. On the one hand, there is a commitment to reappraising the mainstream structures, practices and procedures of the education service in terms of their ability to meet the defined needs of all their pupils, in what is recognized to be a linguistically and culturally diverse society. On the other hand, the brief of this book remains a clear focus on a specific group of pupils, those rather vaguely defined as 'bilingual pupils', and a concern to monitor any specific provision made to support their learning through either of their languages, either in the form of direct teaching support, or in terms of supporting schools and teachers to respond appropriately to a diversity of language backgrounds.

A focus on specific and extra provision does open one to accusations of 'marginalizing' the issues involved in educating children in a linguistically diverse society. However, in a situation in which it is clear, as this report will show, that specific extra funding is made available to education authorities, and is drawn on heavily to support both particular provision and to fund mainstream change in many areas, it would be unrealistic to work blithely from the assumption that educational providers have accepted linguistic diversity as the classroom norm, and that mainstream structures have evolved to accommodate individual bilingualism within societal multilingualism. Indeed, a preliminary study of LEA policy carried out as part of the NFER project indicated that less than half (44) of all LEAs appeared to have a multicultural/antiracist education policy. Of these it is not clear how many explicitly address the need to reappraise structural constraints to equality of opportunity for members of minority groups.

There are two separate questions involved in any study of provision for bilingual pupils in England and Wales. The first is, what provision is being made by LEAs and schools for bilingual pupils as individuals? The second is, how are LEAs and schools responding to multilingualism in their intake?

In the first, the focus is on individual bilingualism and meeting individual needs. The research tends to take ethnicity as a crucial factor in its focus on the particular languages involved, and to look at provision 'added on' to the mainstream, or at separate forms of provision such as bilingual education systems or 'units'.

In the second, the focus is on multilingual institutions, on languages in contact and the effects on learning. Equal opportunities perspectives make the historical background of linguistic diversity, black/white or other structural relationships, societal stratification and institutional racism the crucial factors, rather than ethnicity or cultural diversity. Reappraising structures leading to inequality would lead research to look at curriculum change, structural reorganization, monitoring of the effects of these changes, and the involvement of a wider range of participants in decision making.

The Bilingual Pupils' Project originally focused on the first question, provision for individual bilingualism, with the following basic aims: to provide information on the ways in which LEAs were assessing needs, and providing and deploying resources to meet those needs.

However, in carrying out this aim, it became increasingly necessary to respond to the fact that rather than assessing individual bilingual needs, many LEAs defined bilinguals' needs in terms of the second question, the need for schools which are responsive to multilingualism. Thus, although not in the original brief, it was clearly necessary to take on the second focus.

The Bilingual Pupils' Project

The project was planned in three stages. The first stage involved an in-depth study of six local education authorities in England and a briefer study of one in Wales.

The seven LEAs were chosen on the basis of an initial letter survey of all LEAs in England and Wales, requesting policy documents on language, multicultural education, equal opportunities, and the curriculum. The LEAs selected for study were those where thought appeared to have been given to, and some steps taken to provide for, language development in a multilingual context. The six English LEAs were chosen also to offer a geographical spread, and included a non-metropolitan county, two metropolitan urban districts and three Outer London boroughs. They included both LEAs with and without language surveys; and with a range of languages and percentages of bilingual pupils in their schools. The LEAs have been renamed in this book as Deeshire, Ayton, Beedon, Seabury, Edham and Fordham, since the studies are provided merely as illustrative data for the wider national picture. These LEAs are referred to throughout as the LEAs 'studied in-depth' or 'visited' during the Project.

A number of semi-structured and open interviews were conducted in each LEA with officers responsible in various ways for developing provision for bilinguals, including some Chief Education Officers or Principal Advisers, multicultural education advisers, modern languages advisers, English advisers, primary advisers, leaders of English support teams; race relations officers, ethnic minority group liaison officers, Section 11 administrative officers, local minority group representatives, voluntary community school teachers, and advisory teachers based at teachers' centres. The aim of the interviews was to find out not only what extra provision was being made for bilingual pupils, but what issues the presence of bilingual pupils in schools raised, and how far perceptions of appropriate provision were shared within and across LEAs.

In addition, one bilingual teacher or advisory teacher from each English LEA studied made a visit of between one and four days to one of the other LEAs studied in depth, reporting back to the project on provision for community languages teaching and bilingual support as seen in schools within that authority.

The second stage of the project involved a series of studies of the ways in which LEA policy and provision in the seven LEAs appeared to support implementation at junior/middle school level. One junior school was identified by advisers within each of the seven authorities, as schools which gave some indications of what the advisers felt was evolving good practice in developing support for bilingual pupils. In one authority (Ayton) a school was selected mainly because a specialist language methodology being developed by the local 'ESL' service was being implemented in it. The seven schools studied by the project team were not intended to be a representative sample. The average percentage of bilingual pupils across the six English schools was 64 per cent. Only two schools had less than 50 per cent of bilingual pupils. (Some details of LEAs and schools are shown in the tables A and B in the Appendix.)

The project chose to focus on junior schools for a number of reasons. First, it was impossible logistically to examine schools in any detail across the age range in each authority. It was decided that it was necessary to spend some time in each school to attempt to record ways in which the whole school was attempting to support language development for bilingual pupils; not simply to look at extra provision but to examine it in context. Junior schools are smaller and less complex than secondary schools, and thus appeared to be rather easier to examine in the short time available.

Secondly, co-operative teaching and mainstream in-class support for bilingual pupils is often stated to be both easier and more well-established at the primary level. A junior school placement, therefore, offered an opportunity to look for developing good practice. Finally, since there is very little specific first language maintenance in the junior phase, we were interested to see what 'valuing linguistic diversity' without specific resourcing might mean at junior level – and whether in fact informal ways of supporting first languages between infant and secondary schools could be discerned.

Overall, at least five days were spent within each school by a research officer, observing and talking to pupils and staff, and examining resources.

The third and final stage of the project was the development of a national questionnaire survey, based partly on areas of interest identified in the LEA studies but also designed to update information on basic provision since the last NFER surveys (Townsend, 1971; Townsend and Brittan, 1972).

In the summer term of 1987, all 108 LEAs in England and Wales, including the Channel Isles and Isle of Man, were sent a set of four questionnaires covering (a) statistical information on staffing and Section 11 funding; (b) provision for community languages teaching/support; (c) English language support, and (d) community consultation procedures. Authorities were invited to give details of their provision, giving figures throughout for the year 1986–87.

The project began in October 1985, soon after the publication of the Swann Report. It ended in June 1988, with a brief interruption during that year, just after the publication of the Kingman Committee report (GB. DES, 1988a) on its inquiry into the teaching of English language, and before the English Working Group on the National Curriculum made their first report. All the school and LEA studies were made during 1986 and 1987. The national survey questionnaires were returned between July and December, 1987.

During the project a series of significant documents were released, including Home Office Circular 72, 1986, on the new regulations for Section 11 funding and the CRE report (1986) on English language support. Both these documents influenced discussion and provision during the time of the survey. Two other major factors influenced both observed provision and the questionnaire data. The first was the period of industrial action undertaken as part of the dispute between teachers and their employers during the period of the study, which meant that in-service provision was curtailed, and constraints placed upon teacher meetings out of school time in many LEAs and schools. It was also a period of contracting mainstream education budgets in many LEAs, and the resulting constraints appeared to influence the implementation of policy. It is in this context that this study of the development of educational provision for bilingual pupils post-Swann needs to be placed.

Response to the questionnaire survey

Information on provision for bilingual pupils was received from 83 LEAs in England, Wales, the Channel Islands and Isle of Man (78 per cent of all LEAs).

The total number of full responses to all four separate sections of the questionnaire was lower, at 57 LEAs (53 per cent) (not including those LEAs claiming to make no provision).

Table 1.1:   *Number of LEAs responding to the survey*

	LEAs responding	% of category gp.	Full responses
Greater London	18	(86)	14
Metropolitan	32	(89)	21
Non-Metropolitan	25	(63)	16
Welsh	5	(63)	4
Channel Islands and Isle of Man	3	(100)	2

Table 1.1 indicates that the survey covers a range of different types of LEAs. It is rather weighted towards the metropolitan and London boroughs, but the non-metropolitan LEAs are substantially represented by over half the LEAs in that category.

Although most responses were returned under the signature of one officer, it was clear that a variety of different officers had been involved in compiling the data. The responses were almost equally split between those completed by administrative education officers and those completed by advisers and advisory teachers. Of those specifying their area of interest, the majority were returned by advisers for multicultural education (8); followed by Assistant Education Officers for Special Services (6); Heads of 'ESL' teams (5), with two of these being combined minority languages and 'ESL' teams; advisers for modern languages (4); primary advisers (4); research and information officers (3). Five were signed by directors of education or chief advisers.

Only one was passed down to be signed and returned by a teacher rather than an adviser or inspector or head of service. The returned questionnaires overall, then, indicate an interest in provision for bilingual pupils across a spectrum of responsibilities within LEAs, although still with a base in multicultural education and 'ESL' provision.

The range of LEAs able to offer bilingual pupil numbers were examined to see if they seemed representative of a spread of types of authority.

Table 1.2:   *LEAs with language surveys grouped by percentage of bilingual pupils*

% of pupil population who are bilingual	No. of LEAs
Low – not over 4.2	13
Moderate (5–14)	10
Appreciable (15–24)	6
High (25+)	8
Total	37

Table 1.2, based on the limited language survey data available, suggests that the questionnaire data cover a range of LEAs with both low and high bilingual pupil populations. The findings are not limited only to areas with high numbers of bilinguals.

Twenty-one English LEAs and three Welsh LEAs did not respond to our survey. The non-responding English LEAs were compared as a group with the group responding to the survey, by size, type (London, metropolitan, non-metropolitan) and population of 'New Commonwealth and Pakistan' (NCWP) origin (as defined by the 1981 OPCS Census). It was found that the only statistically significant difference between the groups was in terms of the percentage of the population which was of NCWP origin. The non-responders as a group had just one-third as many residents of NCWP origin as the responders. All the non-responding LEAs had less than the national average of residents of NCWP origin (4.2 per cent according to the 1981 Census). However, five non-responding LEAs included areas with 'moderate' (5–14 per cent) numbers of residents of NCWP origin, and one LEA had 'appreciable' (15–24 per cent) numbers of residents of NCWP origin in some places.

It may be thought that the non-responders were less interested in the content of the survey, probably having fewer bilingual pupils. However, at least three 'non-responders' are known to have approved multicultural education/anti-racist policies, and at least four are known to have some community languages teaching provision. In some cases there appeared to be some political sensitivity on the issue of bilingual provision within LEAs which may have influenced them in not choosing to respond to the survey at that time. The only LEA which refused to take part in the survey (on the grounds that officers were 'too busy') had recently also withdrawn a proposal for ESG grant funding in this area. Other LEAs, when contacted by telephone, offered administrative problems as the reason for 'delay', hoping to send completed papers later.

As the questionnaire was demanding of time and effort on the part of often already heavily overworked advisers and officers, the relatively high response rate indicated considerable interest in the area of provision for bilingual pupils across the majority of LEAs.

All LEAs were asked the following initial question, taken directly from the 1970 NFER Survey (Townsend, 1971): 'Does this LEA make any special arrangements for bilingual pupils which it would not expect to make if no bilingual pupils were on the rolls of its schools?' If the answer to this question was negative, the LEAs were informed that the response would be taken as a 'nil' return, and the rest of the questionnaire could be returned uncompleted.

In 1970, just 49 per cent of all respondents gave a positive answer to this question (Townsend, 1971). In 1987, 82 per cent of the respondents responded positively, indicating a substantial increase in 'special arrangements' across the country.

Only 14 LEAs said that they made no special arrangements for bilingual pupils. On checking by telephone, this number was decreased to 10 LEAs (12 per cent of the respondents) since it was found that three of these LEAs in fact made 'ESL' provision for pupils, and one, the Isle of Man, provided support for Manx in terms of a GCSE Mode 3 exam taken at FE level; some Manx work in some primary schools, resource materials for Manx study and lunchtime and after-school clubs for Manx in some secondary schools.

All 10 of the LEAs making no special arrangements were LEAs with less than the national average percentage (4 per cent) of residents of NCWP origin (OPCS Census, 1981). However, *the response indicates that most LEAs have to respond to the presence of bilinguals in the classroom – it is the norm rather than the exception.* Even of these 10 LEAs making no firm arrangements for bilingual pupils, two LEAs wrote that they found themselves called upon to make small sums available to support schools:

> 'Please note that of course we provide assistance on an individual and *ad hoc* basis to the very occasional pupil who has insufficient English to cope without special teaching.'
> 'From time to time the authority authorises small amounts of "extra teaching time" when required by schools, to support staff, rather than provide EFL.'

The two very different approaches suggested in these last two comments indicate alternative ways LEAs react when they very occasionally receive pupils who speak little English. The first indicates that it is thought that 'specialist' teaching is required. The second indicates that the busy class teacher will need to be relieved to enable the new pupil to receive some individual or smaller group attention. These different approaches to language support provision will be discussed in more detail in the section on English language support. However, the response shows than even those few LEAs who see themselves as making no special arrangements for bilingual pupils need to think through the issues raised in this report in order to reach a policy both for supporting the occasional child's immediate needs, and for the longer term school response to multilingualism both in the wider society, and within the school community where it exists. Even where there are no 'new arrivals', children's first languages are the languages of their parents and do not necessarily disappear as they become fluent in English.

LEA language surveys

There are no national census figures for the numbers of speakers of other languages than English within England. Details of Welsh speakers are only collected within the borders of Wales. The 1981 Welsh Census figures indicate that 19 per cent (503,549 people) of residents in Wales were said to speak Welsh. Baker (1985) discusses the problems of census data collection in giving a full picture of language use. However, analysis of the census data can offer a more detailed picture of the distribution of speakers within Wales, of generational differences, and of literacy in the language, allowing tentative predictions to be made of future language use and providing indications of the extent of future provision required by alternative language policies.

No such overall national data is available within England for other languages, nor for languages other than Welsh within Wales. The Inner London Education Authority (ILEA) has, since 1978, been compiling a picture of the languages of the capital, and their distribution. The Linguistic Minorities Project (LMP, 1985) developed a detailed analysis of languages and languages use within three local authorities in England, and a briefer analysis of the languages of school pupils in a further two areas; providing rich data, but from just five local areas in all. However, a Schools Language Survey 'Manual of Use', developed from the LMP Project, did offer LEAs a tool for carrying out their own analyses, which might form the basis for a deeper consideration of the needs of bilingual pupils within their own LEAs. The NFER questionnaire therefore asked all LEAs whether they had completed a language survey, and if so, at what date.

Just 29 English LEAs responding had carried out a language survey of pupils, with three more LEAs having carried out a partial survey in certain districts only. In addition, five LEAs (three in Greater London and two Metropolitan districts) provided detailed estimates of bilingual pupil numbers. Twenty-seven LEAs reported having carried out no survey. Three Welsh LEAs collected details of Welsh and English speakers only. The Welsh data will be examined in a later chapter since the data available is more detailed than that currently available in England and is able to offer a richer picture of language use, and the practicalities of bilingual educational provision. The remainder of this chapter will focus on language surveys in England.

The language background of pupils

Language survey data were received from:
• 13 LEAs in Greater London (3 'estimated')
• 14 LEAs in Metropolitan Districts (2 'estimated')
• 10 LEAs in non-Metropolitan districts, or shires

suggesting a wide range of contexts, although proportionately to all LEAs, weighted towards the urban areas. Again, it should be recognized that these LEAs are 'self-chosen', not a random sample of all LEAs, and so provide an incomplete picture of bilingualism in the UK. It is vital to stress that it is impossible to extrapolate from a picture drawn up from 37 random LEAs, each using one of a variety of data collection methods, to a national picture of the languages in use in the UK.

In recent years, since the publication of Rosen and Burgess' (1980) study of 'Languages and Dialects of London School Children', it has become customary to stress diversity. There were good reasons for this, not least among them being the need for educationalists and teachers to accept that the multilingual situation required a major response from mainstream structures and teaching methods, not simply an 'add-on' of extra provision for a few. Thus Rosen and Burgess identified 55 languages in a sample of London secondary schools in 1978; the ILEA Census recorded 147 languages in 1983, while increased awareness led to a total of 161 languages recorded within the same authority in 1985.

However, the danger of too great a stress on the numbers of languages involved in multilingual situations is that it can make the idea of more planned provision appear impossible; and suggest that the school system can only 'value' the languages pupils bring to school. Thirty-seven languages in the ILEA (1985) survey had just one speaker each within London schools. However, Bengali was spoken by as many as 22 per cent (12,627) of the ILEA bilingual pupil population and Chinese was spoken by 6 per cent (3,546). It seems that other educational responses to bilingualism could be feasibly planned alongside a response to multilingualism, at least for the more widely spoken languages.

Two different strategies may be indicated by examining the range of languages and numbers of speakers in UK schools:

(a)   The need to prepare schools and teachers for multilingual classrooms; to develop strategies for helping all pupils to feel able to draw on languages in learning as they wish.

(b)   As part of (a) above, make provision where possible for the development of literacy and more positive curriculum support in other languages.

This section is an attempt to look at available data to see if planned provision for bilingual pupils' language support and teaching is practicable, bearing in mind that this provision would need to be seen within a wider educational response to linguistic diversity as the classroom norm rather than the exception.

Bilingual pupils in 37 English LEAs

LEAs were asked in the NFER questionnaire if they had carried out a language survey. If they had, they were asked 'according to this survey, how many pupils speak a language other than English at home?' This question reflected the wording of the LMP questionnaire, but there is no guarantee that all LEAs responding had used a similar form of question to pupils in their surveys. Very different results may be obtained, for example, by asking pupils 'Can you speak a language other than English?' than by asking 'Do you yourself ever speak a language other than English at home?' (LMP, 1985: pp. 312-327). This should be kept in mind in examining the data below presented on 'bilingual' pupils.

In the LMP format (LMP, 1985) which had provided a model for a number of surveys, class teachers or tutors briefly interview each pupil individually, using a carefully prepared standard questionnaire, and with central back up and advice available at a local centre. While this methodology has itself been criticized (Alladina, 1985b; Nicholas, 1988) at least it is explicit and systematic. In some LEAs, however, it appears that teachers answered the questionnaire themselves on the basis of their own knowledge of pupils' languages; in others it is understood that the ESL service was responsible for carrying out the survey in schools, and not all pupils were interviewed.

The responses to language surveys are likely to be dependent on the linguistic awareness and sensitivity of the teachers who undertake them, the thoroughness of the surveys, and the nature of the school and classroom contexts in which they take place, which may be more or less hospitable or hostile to home languages use. Nicholas (1988) explains:

> The presence and use of languages in addition to English in Britain cannot be measured as neutral, demographic, 'hard facts,' primarily because they exist in a hostile environment, a part of which is the monolingual English hegemony ... It is evident from the experience of performing language diversity surveys that they swiftly reveal and draw out racist antagonism.

One of the full LEA language survey reports submitted to the NFER in response to the questionnaire explicitly referred to racist reactions within some schools hampering the carrying out of the survey.

The presentation of language survey data in this book must therefore be seen as simply illustrative of the nature of linguistic diversity in the LEAs responding, *as perceived by the respondents*. With these points in mind, a brief study of the data collected in the questionnaire will now be cautiously undertaken.

The total number of pupils identified by the 37 LEAs on the basis of their own surveys as speaking a language other than English at home was over 209,000, a substantial number, although probably an underestimate (Alladina, 1985b; Nicholas, 1988).

As one objective of the questionnaire was to identify possible local authority provision for languages, the purpose of collecting language survey data was to identify those shared or common languages among large groups of pupils which might practically be provided for by LEAs. LEAs were therefore asked to list only the first five most widely spoken languages in their areas. From 53 LEAs responding to this question, 19 languages were listed altogether, with the addition of 'European languages' (six LEAs) and 'S. Asian languages' (three LEAs). This response is impressionistic since 16 of the LEAs responding had carried out no language survey.

The examination of the languages reported by 53 LEAs (see Table 1.3) indicated that although most individual LEAs have distinct linguistic profiles, there are a small number of languages which frequently form a substantial part of that linguistic profile, and which when actual language survey figures are amalgamated, are shown to account for large numbers of bilingual pupils. The languages most frequently mentioned by these 53 LEAs were Panjabi, Urdu, Gujerati, and Bengali, then Chinese, Hindi and Italian.

Chinese was reported as widely spoken by seven LEAs, with nine others specifying Cantonese, one specifying Mandarin, and one 'Cantonese/Hakka'.

Table 1.3: *Languages listed by LEAs as one of the five most widely spoken languages within them*

Language	No. of LEAs	Language	No. of LEAs
Panjabi	40	Turkish	3
Urdu	38	Vietnamese	3
Gujerati	31	Portuguese	2
Bengali	30	Polish	2
Chinese	18	Spanish	2
Hindi	13	Japanese	1
Italian	13	Farsi	1
Greek	6	German	1
Arabic	4	Pushto	1
Creoles	4		

Panjabi was another complex category. While 40 LEAs reported Panjabi as one of their five most widely spoken languages, five LEAs specified that pupils speaking Panjabi belonged to that section of the linguistic minority group for whom the language of literacy was Urdu, as is usual with Moslem Panjabi speakers. One LEA indicated that its largest Panjabi speaking group would use the script common to Sikh Panjabi speakers, and 34 LEAs did not specify towards which script the Panjabi communities in their areas would have affiliations. (Some Sikh informants have indicated strongly that the description of the script they use in writing Panjabi as 'Gurmukhi script' rather than simply 'Panjabi' was deeply offensive to them. Although frequently met with in sociolinguistic studies, the description seems clearly an 'outsider's' categorization, and so will not be used in this study.)

Three Greater London LEAs and one non-metropolitan LEA reported the presence of speakers of Creoles. One LEA specified that these were English-based Creoles, two did not specify. The fourth reported that while English-based and 'other non-French-based' Creoles accounted for 9 per cent of the LEA's pupils speaking languages other than English, 4 per cent spoke French-based Creoles. Most LEAs obviously had problems in dealing with the boundaries of Creoles and varieties of English dialects. The ILEA after its 1978 Census decided no longer to record details of 'Caribbean English dialects and Creoles' since 'some teachers confused ethnicity and language and recorded all pupils of Afro-Caribbean origin as speaking Caribbean dialects' (ILEA Language Census report, 1986: p. 2). (For analysis of Creoles and their current use see Dalphinis, 1985.)

The 'naming' of languages

The naming of languages in any list for language diversity surveys is always problematic. LMP (1985) devote 11 pages to discussing the 'boundaries and definitions of linguistic minorities'. The basic problem is that the 'boundaries of particular languages cannot in reality be easily established' (LMP, 1985: p. 19). Language boundaries are politically and socially, rather than linguistically, defined. Language is not only a system of communication, but a marker of identity and ethnicity, and as such is closely bound up with a number of other ethnic markers such as national original, nationality, and religion. People speaking closely related and mutually intelligible languages may categorize these as either different 'languages' or 'dialects', depending on the perceived importance to them of national and ethnic boundaries.

Where different scripts are involved, there is a further complication. People may have a different language of literacy from the language actually spoken at home, which may nevertheless be a crucial part of their lives and that of their ethnic community.

In many communities it may be common for an individual to use a number of different languages, so that language surveys which allow pupils to mention only one language other than English may already lead to distortion.

Readers who would like further discussion of these issues are referred to LMP (1985) as a starting point. However, it is important to note that the definition of languages by people outside the linguistic communities involved (whether academically agreed or part of 'folk' knowledge) may be very different from the linguistic boundaries perceived by group members themselves. 'Outsider' definitions may be oversimplistic, miss valuable differences between language users, and at worst may be downright offensive to the speakers concerned. Ultimately, definitions of language boundaries must 'rely on subjective information provided by members of the minority in question, rather than on criteria of actual linguistic behaviour adopted by researchers' (LMP, 1985: p. 18). Essential to any future school survey, then, would seem to be the active participation of linguistic minority groups (Alladina, 1985b; Nicholas, 1988).

The language survey data presented here should therefore be viewed only as a record of current knowledge and awareness of language use among educationalists and within LEAs. Members of linguistic groups who would wish to challenge the language labels used should do so, since these are the labels now widely being used in practice.

Figure I: *Percentages of bilingual pupils in LEA areas where information has been provided on the five most widely spoken languages*

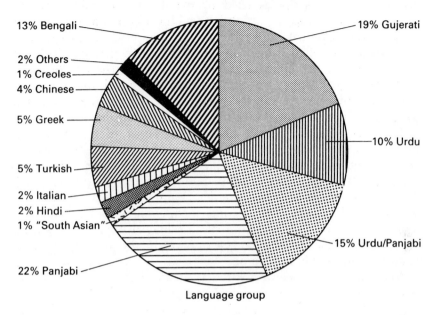

Language group

The pie chart (see Figure 1) illustrates the comparative sizes of the pupil populations identified as belonging to the five largest language groups in the 32 LEAs with surveys. All the groups identified separately had at least 1000 members, smaller language groups being grouped in the category 'others'. 'Other' languages included German, Polish, Arabic, Farsi, Japanese, Vietnamese, Spanish and Pushto as well as unspecified 'European' languages, and Portuguese in the Channel Islands.

In this smaller sub-group of LEAs with language surveys, the largest language groups were the same as those most frequently mentioned by the 53 LEAs: Panjabi, Urdu, Gujerati and Bengali; in numerical terms Chinese speakers appeared to be a very much smaller linguistic group than the others, although their presence had been frequently reported by LEAs.

Although pupils speaking Panjabi with Urdu as the language of literacy were reported by only five LEAs as a large linguistic group, these pupils accounted for as much as 15 per cent of the bilingual pupil population in the 32 LEAs. This suggests that LEAs with large numbers of any one language group may tend to be more specific about the language varieties involved. Similarly, just one LEA specified the presence of Panjabi speakers who were specifically said to write Panjabi script as used by mainly Sikh Panjabi speakers; however, this group in just this one LEA accounted for one per cent of the bilingual pupils identified. This group is included in the category labelled Panjabi in the pie chart, which also includes 21 per cent of the bilingual pupils identified whose use of script and language of literacy was not specified, and which may therefore include a number of Panjabi speakers for whom the traditional language of literacy would be Urdu rather than Panjabi.

Languages listed by each LEA as the *largest* of the five most widely spoken languages had a range of from 22 per cent to 91 per cent of all the bilingual pupils in the LEAs reporting. The languages were (in order of most mention) Panjabi, Urdu, Gujerati, Bengali, Greek, Italian and Creoles. Portuguese was reported in the Channel Islands. The second most widely spoken language never had more than one-third of all bilingual pupils in any LEA; this group included the languages already mentioned, together with Turkish, Arabic and Hindi.

No further languages were listed as the third most widely spoken. The fourth most widely spoken language was spoken by less than 20 per cent of the bilingual pupil population in any LEA. At this point Farsi and Vietnamese were reported. Polish, Pushto, Spanish and German were mentioned only by one LEA each as a fifth language, never spoken by more than 10 per cent of the bilingual pupil population in any of these 32 LEAs.

These findings appear to be supported by past research reports. Tansley and Craft (1984) found the most frequently mentioned languages by 63 LEAs were Urdu (46 LEAs), Panjabi (43), Bengali (36) and Gujerati (35). In the surveys of pupils' languages in five LEAs carried out by the LMP (1985), Urdu, Panjabi and Gujerati were the languages of the three largest linguistic minority groups in three of the five LEAs surveyed, among the four most widely spoken languages in the fourth LEA, and among the languages listed as found within the fifth LEA, which had a more hetero-geneous bilingual population. The LMP noted that although in each area surveyed there was a range of languages in use:

> From the point of view of potential educational support for
> minority languages this suggests that the kind of objection
> which is based on logistic problems arising from extremely
> large numbers of different languages in particular areas has
> only limited force (pp. 330–1).

The NFER amalgamation of the results of 32 language surveys reflects these conclusions. The study of 32 LEAs revealed no other large language groups than those revealed by the LMP study of just five LEAs.

However, the proportions of the less widely spoken but still frequently mentioned languages seem more likely to vary according to the numbers of LEAs involved in any study. With only 32 LEAs involved, the addition of a small number of other LEAs is likely to alter the proportions of the smaller linguistic groups shown on the pie chart. Similarly, additional LEAs may alter the order of size of the four largest linguistic groups. These relative proportions remain specific to the particular group of 32 LEAs involved and cannot be extrapolated from to form a national picture.

The use by pupils of more than one language was excluded from the data. The inclusion of second, third and fourth languages might alter the picture of language speakers, for example in swelling the number of Hindi speakers, although LMP (1983) indicated this made little difference to the overall picture. Clearly, closer investigation of the language attitudes and educational goals of any particular group would be required before appropriate educational provision could be developed.

A larger scale study of more LEAs would be likely to reveal an accumulation of more speakers of the more scattered language groups, such as Chinese speakers, for example, for whom more centralized educational provision (perhaps through distance learning) could be made available should bilingual language development become policy. A combination of central and local policy formation and resourcing would seem essential to respond to both the more widespread languages and to localised 'pockets' of large numbers of a particular linguistic minority group, which for historical reasons was largely confined to certain LEAs and areas.

The point of this section has simply been to suggest that language surveys, as well as revealing diversity, are able to provide a starting point in indicating the practicalities of more substantial provision within England and Wales for large numbers of bilingual pupils speaking a relatively small number of languages widely spoken in local communities.

It is necessary to stress that school language surveys are seen as a very crude form of data collection on language use in complex social settings by sociolinguists. Unless minority linguistic group communities themselves are centrally involved in the process of data collection, the results are likely to be unreliable, in terms not only of numbers collected, but in language classifications and details of more complex language use, such as the use of second, third and fourth languages, languages of literacy, and languages of historical and religious affiliations.

Minority linguistic group participation is not only necessary for information gathering, however, but essential in policy formation. Research into bilingual education indicates that the wishes and perceived needs of language users themselves are crucial to the success and viability of arrangements for language provision or bilingual education. While central resourcing may need to be made available, provision would need to be carefully assessed both at central and at local level in cooperation with linguistic minority groups.

Finally, it is important to stress that provision for bilingual pupils is not an unusual issue, one for a few, rare LEAs, or an 'inner city' issue alone. The mean percentages of bilingual pupils in each of the LEA category groups were as follows:

- ILEA: 19%
- Outer London: 26%
- Metropolitan: 9%
- Non-Metropolitan: 4%

Although there were areas of high concentrations of bilingual pupils, the majority of bilingual pupils go to school in areas of 'moderate' or 'appreciable' numbers of bilinguals (from 5 to 24 per cent).

Another conclusion of this study, then, must be that in talking about bilingual pupils one is not talking about exceptional cases in a few urban authorities, but about a substantial proportion of the school population. The implications of this bilingual presence need to be clearly considered in national policy making, and in the national curriculum.

In the next chapter we will draw on the NFER survey data to examine the extent of extra provision for meeting the educational needs of bilingual pupils, and go on to analyse special funding for this provision.

In Chapters 3 to 6 the use of extra staffing will be examined in more detail; for English language support, bilingual support and community languages teaching, with the survey data supplemented by more detailed in-depth studies of LEAs and schools. Separating English and other languages support provision in this way is not ideal; however this editorial decision was practically imposed by the nature of the data, which mostly, although not always, involved different staff and different structures. Similarly, the very different educational structures in Wales could not easily be treated alongside a discussion of provision in England, and will be discussed in Chapter 7.

In the final chapter, some threads from the Welsh and English situations will be brought together, and the implications of changes in the education system following the Education Bill (1988) for bilingual provision will be charted.

2 Extra Staff and Special Funding

Provision of staffing

In a survey of all English LEAs in 1970, Townsend (1971) found that 2447 extra staff were employed by LEAs to meet 'the additional needs of immigrants'. Most of these teachers were involved in teaching English as a second language, although some were used to lower teacher/pupil ratios in schools, such as 'by increasing a school staff by 0.1 teachers for every 10 immigrant pupils on roll' (p. 92).

By 1987, rather than numbers of 'extra' teachers decreasing as schools adopted mainstream structures for linguistic and cultural diversity, data from 74 LEAs showed that there were over 5250 teaching staff 'extra to normal staffing', specifically to meet the needs of pupils of 'Commonwealth origin'. This was well over twice as many as in 1970. However, only 2975 staff were involved in language support. The increase in staffing was largely in areas other than language support, such as multicultural education posts, various other curriculum development posts and home/school liaison.

The 1987 figures for language support, like the 1970 figures, include teachers identified for bilingual support and community languages teaching. Townsend (1971) identified 137 teachers in 20 LEAs employed 'primarily to teach pupils from the same country of origin', mainly working in reception language centres and as 'ESL' teachers. Community languages teaching was scarcely in evidence (found in less than 3 per cent of LEAs). In the 1987 study, the total number of language support teachers identified included 417 bilingual teachers providing bilingual support and community languages classes. If teachers of these new and developing forms of language provision are subtracted from the total number of language support teachers, it would appear that the numbers of English language support staff have not expanded greatly over the past 17 years.

While community languages teachers are sometimes members of modern languages departments in secondary schools, and courses are often open to all pupils and not simply to pupils bilingual in English and the language concerned, to date community languages appear to be *additional* to the more traditional school language choices. Thus community language teachers are usually additional to rather than replacing other languages staff. For this reason, community languages teachers have been included in this section as 'extra provision' made in response to the presence of bilingual pupils.

It is not intended to suggest that language support staff are deployed specifically to work with bilingual pupils. Both English language and bilingual support staff have varied ways of working within different LEAs, classrooms and schools, and in some cases are responsible for developing strategies to support teachers in responding to multilingual classrooms, rather than focusing on particular children or specific language needs. The actual roles of staff will be discussed in detail in later sections. This section merely attempts to look at overall numbers and patterns of provision.

LEAs were asked to give the total numbers of qualified teachers employed as full-time equivalent figures (f.t.e.) whose duties were primarily concerned with: (a) English language support (or 'ESL'); (b) the teaching of community languages; (c) bilingual language support. After checking that the same teachers were not listed more than once in the three categories, analysis of the results showed that of the 2975 (f.t.e) qualified teachers deployed altogether across the 74 LEAs responding to the question: 86 per cent of the teachers were deployed as English language support teachers; 9 per cent as community languages teachers, and 5 per cent as bilingual support teachers.

Fifty-four per cent of all language staff were based in primary schools, with 31 per cent in secondary schools, and the rest either working across the age range, or with age phase unspecified in the returns.The numbers involved in bilingual support do not include members of 'ESL' teams who may or may not themselves be bilingual. (A few LEAs claimed that all 'ESL' teachers carried out bilingual support whether they were bilingual or not.) They do include bilingual members of 'ESL' teams where these were clearly identified as also carrying out bilingual curriculum support for part of their timetable.

The figures indicate that despite increased interest in supporting and maintaining the languages other than English of bilingual pupils, resources remain directed towards English language development, especially focused on the primary phase.

Next, it should be made quite clear that the proportions of extra language support teachers (of whatever kind, – ESL, bilingual support, community languages, etc.) to the numbers of bilingual pupils in schools was very low. Data from the 37 LEAs which provided language survey data showed that only four LEAs had ratios below 50 bilingual pupils to one language support teacher. Twenty-four LEAs had over 75:1, with six of these having more than 200:1. The highest ratio was over 530:1; the lowest was 30:1. (This, of course, takes no account of the distribution of pupils across schools within LEAs.)

Extra language support staff in these numbers would not, then, be able to work with all the bilingual pupils in UK schools, nor could all bilingual pupils expect much contact with language support teachers.The staff were likely to have special duties, for example, to monitor and support 'first stage' English learners; to provide 'option' languages classes; to enable and support class teachers in an inservice role, to provide translation or interpreting services. Any recommendation for practice which involves or expects a high level of extra staffing in schools is unlikely to be practicable in the current context.

Although there is no central policy on the numbers of extra language support staff that should be provided in relation to the numbers of bilingual pupils in schools, the distribution of extra staffing was found to be statistically related to the presence of bilingual pupils. An even clearer relationship was found between the number of language support staff as a percentage of all pupils and the grouped percentage of population of NCWP origin (OPCS Census, 1981), which was based on a larger number of cases for analysis (data from 65 cases compared to 36 cases offering

Table 2.1: *Density of language support staff as a percentage of all pupils to the percentage of the population of NCWP origin (OPCS, 1981 Census) in LEAs in England*

Density of language support staff (as % of all pupils) per 10,000 pupils	No. of LEAs by % NCWP population			
	Below 4%	*5–14%*	*14–24%*	*25%*
None	10			
1 to 3	24			
4 to 7	4	5		
8 to 15	2	2	1	
16 to 25		6	2	1
26 to 35		1	3	2
36 and above		1		1
Total no. of LEAs	40	15	6	4

($p < 0.00005$)

bilingual pupil numbers). This last relationship can be seen in Table 2.1.

There were significantly fewer language support staff when weighted for size of the LEA in areas with few residents of NCWP origin, and proportionately more as the numbers grew larger.

The provision of language support staff was more than proportional to the density of pupils of NCWP family origin even when LEAs were weighted for overall size. In areas with a high concentration of pupils with NCWP family origins, the ratio of language support teacher to population of NCWP origin was as low as 1:300. However, in areas of 'moderate' or 'low' percentages, the ratio was as high as 1:600 and 1:6000 respectively. Extra provision per pupil is therefore focused more on areas with a considerable presence of bilingual pupils of NCWP family origin rather than on extra support for areas where there are few, possibly scattered, bilingual pupils.

The data show considerable consistency, with comparatively little variation within the defined categories: the relationship of density of language staff to percentage population of NCWP origin is one of the very few 'within group' consistencies found in this survey, which elsewhere reveals great variation within category groupings of LEAs.

(As a note on methods of analysis used later in this book, the consistency of provision to percentage of residents of NCWP origin indicates that the categories based on the 1981 Census data are useful in practice. For this reason, they can be used as reference points for the comparison of different types of provision across LEAs in the absence of full language survey data.)

The relationship of language provision to percentages of population of NCWP origin can be partly explained by reference to the language survey data in the last chapter, which indicated that the large majority of bilingual pupils in the 37 LEAs giving language survey information used languages that were themselves of South Asian, and therefore NCWP origin: Urdu, Panjabi, Gujerati and Bengali in particular.

The close relationship between language staff provision and patterns of established populations of NCWP origin may indicate either that the language survey data may be generalized to conclude that the majority of bilingual pupils overall in England speak languages of South Asian origin; or to conclude that bilingualism and bilingual language needs have only become salient within the English educational context where there are populations of NCWP origin, with other linguistic minorities having been overlooked in terms of provision.

Either conclusion is possible within the terms of the data so far available, but while there is no source of extra funding for language provision per se, Home Office Section 11 funding for language provision (see below) would clearly encourage provision for pupils of NCWP family origin, so the latter conclusion might be more strongly supported.

The consistency of language support staff numbers to bilingual pupil numbers and percentage population of NWCP origin across LEAs indicates that once numbers of staff are recruited for identified language support needs, they may not be reduced or redeployed in the mainstream as the years go by, but stay within language support roles, although those roles themselves may be redefined and their terms of reference altered. Thus, although different expertise (e.g. bilingual skills) may be added to the support teams, the overall numbers appear to remain consistent across LEAs, when weighted for size, according to the concentration of the bilingual pupil or NCWP origin population figures.The situation overall does not appear to be one of flux and *ad hoc* temporary arrangements in response to the specific needs of the localities, as this would be signalled in inconsistency between LEAs responding to particular local pressures and needs.

Differences in political commitments towards supporting provision for bilingual pupils in different LEAs do not appear to be enough to alter the consistency of the relationship of provision to proportions of NCWP origin residents. *Again it is likely that central government resourcing through Home Office Section 11 is responsible for this consistency in response in relation to NCWP population size.*

The fairly static picture of language support in terms of numbers of extra staff may reveal an interesting trend within LEAs. Many LEAs in our survey (see Chapter 3) described increasing the numbers of their English language support teams; few described a decrease in numbers, although a number mentioned changing roles. *Overall, it would appear that rather than increasing Section 11 English language support provision, the last few years have seen Section 11 redirected from posts lowering teacher/pupil ratios (indirect English support) to specific identifiable English language support posts. The new Section 11 regulations for funding have obviously been influential in this area.*

Funding provision for bilingual pupils

The main funding for the education service in England is received through the rate support grant from central government. This funding is allocated as a block grant for each local authority's spending as a whole, with no part specifically set aside for education, although central government gives 'advice' on national expenditure policies.

As most of the rate support grant allocations to education are tied up in capital costs, maintenance and staff salaries, the role of additional, specific grants, although small in comparison, is extremely important in setting new priorities for the development of education and enabling curriculum change.

There are just two central government grant schemes specifically for the education service in England and Wales, the in-service teacher-training grants scheme (GRIST), and the education support grants (ESG) scheme. Both of these have the potential to bring central government influence to bear on the development of education for bilingual pupils.

Within GRIST, while training related to locally assessed needs and priorities is supported by grant at a 50 per cent rate, expenditure related to *nationally* set priority areas is supported by grant at 70 per cent, thus encouraging local authorities to give weight to national priorities. For 1988/9, fifteen national priority areas for school teacher in-service were listed; these included one priority called training in 'teaching and the planning of the curriculum in a multi-ethnic society'. Circular 9/87 (GB. DES, 1987b) elaborated on this last priority:

> Courses for teachers from ethnically mixed schools will give priority to monitoring and assessment of pupils' achievements and needs, appropriate teaching methods for linguistically and culturally mixed groups and pastoral issues (para. 11).

At the time of the survey, funding for this national priority was not yet in force. In addition, the industrial action relating to teachers' pay and conditions made very little in-service activity possible within many LEAs. The survey data, however, rarely referred to future plans for major GRIST in-service activity in this area.

The Education Support Grants (ESG) scheme offered short term extra funding for LEAs to enable the development of specific new projects.The central government set priorities for each year, limiting the budget for each accordingly. In 1986/7, three LEAs received grant funding relating to (a) the development of English language support (one LEA) or (b) 'mother tongue' support (two LEAs). In 1988/89, 14 LEAs had received approval for grant aid related to the development of materials and resources to support Section 11 funded 'ESL' staff (see below); one LEA to support teachers working with ethnic minority pupils outside the scope of Section 11 ('mainly Japanese') and just one programme to develop bilingual support (for pre-school age children).In addition, there were two grants specifically for initiating after school study programmes for Afro-Caribbean pupils, focused on examination achievement.

In Wales, Welsh Office funding is available for grants to local education authorities for the teaching of Welsh, and for the teaching of other subjects in Welsh. Other grants are made to maintain the Welsh Books Council (a central Welsh resources centre), and to Welsh medium nursery schools (Ysgolion Meithrin) as well as to voluntary bodies for the maintenance of Welsh, such as Yr Urdd, the Welsh youth league. A number of research projects into Welsh education have also been supported through the Welsh Schools Council or later, Schools Curriculum Development Committee, and a Welsh National Language Unit was established in 1968.

No specific educational funding arrangements are made for other languages or for English language support for bilingual pupils by the Department of Education and Science in England and Wales. The DES have funded research into bilingualism in the school population ('The Linguistic Minorities Project', 1979–83, University of London and the short Bradford College 'Mother Tongue and English Teaching Project' (MOTET), 1978.) A special division within the DES was set up in 1975 for consideration of issues relating to minority ethnic group needs, which liaises across the DES, with HMI and with other government departments, including, most importantly as far as funding goes, the Home Office (see below – Section 11 funding).

No direct funding for provision for bilingual pupils is currently received from the European Community towards the implementation of the 1977 Directive. The EC does, however, also provide funding into research into curriculum development, having supported recently the pilot project on 'Community Languages in the Secondary Curriculum (1984–87)', University of London; the 'Linguistic Diversity in the Primary School' project (1986–89), University of Nottingham; and the Schools Curriculum Development Committee 'Mother Tongue Project' 1981–85. All these projects were designed to have a direct impact on developing school practice, and in this way EC funding has contributed to curriculum development. However, no substantial funding has been made available to enable the recruitment of staff with the bilingual skills needed to provide a coherent structure for bilingual support within authorities. The European Social Fund at one time contributed to Home Office Section 11 Funding (see below), but this EC funding was withdrawn from the Home Office in 1983, since it was felt that many Section 11 posts did not meet the EC criteria which were directed at combating unemployment in the inner cities.

EC funding for bilingual provision was made indirectly, however, through some European embassies in the UK which provided after-school classes and/or peripatetic teachers to work in schools with children with family origins in those countries. This provision is not examined here, as the focus is on local authority provision.

Central government funding did reach some projects for bilingual pupils through indirect routes such as Inner City Partnership Project funding in some LEAs, and through Manpower Services Commission (MSC) employment training schemes with bilingual trainees working in schools in some areas. However, the bulk of support for provision for bilingual pupils has been made via the Home Office.

'Section 11'

Extra Home Office funding under 'Section 11' of the Local Government Act 1966 to local education authorities has been a major factor in influencing the way in which the educational service has developed in response to linguistic diversity in schools. Townsend (1971) reported 49 LEAs claiming Home Office grant funding in 1970. Home Office provision had greatly increased in 1987. Some explanation of 'Section 11' is therefore necessary to understand the background to provision for bilingual pupils.

Under Section 11 of the Local Government Act 1966, special funding is made available to local authorities, at the discretion of the Home Secretary, for the employment of staff 'in consequence of the presence within their areas of substantial numbers of immigrants from the Commonwealth, whose language or customs differ from those of the rest of the community' (GB. Statutes, 1966). The law itself reflects the dominant perceptions of the time in which it was enacted. By contrasting a homogeneous group, 'the rest of the community', to the 'immigrant population', Section 11 operates in contradiction to multicultural education as expounded by Swann, for example, which reveals diversity within the society as a whole.

Section 11 remains in force today in its original terms of 'immigration', rather than as funding for the development and protection of minority group interests and minority group participation in society. It has therefore been a focus of controversy for many years; some reject it as inherently racist; others are willing to use it in the absence of more appropriate funding.

Although the law itself has not been changed since 1966, regulations for the administration of funding and for the scope of its interpretation have changed over the intervening years, most radically since 1986 when more stringent rules for its application came into force.

Under the law, funding is restricted to a percentage (currently 75 per cent) of the cost of staff posts only. No funding is made available for initial training or in-service secondments, equipment or materials under the Act. This focus on extra staffing has had a distinct influence on provision, as will be examined later in this book.

Funding is available for *any* area within a local authority, whether housing, social services, or education, etc., provided the post meets two underlying principles. First, the post must be *extra* to 'normal' staffing needs; secondly, the posts must be designed to meet the *specific* needs of 'Commonwealth immigrants'. 'Commonwealth immigrants' in 1986 was interpreted to mean those who were born in a country of the Commonwealth (including Pakistan prior to 1972, when it left the Commonwealth) and 'their immediate descendants'. The 'target' group therefore, though vague in definition, is mainly in practice focused on Black residents with family origins in the New Commonwealth and Pakistan (NCWP) and may in practice include third and even fourth generation children with family origins in the NCWP.

However, Section 11 funding is available with reference to posts meeting needs due to 'differences in language or culture' of pupils with family origins in any one of the 47 countries of the Commonwealth. It would therefore be applicable, for example, if there were specific needs due to language and cultural differences, not only to pupils of South Asian and Afro-Caribbean origin, but also to Greek and Turkish speaking pupils with family origins in Cyprus, but not from the mainland states; or to Chinese speakers with origins in Singapore and Malaysia, but not from Vietnam or mainland China.

For example, Home Office funding was provided to one outer London borough after the 1974 Turkish invasion of Cyprus. The LEA used Section 11 at that time to fund part-time classes in English for newly arrived Greek speaking pupils.

So far as defining the 'target' group for Section 11 funding is concerned, the onus appeared to be on LEAs themselves to make the case for special funding for provision for any group with reference to its own local situation.

The particular needs the Section 11 posts should meet are left open to wide interpretation by local authorities and the Home Office, with educational advice from the DES; the only stipulation is that the 'target group' should have needs 'different from or the same but proportionately greater than' the mainstream of society (Circular 72/86, Home Office, 1986).

Funding is not allocated proportionately to the numbers of people of Commonwealth origin within an authority. LEAs can choose whether or not to apply for funding, and decide what posts would be most suitable to meet specific needs, within certain limits.

Any 'points' allocation of staffing to schools by local authorities is locally determined, not a necessary requirement.

In 1983, a three-year review of the use of Section 11 in LEAs was undertaken by the Home Office. In 1986 new criteria for funding were brought into operation. In addition to the principles of 'extra' and 'specific' provision (above), applications had to be accompanied by an analysis of the needs that the local authority intended the post to meet; show how these related to an overall LEA strategy for meeting the needs of the 'target' group; and describe how the needs had been identified. The local authority was also required to show evidence of having tried to consult, in detail, on the appropriacy of the posts a cross-section of the community whose needs they were intended to meet.

Turning to staffing, Circular 72/86 asked authorities to reappraise the qualifications required for Section 11 postholders, emphasizing that membership of the minority ethnic group in question might in some circumstances be more important than academic or professional qualifications.

From 1986, every post was to be identified both by the name of the postholder and by its location, and each postholder was to have a detailed job description outlining the duties involved; and this job description also to be part of the community consultation process.

In addition to job descriptions, each post was also to have negotiated 'output measures and performance indicators', by which the effectiveness of the post could be regularly reviewed. These measures were intended to come into operation as early as possible; however, recognizing the difficulties of establishing these criteria, some time had been allowed authorities by the Home Office to get assessment measures operationalized.

The types of post able to receive funding, provided the Home Office criteria were met and determined on the basis of evidence of need from the local authority and evidence of support from the local communities, were open to negotiation between local authority and Home Office, with advice from HMI. Examples in education where the need for support was recognized were teachers of English as a second language; bilingual teachers 'in the nursery and early primary years', 'teachers concerned with improving access to the school curriculum for pupils of Commonwealth origin'; and 'trainers and advisers with the particular knowledge, skills and experience to assist schools and colleges to respond effectively to the special needs of pupils and students of Commonwealth origin' (Circular 72/86, Home Office, 1986).

Simply providing 'enhanced staffing' to schools with large numbers of pupils of NCWP origin was no longer to be permitted. This ruling had far-reaching effects on provision, as LEAs attempted to name, redeploy and reorganize staffing, in order to avoid losing grant funding, as this study will show in more detail.

In the past, posts for teachers of community languages were also regularly accepted for Section 11 funding. However, since 1986 the Home Office interpretation appears to have changed. Where community languages teaching was to be provided as mainstream modern languages options, open to all, more recently the Home Office has pointed out that these were not specifically targeted posts, and should therefore receive mainstream funding, a position that it is hard to dispute. However, without the substitution of another source of funding for new language posts, the development of this area of education may be constrained.

The deployment of Section 11 funded English language support teachers in the mainstream classroom, however, was not disputed by the Home Office, which appeared to have adopted the Swann Report recommendations as its baseline for evaluating proposals. Thus bilingual support in the classroom to give bilingual pupils equal access to the curriculum was also still open to funding even in the later age range, if a case could be made for its value in enhancing achievement.

The use of Section 11 across LEAs has always been something of a mystery. There were no official documents circulated to inform LEAs of the amounts that other LEAs were claiming, nor of the range of posts and their pay scales, that others were applying for and developing. Advisers interviewed seemed to rely on informal meetings and discussions with other officers for information, alongside a sort of rumoured 'case law' of what posts had been approved or rejected in other LEAs. However, HMI provided advice to LEAs, based on DES policy on 'good practice', and also made recommendations to the Home Office in support of bids.

An important feature of current extra provision for developing the curriculum to respond to bilingual pupils (whether ESG or Section 11) is that making bids was a voluntary exercise on the part of local authorities. LEAs had to submit proposals both to the DES and the Home Office for extra funding. Provision would seem likely, then, to depend greatly on (a) LEA commitment, willingness, and ability to allocate a percentage of funding from mainstream budgets; (b) LEA officers' knowledge of all the types of funding available, and skills in negotiating approval for bids; (c) the strength of bilingual community group pressure and ability to mobilize opinion and vocalize demands for specific types of provision. One would therefore expect wide variation within authorities in the overall amount and deployment of provision made. This expectation, as this book will show, is not altogether met.

The next section will look at the use and deployment of Section 11 in provision for bilingual pupils. The issue of the effects of specific 'special funding' on the movement to developing mainstream structures accessible to pupils from diverse linguistic backgrounds will be examined in more detail later in the book.

It is important, however, to clarify at this point the comparative magnitudes of specific section 11 funding and ESG mainstream curriculum development funding. ESG funding for 1988/9 was set at £125.5m, with £10m allocated for National Curriculum implementation, £4.8m for English in the Curriculum (mainstream) and just £2.7m for 'Education for a Multi-ethnic Society'. With most funding allocated to the development of the National Curriculum and new school management programmes in the near future, it seems essential that a bilingual perspective is included in these 'mainstream' programmes, not simply within the 'multiethnic' programmes which have limited funding available.

Funding to support the Welsh language (see Chapter 7) was £3m in 1988/9. The rate for Section 11 take up in 1988/9 was estimated to be £107m in grant funding, making an expenditure of £140m on Section 11 posts overall. In contrast to ESG funding, Section 11 funding had no official limits on allocation. *The impact and influence of this massive source of funding is therefore potentially crucial for current provision. Almost all language support teachers are in fact part of a Section 11 service operating within although not only accountable to the education service.*

One fear regarding the impact of the new Section 11 regulations is that the complexity of the administrative demands entailed in setting minority group provision in the context of mainstream education, which rightly require an overall LEA policy, may deter just those LEAs where commitment is lacking from developing provision. Others would argue that in such a context, extra provision is a negative influence anyway, merely providing a 'buffer' between minority needs and an unchanged educational system. Without extra staff and structures, this view would maintain, the mainstream system would be forced to consider its practices and adjust. This would, however, be a bleak prospect for many pupils currently at school.

The implementation of the National Curriculum and assessment procedures could offer an unprecedented opportunity for central direction of the curriculum and the resources needed to support it in favour of responding to multilingualism and bilingual educational needs. Whether existing national curriculum documents imply such a move will be examined briefly in the conclusion to this book.

Section 11 uptake

The figures from the 1987 survey clearly show that 85 per cent of *language support staffing for minority linguistic groups in England was supported by the Home Office through Section 11.* While the survey identified 2975 language support staff across the 77 responding LEAs, 2532 of these were Section 11 funded posts.

These language support posts were, therefore, explicitly targeted towards meeting the needs of a specific number of linguistic minority groups, those of NCWP family origin. Little mainstream funding was apparently being made to meet the needs of other linguistic minority groups, for whom there is no source of *extra* funding (except for Welsh within the borders of Wales). Paradoxically, any moves towards mainstream support for bilingual language development which required extra staff, must therefore have been taking place largely on the basis of extra and special funding based on a response to 'immigration' – a picture very little changed since Townsend's 1970 survey.

While figures indicate that a small number of language support staff (15 per cent) were not funded by Section 11 in 1987, these seem to be mainly the one or two 'ESL' staff in authorities making little provision for English support, for whom, presumably, Section 11 was not available (in consequence of low numbers of the population of NCWP origin).

There were also a few LEAs who 'topped up' the numbers of English language support staff with mainstream funding to permit the use of staff to work with pupils of other than Commonwealth origin (e.g. Vietnamese, Morroccan). These LEAs claimed Section 11 for just a percentage of each support staff member's time, basing the percentage on language survey figures for the various linguistic minority groups. For example, in one LEA with a very diverse linguistic population, Section 11 was claimed for just 58 per cent of each post; in another for just 83 per cent. In this way the LEA was enabled to continue to deploy its staff flexibly in the school among all bilingual pupils, while not flouting the 1986 Section 11 regulations. Manipulation of total numbers of posts claimed for was undertaken at LEA level, leaving schools free to deploy staff among bilingual pupils without regard to their specific ethnic minority group background.

However, most LEAs appeared not to make proportional claims. Few, if any, of the other LEAs appeared to restrict language support staff to working with pupils of NCWP origin only in any case, and no adviser interviewed suggested staff should be so limited, nor did Home Office officials or their HMI advisers.

From our data, Section 11 staff appeared to make up around 2 per cent of all teaching staff in England in 1987. The survey indicated that overall Section 11 provided for eight per cent of teaching posts in Greater London (4 per cent in the Outer London boroughs), 3 per cent in the metropolitan areas, and just 0.6 per cent in the counties.

Section 11 posts seem to be rarely separately identified in educational documentation. Most teacher/pupil ratio comparisons include staff in posts funded by the Home Office under Section 11 although these should be 'extra' to normal staffing. Overall pupil/teacher ratios for 1986/7 were: Greater London: 19.6 (primary), 13.8 (secondary); metropolitan: 21.8 (primary), 15.3 (secondary); and non-metropolitan: 22.5 (primary), 16.2 (secondary) (GB. DES, 1988d). Staffing levels overall across types of LEAs appear then to reflect the weighting of Section 11 funds, which appear to account for about half the difference between the three categories of LEAs.

Analysis of the distribution of all Section 11 teaching staff across LEAs confirmed that the numbers of Section 11 teachers in each LEA were significantly related ($p < 0.001$) to the size of its population of NCWP origin, according to 1981 census figures. This level of significance points to so clear a relationship between the distribution of Section 11 posts and the size of 'presence' of people of NCWP origin that it is hard not to conclude from the figures that, despite official Home Office policy, Section 11 staff are allocated so as to be proportional to NCWP population census figures.

(The relationship of numbers of Section 11 staffing to overall LEA population size (mid-1986) was statistically significant ($p < 0.02$) with larger LEAs having more section 11 staff than smaller LEAs, despite variation within groups of LEAs of the same overall size. However, a much closer statistical relationship ($p < 0.0004$) is found between Section 11 staffing and the grouped percentage of residents of NCWP origin (OPCS, Census 1981), despite wide variation within groups. This indicates a 'fair' distribution among LEAs if allocation is based simply on 'presence', despite the voluntary nature of Section 11 bids.)

Section 11 language provision

The survey indicates that, so far as the responding LEAs were aware, there was very little uptake of Section 11 outside education. Some posts that might be covered include Race Relations officers, race advisers to the Chief Executive; housing officers; social workers; translators and interpreters, all with special responsibility for people of 'Commonwealth origin'. However, only 123 such posts were identified by LEAs in the survey.

Section 11 in 1987 covered a wide range of multicultural advisory posts, curriculum development posts, home-school liaison posts, NNEBs and classroom assistants as well as language support staff. Multicultural advisers and inspectors, clerical staff, wardens and caretakers attached to multicultural centres seemed also to be funded by Section 11, as were local authority officers co-ordinating voluntary community classes, some FE provision, and even the officers with responsibility for making Section 11 bids. Under half of all Section 11 posts in LEAs were for language support.

The use of Section 11 to fund language posts again appeared to vary according to the percentage population of NCWP origin. In LEAs with a low percentage of population of NCWP origin, most Section 11 posts were for language support (75 per cent of all Section 11 posts). In areas with 'appreciable' and 'high' concentrations, less Section 11 posts were used for language support (41 per cent and 47 per cent respectively). Areas with 'moderate' percentages of the population of NCWP origin had their Section 11 service equally split between language support and other provision.

Uptake of Section 11 to fund language posts was generally high. The survey found that the LEAs responding which had no Section 11 language support staff were usually LEAs with just one or two language support teachers. Twenty-seven LEAs, 50 per cent of those responding who made provision for bilingual pupils, had *all* their language support posts Section 11 funded. A further 11 LEAs had over 90 per cent Section 11 funded. Just three LEAs had under 50 per cent of their language support posts funded by Section 11.

Different responses to Section 11 use appeared to be made in different categories of LEAs, as Table 2.2 illustrates.

Table 2.2: *Section 11 Language support posts as a % of all language support*

	Mean %
Greater London	75
Outer London	94
Metropolitan districts	95
Non-metropolitan districts	58
(Total LEAs: 67)	

Section 11 bids are voluntary, and LEAs may choose whether or not to submit a proposal for Section 11 funding, so there could be wide variations between LEAs with similar numbers of pupils with Commonwealth family origin. Also, Section 11 funding is now meant to be for specific identified needs relating to differences in 'language and culture', not simply to be drawn on according to 'presence' of large numbers of people of NCWP origin. However, there was a clear pattern shown in the survey data. LEAs with a population of NCWP origin below the national average as a group only received Section 11 funding for 45 per cent of their provision, in contrast with those with 'moderate' or 'appreciable' numbers, which received Section 11 funding for 91 per cent of language support posts, and LEAs with a 'high' concentration, which received funding for 94 per cent of their language posts.

It is important to note, however, that there was high variation between LEAs 'below national average NCWP population' and their use of Section 11 funding for language support staff. In contrast, there was very little variation in uptake between LEAs in the 'High' category. Political will and officer expertise in developing bids for Section 11 posts may be more crucial in areas with fewer pupils of NCWP family origin.

Using the data on percentage bilingual pupil population found in the 1987 survey, no statistically significant figure is found between the total number of Section 11 teaching posts and the percentage of bilingual pupils in each LEA. But a statistically significant relationship (< 0.005) is found between the number of Section 11 *language support* posts and the percentage of bilingual pupils within each LEA. The survey therefore indicated that while all Section 11 teaching posts appeared to be distributed more closely according to numbers of the target NCWP origin population, Section 11 language support posts appeared to be distributed according to the percentage of bilingual pupil population, which does not quite match that of NCWP origin, although the relationship is strong.

This suggests a not unfair distribution of staff among LEAs according to *presence* of bilingual pupils, although it gives no indication of whether it is a sensitive response to the identified *needs* of the bilingual pupil population. The strong overall relationship between language support provision and overall size of bilingual pupil population may, again, lead one to question whether provision is flexible, changing according to demand.

However, the data available cannot be used to examine whether provision is flexible. That would require the collection and comparison of data over time. Comparison with Townsend (1971) indicates that while there have been considerable changes in deployment (see later sections), overall numbers of language support staff were fairly constant in 1970 and 1987. Changes in higher scale posts and in responsibilities would not be recognized in these overall numbers of posts, which appear to have remained constant.

Community languages and Section 11

With 86 per cent of language support posts covering English language support, it is clear that most Section 11 funding is used to subsidize the employment of English language teachers. However, survey data showed it was also used to fund community languages posts. Section 11 was more often used to fund community languages teaching posts than posts for bilingual support for the curriculum in 1987. Indeed, few bilingual support posts seemed 'official'; there was a degree of uncertainty over how many teachers were involved and how they were funded, which probably confirms that few were Section 11 funded established posts, but more informal, even temporary arrangements.

Looking first at community languages teaching, 13 LEAs received Section 11 funding for all their community languages teachers (100 posts, both primary and secondary). Four LEAs funded all their community languages teaching posts themselves, just nine posts in all, from mainstream budgets. Three LEAs received Section 11 for the bulk of their more generous community languages teaching provision (83 teachers), while claiming to supplement these with a further 24 mainstream funded (mainly secondary) posts.

Turning to bilingual support, 10 LEAs received Section 11 funding for all their bilingual support posts (63 posts); three LEAs provided eight bilingual support posts from mainstream budgets and two LEAs supplemented nine Section 11 funded posts with eight mainstream funded posts. Four respondents had no information as to whether their bilingual support was Section 11 funded or not.

These results show that community languages teaching provision in 1987 was still largely supported by Section 11 funding, especially formal community languages teaching, while bilingual support, although heavily Section 11 funded, tended to be more 'ad hoc' in some LEAs.

There appeared to be considerable confusion among some LEAs over the new interpretation of Section 11 criteria, some LEAs indicating a belief that no Section 11 funding would be permitted for any type of bilingual support – a position which was not correct. Section 11 funding was still being granted for bilingual support for the curriculum where LEAs justified provision. The uncertainty over interpretation may have meant that some LEAs were deterred from making claims for such posts.

The effects of the withdrawal of Section 11 funding from secondary community languages options is likely to shift the picture radically in favour of more bilingual support posts being Section 11 funded, perhaps with community languages teaching posts being redesigned to incorporate bilingual curriculum support as well, to gain at least partial funding. In the present economic climate for schools, it is unlikely that many LEAs or schools will be able to support new posts themselves, unless the languages offered as modern languages are gradually replaced with the languages of the local communities. This latter scenario seems unlikely with the emphasis of the National Curriculum on EC languages, the 1992 Single European Act approaching, and economic reasons stressed for developing the languages of European Community partners. If community languages teaching posts are to be maintained and extended, some additional financial support to replace Section 11 funding seems necessary.

Section 11 advisory teachers

One hundred and eighty-seven Section 11 funded advisory teachers were identified in the 1987 survey. Of these, at least 26 per cent (49 advisory teachers) were themselves bilingual. This represents a higher proportion of bilingual staff than would be expected within the teaching force as a whole, but remains a minority of the management of Section 11 services.

These bilingual advisory teachers were to be found in small numbers in the non-metropolitan areas as well as in the metropolitan and London boroughs. The figures indicate the existence of a small core of bilingual specialist advisory teachers within LEAs. Not all of these were necessarily involved primarily in language support work, but their bilingual skills and in-service experience suggest a potentially useful role in reappraising school provision.

However, the mean numbers of all Section 11 advisory teachers (whether bilingual or not) were low, with an average of just five in outer London boroughs, three in metropolitan areas, and just one advisory teacher per non-metropolitan LEA on average. These figures indicate small career opportunities within 'Section 11 services' overall.

Section 11 – the case studies

In the six LEAs studied in depth, a variety of provision was found, the Section 11 'profiles' of each of the six LEAs being very different from one another. Differences in the take up of Section 11 funds varied widely; of three outer London boroughs visited, sums of £1m, £4m. and £7.5m. were said to be claimed annually. One Outer London borough had a ratio of 36 bilingual pupils to one Section 11 teacher, another 68 to one.

Nevertheless, all six LEAs visited claimed Section 11 funding for 100 per cent of their English language support ('ESL') provision. Five out of the six LEAs claimed Section 11 for the majority of their community language teaching and bilingual support provision as well. One LEA claimed for 100 per cent of its language support posts of all kinds.

Very few language support posts were not funded by Section 11. The only posts that were identified as mainstream funded across four LEAs were: one advisory community languages teacher, three community languages teachers employed by schools under their own capitation and one Italian primary community language teacher, ineligible for Section 11 funding.

In the sixth LEA, Section 11 funding for community languages teaching had been rejected as inappropriate by local community consultation prior to changes in Home Office interpretations: 'We want the language teachers in schools but we want them on mainstream rather than Section 11 funding' (LEA Committee papers, 1986). However, a decision had been made by this LEA during the study to apply for Section 11 funding for a number of bilingual support teachers and instructors – so in the future all six LEAs would be likely to be using Section 11 funding for at least some community languages teaching or bilingual support provision.

Other posts with Section 11 funding in the six LEAs studied included a number of bilingual special needs teacher posts (3 LEAs), focusing on diagnostic assessment but also on 'delivery of service' and monitoring of provision (one LEA); an educational psychologist (one LEA); multicultural and antiracist curriculum development in-service teams (four LEAs); Afro-Caribbean support and curriculum development teachers (two LEAs); bilingual learning support teachers ('remedial' provision) (two LEAs); home/school liaison teachers; bilingual and monolingual classroom assistants or 'helpers'; NNEBs; multicultural education advisers and an adviser for bilingualism. In one authority, the number of LEA advisers funded by Section 11 was doubled in 1986 to eight Section 11 advisers altogether. LEA officers identified as funded by Section 11 were, for example, supplementary school officers and bilingual information officers.

In three LEAs, the emphasis appeared to be shifting strongly away from individual support for pupils to a Section 11 role of monitoring effective delivery of the whole education service to pupils of Commonwealth family origin. Here structures for Section 11 postholders tended to be reorganized away from special services into more diffuse 'key' positions within mainstream structures, but with clearly defined job descriptions and specific duties, including monitoring the services they were involved with.

Thus in one LEA, some Section 11 postholders were placed as school advisers, responsible for implementing whole school strategies for equal opportunities; others as curriculum advisers, developing policy across a horizontal cross-curriculum advisory structure. In another LEA, a Section 11 educational psychologist and a special needs advisory teacher were part-time Section 11, part-time mainstream team based, to avoid 'marginalization'. In a third LEA, a new team of Section 11 staff was being set up, replacing a multicultural curriculum development team, to work alongside advisers 'to guide overall policy; maintain consistency and co-ordination; ensure accountability and evaluation; assist in appointing staff and manage them, and allocate them to schools and teams'. Other Section 11 team staff would be based in schools 'to assist...senior management in the implementation of race equality strategies'. The 1976 Race Relations Act had been used in all of these three LEAs in the positive recruitment of Black staff, some from specific linguistic minority groups, for a range of Section 11 and mainstream posts within the authorities.

Two of the LEAs reported concern that Section 11 funding was not eligible for staff undertaking training, as there were problems in recruiting sufficient qualified staff in these LEAs. However, Home Office Circular 72/86 does state (para. 22) that while not usually granted for trainees, Section 11 may be applicable 'where the Secretary of State decides from time to time that a particular need exists for training for members of the Commonwealth community'. At the time of the survey, it was understood that the Secretary of State had not yet made such a decision regarding the training of teachers.

The case studies indicated what appears to be a wider, more national division between LEAs with clearly identified, separate Section 11 services, and LEAs that are moving towards placing Section 11 service postholders into mainstream structures, but with well defined roles and responsibilities, and an alternative line management structure. Where for one group the Section 11 service was seen as specifically for Black and/or bilingual pupils, for the other group of LEAs it was seen, at least in part, as central to reappraising and restructuring the whole education service to provide equal access and opportunities.

The developing use of Section 11 postholders as 'change agents' is an interesting strategy. However, in the three LEAs focusing on institutional change above, the strategy was recognized to require new skills and additional staffing. In other LEAs there were indications that existing 'ESL' teams were being retitled 'multicultural services' with very little change in either staffing or retraining programmes. It may be less realistic to expect these teachers to become 'change agents', but this appeared to be the expectation in two LEAs visited. Again, this reflected a shift away from a language focus to new multicultural education curriculum posts, but with rather a different perspective from those LEAs attempting to reorganize mainstream structures.

There was clearly concern in three LEAs studied which were involved in secondary community languages provision, that the new Section 11 interpretations would impede the expansion of their languages teaching services. It was understood that Section 11 funding would not be removed from existing posts, but it was unclear for how long these would be secure. However, with new posts unlikely to be funded as secondary option choices by the Home Office, one LEA had made a bid instead for a number of 'ESL/Urdu' posts, justifying these as necessary for access to the curriculum and pastoral/social reasons in schools with numbers of pupils more recently arrived in the UK. Another LEA had shifted its focus for new provision downwards to enlarging bilingual support in middle schools, still allowing for some community languages teaching on the timetable.

The experience of another LEA, which had never claimed Section 11 for community languages teaching at secondary level, was not encouraging, as very few schools there had responded to LEA encouragement to employ their own community languages teachers within modern languages departments. (This issue will be returned to in the section on community languages teaching.)

Few LEAs appeared to be responding to Home Office suggestions that secondments or detached duty posts might be made for teachers to work within community organization teaching networks for after school provision. The main problem here appeared to be concern about redundancy payments, should funding later be withdrawn. Nor was any evidence seen of LEAs 'sharing' Section 11 posts to meet the needs of 'smaller' minority groups, such as Chinese speakers, as recommended by the Home Office (1986) (72/86).

There was some evidence that Section 11 funding was being refused for in-service training posts for RSA Diploma tutors for the course in English across the curriculum in multilingual schools, on the grounds that these should be mainstream funded since not specifically to meet the needs of the population of Commonwealth origin. Other reasons for refusal of posts were based on the lack of a coherent overall LEA policy and structure for Section 11 use, or the lack of community consultation before bids were submitted.

Section 11 job descriptions and Section 11 abuse

Although all Section 11 postholders were required by the Home Office to have clear job descriptions, in the NFER study a number of teachers listed as Section 11 by their LEAs had never seen their job descriptions. Most staff appeared to know that their post was funded under Section 11, but fewer understood what this meant for them in practice. One Section 11 teacher, deployed as a classteacher, commented: 'No one's specifically Section 11 – we feel we've gone beyond that, we're all responsible. I'm 'named', but I don't hold any special responsibility.' The bilingual instructor at the same school, also funded under Section 11 had never been told of her status, nor seen a job description. Other Section 11 postholders knew they were 'named' but had seen no job descriptions.

This was the most extreme example indentified. In four of the other schools visited, Section 11 postholders were English language support staff from central language support teams, and thus clearly 'extra to normal staffing'. Not all, however, had seen a Section 11 job description. In the sixth school, the English language support staff had recently been informed of their Section 11 status, and were to receive in-service on the nature of the requirements of their role.

LEA monitoring of the role and effectiveness of Section 11 staff was mainly carried out informally by the responsible advisers except where staff belonged to a central team. Where there was a team structure, 'heads' of services appeared to collect information on the number of pupils each teacher worked with, and, in the case of language support, the number of hours spent in-class compared to withdrawal. Examination entries and results were the sort of data collected by the community languages co-ordinator. Details on language background were collected by some service heads, while another LEA collected data on pupils supported in terms of whether of 'Commonwealth' or 'Non-Commonwealth' origin, with a special section on work with pupils of 'Caribbean origin' – teachers being required to state the percentage of teaching time spent on both those of 'Commonwealth' and 'Non-Commonwealth' origin.

The alternative 'special service' or 'mainstream' change perspectives on the use of Section 11 funding can be seen in LEA responses to the use of Section 11. One LEA had since 1983 provided all the (Scale 2) teachers in the 'ESL Service' with the same job description, listing 22 separate points, including duties out of school hours, staff development responsibilities, responsibility for the promotion of multicultural education, and responsibility for curriculum development in at least one other area than 'ESL'. This LEA required teachers to account for the time spent with specific groups of pupils, and to sign these returns as accurate. Another LEA, in contrast, attempted to balance an educational concern for language provision to be made, irrespective of pupils' background, in the mainstream by supporting teachers, with its need for extra funding which was limited to a specific group. Its job description for language support teachers was addressed to the Home Office rather than the teachers:

> The teachers who are teaching English as a second language
> are an addition to the staffing allocation of schools so that
> staff throughout the school can pay more attention to the
> linguistic and other academic needs of ethnic minority children
> in particular, but their specialist function still remains that
> of teaching, or advising on the teaching of, English as a
> second language in particular and multicultural education in
> general.

Since 1986, a few LEAs have avoided the necessity under the new Section 11 criteria of 'targeting' their language support provision *solely* at pupils of NCWP family origin where pupils from other minority ethnic groups are present in schools, by claiming for just a percentage of each post based on the percentage of pupils of NCWP origin within the total bilingual population. However, the NFER study came across no cases where this had led to a drop in claims for Section 11 funding. Nor did the removal of funding for 'enhanced staffing' create a drop in the amount claimed. It appeared that posts or percentages of posts were created in order to maintain the level of funding.

Whether enhanced generalist staffing should be Section 11 funded or not has been subject of continued debate since the 1970s. However, in the 1986 criteria such use was no longer acceptable. There was some evidence from two authorities which suggested that understaffed Section 11 services were being used by some LEAs as a means of redeploying staff who would otherwise have been made redundant as part of 'rate-capping' exercises. This indicated that rather than developing an overall strategy to meet specific educational needs, and recruiting staff with the most appropriate skills to meet them, Section 11 funding was being diverted in those LEAs to manage an immediate financial crisis.

Section 11 reviews

The review of posts which had begun in 1983 had raised issues in most authorities which were likely to change the nature of

Section 11 use. Some authorities in developing consultation with local community groups found strong reactions to the use of Section 11 at all. One community group reported of Section 11:

> It segregated us as special people with special problems in
> need of special treatment backed up by special funding. Except
> we were not even aware of the existence of the section
> and what it stood for. In our judgement it is a racist Act
> (Indian Workers Association, 1987).

Local authorities themselves sometimes took on this perspective in writing consultative briefing papers for their local communities. One paper (dated 1986) for a consultative meeting on the use of Section 11 funds from a local authority not known for a radical approach to local government, stated:

> [Section 11] funding was used by boroughs all over the country
> to subsidise the employment of ESL teachers, so the problem-
> centred view of ethnic minority pupils was institutionalised.
> Separate provision was seen to be necessary, rather than an
> integrated approach from within the education system.
> In retrospect, this thinking can be seen as an example of
> institutional racism, although at the time it was thought of
> as 'positive discrimination'.

However, most authorities, including that quoted above, recognized a continuing need for some source of extra funding. A different LEA explained its continuing use of Section 11 in an open document in this way:

> The long term objective is to provide for the differing needs
> of the various communities within the borough within its
> overall service provision and to fund them by the normal
> funding sources. . . However, in order to develop or tailor
> services as comprehensively as possible, at a time of severe
> financial restraint, it must look to outside help.

Section 11 provided that help.

It was clear that for most authorities, and for the community groups consulted where their reports were also received, the need for extra funding to bring about changes in schools was strongly recognized. In these circumstances, however, it sometimes appeared as if Section 11 restrictions were the starting point for some LEAs' identification of needs:

> In view of the shortfall in funding between current expenditure
> and estimated costs of the proposed service, priority would
> be given to identifying posts for which some Section 11
> funding would be appropriate, and preparing applications for
> that funding.

Despite being a source of specific funding, then, the 1986 review documents suggest that Section 11 has been seen as essential funding for bringing about change in schools in recognition of changing perceptions of society, and the need to provide equality of access to the curriculum.

Six LEAs sent 1986 Section 11 review papers in answer to our request for documentation on the monitoring of Section 11 provision. One document listed the concerns of Section 11 postholders about the funding. These included the 'marginalization' of pupils and teachers where their work was not seen as an integral part of the school as a whole. There was concern that Section 11 funding identified one section of the community as a 'problem', and implied the LEA did not have a responsibility to meet the needs of the whole community. There was also concern about promotion and career prospects within a 'Section 11 service'. On the other hand, there was a recognition that safeguards had to be made to ensure the needs of bilingual pupils were met, and that pupils were not absorbed into 'special needs' structures, for example. Section 11, it was thought, might play a continuing role in curriculum development and in-service training in the field of antiracist education, providing a context in which language needs could be met within the mainstream.

One of the most important outcomes of the Section 11 review appeared to be the impetus for some authorities to bring together in one document a full description of all the posts for which Section 11 funding was claimed for in the authority. Scattered provision, made over a number of years, from differing ideological perspectives in some cases, could be seen as a whole, for reappraisal. Where these documents were put before community representatives, who often learnt about the existence of many of the posts for the first time, there was added impetus to make changes in the service.

One LEA Review Committee whose Section 11 service included a large 'ESL' team, reported back after consultation that while it recognized a continuing need for English language support teachers, it 'recommends that such specialist teachers should operate within a whole school policy recognizing English as a second language needs, and that the existence and monitoring of such a policy should be one of the factors considered in the deployment of Section 11 staff to multiracial schools.' There was commitment to 'changing the role' of the original Section 11 teachers 'from exclusive concern with English as a second language teaching in small withdrawal groups to support for the classroom teacher in developing their skills and to promoting multicultural and antiracist ideas throughout the schools' curriculum and organization.'

A frequent theme was the necessity to employ Black staff, who were seen as under-represented in the education service. Black representatives were called for at all levels, intervening across the service from monitoring the service to sitting on interviewing panels. Bilingual staff were thought to be needed not only for the teaching of community languages, but within the mainstream curriculum.

Overall, the emphasis on Section 11 posts was to see these staff as 'change agents', one LEA suggesting their role should be 'to influence the way in which teaching is provided and what is taught over the whole curriculum'.

Monitoring and consultation

The new Section 11 Criteria (Home Office Circular, 72/1986) stated: 'It is essential that local authorities should, if they are to meet special needs properly, set clear objectives for their posts and that they should monitor their effectiveness in meeting those objectives.' All new posts were to be monitored and regularly reviewed, and all posts established before 1986 were to be brought within the review system set up by each authority as soon as possible.

By 1987, little progress appeared to have been made in establishing actual structures for monitoring the effectiveness of Section 11 posts. Of those LEAs responding to the NFER survey who received Section 11 funding, as many as ten LEAs had no documentation at all relating to Section 11 monitoring. Fourteen LEAs replied that they were in the process of making plans for such monitoring, one commenting 'but it is problematic'. Twenty-three LEAs sent documentation or wrote notes on new procedures.

Only two of these LEAs confirmed that their procedures were already 'accepted' by the Home Office. One of these described the procedure as consultation via the local Community Relations Council (CRC), with a monitoring system previously negotiated with school heads, based on the job descriptions drawn up for each post. This model, which was the most common one described by LEAs, appeared to rest on the Section 11 postholder's self-appraisal in terms of the job descriptions, with a regular report made to the school head or head of service. This self-appraisal would in some cases be placed in the context of the mainstream school appraisal systems being set up by authorities, so that the head and advisers would jointly negotiate an annual report to the consultative committee.

One LEA used the monitoring requirement to ask schools to draw up 'contracts' with the Section 11 service. This involved reappraising the needs of the whole school, and in negotiation with the service 'management team', deciding on the roles of the extra staff required. Schools would then make bids to the Section 11 service, and have a temporary contract drawn up, which included details of the ways in which the school *itself* would review and assess its needs.

The major impact of the change in funding on the role of Section 11 teachers would appear to be a new emphasis in their work on monitoring, while at the same time having their own work monitored. Depending on the position their authorities adopted, there may be either more emphasis on monitoring the work of individual pupils in order to provide individual support, or more emphasis upon monitoring the delivery of the curriculum by the whole school on linguistic minority pupils' progress, in order to support staff in creating new strategies.

In the context of the new National Curriculum assessment procedures for all pupils, it would seem that the responsibility for the first type of individual monitoring must rest with the mainstream class and subject teacher, and that, therefore, the trend towards extra funding being used to monitor school processes for their effects on minority ethnic group pupils should continue, if Section 11 funding remains available.

Overall, the responses to Section 11 monitoring indicated that the two co-existing perspectives within current educational practice identified earlier in this book, between an 'individual, problem orientated' perspective and a 'whole school change' focus, were also played out within responses to Section 11. Where job descriptions were related to special and specific needs, they were being monitored with reference to records of pupils numbers, and drawn up by agreement with a specific 'ethnic minority' consultative group. However, where the wider perspective was taken, the need for a whole classroom change perspective at the school level appeared to be matched by LEA structural reappraisal at the administrative level, raising questions about how agendas were being set; about democratic participation in decision making at local authority level; and about accountability.

Thus for some LEAs (13), the priority for Section 11 funding appeared to remain as special provision in terms of extra staff to meet the 'special needs' of ethnic minority pupils; with, for at least one LEA, effectiveness measured by 'total integration without any additional support'. There was to be no apparent reappraisal of the mainstream. However, eight other LEAs were attempting to readdress Section 11 needs within a mainstream system which took cultural and linguistic diversity as a classroom norm, while attempting to identify and remove structural barriers to equal opportunities. There were indications in some of these documents that review might lead to more temporary Section 11 posts in future, related to specific short-term curriculum development projects, and more 'part-funding' of posts by Section 11 together with mainstream budgets in order to prevent 'marginalization'. The main thrust of these documents focused on ways to start to develop consultative procedures which allow for genuine participation by a wider range of minority ethnic group representatives, and for the power to influence provision.

Summary

This chapter has attempted to clarify the nature of extra funding to support LEAs in making provision for bilingual pupils. It has revealed the extent of the influence of Home Office Section 11 funding, which has led LEAs to emphasize the appointment of considerable numbers of extra staff, but which had, until recently, provided little direction for such staffing, nor demanded any clear overall policy from LEAs on how such staffing could most effectively be deployed. It has suggested that recent changes in the funding criteria would have far-reaching effects on the LEAs making use of Section 11 funding, effects that will be illustrated in later chapters.

The responses to the survey indicated uncertainty over the future use of section 11; *with a consensus that some form of extra funding was required if the needs of minority ethnic groups, however defined, were to be adequately met within the education system.* It was also suggested that although minority ethnic group perspectives had begun to make an impact on the ways in which provision for bilingual pupils was being perceived and defined, there was as yet little encouragement of participation by those groups in active decision making and policy formation.

3 English Language Support

The background

In this chapter we will look at policy for English language support in 1985–7, and the ways in which the extra teachers for English language support identified in the last chapter were actually being deployed in schools.

The Swann Report (GB. DES, 1985) both reflected thinking among educationalists and legitimated the approaches that were tentatively being developed in schools: approaches which emphasized non-exclusion, and the redefinition of existing norms of language assessment. As discussed in the introduction to this book, Swann did not question the importance of the acquisition of English as a second language in the school system, but was concerned to place language learning within the wider context of access to learning across the curriculum. At local authority level, too, language issues in 1985–7 were being recontextualized within the wider educational issues of 'the extension of equal opportunities and...the raising of the level of educational achievement' (ILEA, 1986).

Alongside a stress on educational achievement, there was a growing emphasis on not seeing English development in isolation, but as part of the development of bilingualism. But while some effort was being put into recruiting teachers of the languages of minority ethnic groups in a number of LEAs, advisers stressed their continuing recognition of the importance of each child's access to English.

A 1986 advisers' action plan stated:

> We continue to develop the nature of language support work. Whereas in the past there was an emphasis on 'withdrawal' work, we are now moving towards minimising that type of provision and shifting towards offering English language support

within the mainstream wherever possible.

This passage contains two key words in English language provision in the mid-1980s, 'mainstream' and 'withdrawal'. Debate has at times raged so fiercely over the *location* of extra English language support for pupils, that its content and procedures have seemed scarcely examined (Ellis, 1985, pp. 12–18). Yet the argument about where bilingual pupils who were still at an early stage in learning English should be placed is in essence an argument about pupils' rights to a full curriculum and continuity in education.

In 1986, the Commission for Racial Equality (CRE) in its report on 'Teaching English as a Second Language' had found that in Calderdale LEA, provision for 'ESL' had been discriminatory in effect. The CRE asked the Secretary of State to take action, including the recommendation to the Home Office for a cessation of Section 11 funding for similar provision. The effect of this report was to focus attention on details of 'ESL' provision previously often overlooked, including the effects of losing school time by 'bussing', lack of continuity in education, lack of parental choice of school, lack of parental involvement in electing the governing bodies of centres as opposed to schools, a narrowing of the curriculum open to children receiving special language teaching, and criteria for testing some children and not others.

While the immediate effect of the report was concentrated on the phasing out of Language Centres, where these still existed, there were many elements that might also be used to reappraise separate language units within schools, and to open up questions about how pupils are selected and grouped for special language teaching – its timetabling, content and duration.

It is clear that the CRE report put 'ESL' provision on the political agendas of a number of LEAs, either hastening reorganization, or beginning a reappraisal. Politicians in one LEA studied called for advisers' reports on 18 items relating to the language needs of ethnic minority children. It should also be noted that Calderdale authority itself had already approved a move to a Swann-type mainstream support model in principle. The argument was not over principle, which seemed generally agreed, but the physical arrangements made for, and the speed of, the change. Since Calderdale, the debate over the continuing use of Language Centres has more or less ceased. Centres were no longer thought to be an effective form of provision except within a few authorities, most of whom were actively reappraising their provision.

The Calderdale Report does not close the question of the location of the bilingual pupils still in the process of learning English. While it strongly supports the placement of these pupils in mainstream schools, it leaves open to discussion the possibility of *extending the range of types of mainstream schools available.* It is open to us in principle to conceive of the possibility of schools offering bilingual education, open to all who choose to enter them, teaching a full curriculum in the medium of at least one other language in addition to English, either completely separate from or attached to an English medium school, perhaps on the Welsh model (see Chapter 7). The nature of the English language provision which would be appropriate in such a bilingual institution has, again, received little attention in current discussion.

However, in this chapter the focus will be on the nature of English language support within the mainstream English medium school, since that is the provision currently available to bilingual pupils in state schools in England.

Projects which had been influential in developing language support at the time of the NFER study had gradually developed models of practice which were based on temporary and flexible groups of children from a variety of linguistic backgrounds working on collaborative problem solving activities in a number of curriculum areas. They attempted to offer pupils access to the language of the curriculum both through participation in peer discussion and through carefully structured models for recording activities, leading to continuous written prose where appropriate. Examples can be found in the videos and materials developed by the Schools Council Project 'Language in the Multicultural Primary Classroom'; and the ILEA projects: 'Second Language Learners in the Mainstream' and 'Bilingual Learners in the Secondary School'.

The main principles of these approaches can be briefly analysed as follows:

(a)   Learning is best achieved through enquiry-based activities involving discussion.

(b)   To learn a language it is necessary to participate in its meaningful use.

(c)   The curriculum itself is therefore a useful vehicle for language learning.

(d)   Some curriculum subjects are structured in such a way that they themselves give support to children learning English (e.g. through the patterning of certain activities and thus of certain linguistic structures).

(e)   A main strategy then for both curriculum learning and language learning is the flexible use of small group work.

(f)   This way of working allows also for the development of bilingual children's other languages if encouragement is given for their use in curriculum areas where there are other children who are speakers of the same languages, and especially if a bilingual teacher sharing the same languages is also present.

(g)   By starting from encouraging children to apply their personal and already acquired knowledge to solving group problems, and from observing their efforts in a collaborative situation, to identify and provide any support that might be needed by individual children to acquire curriculum concepts and the languages needed to express them.

It is clear that these models did not suggest that pupils should simply be incorporated into mainstream classrooms, but that mainstream classes needed to be carefully reorganized to meet a range of linguistic backgrounds and needs. The strategies offered for co-operative peer group learning could be developed by class teachers alone, as well as by those working within team teaching structures.

Through the development of these approaches, English as a second language learning has come to be perceived as part of a continuum of language development, not in itself a very different process from extending the repertoires of a first language across an increasingly differentiated range of domains. In this way, it has become possible to incorporate English as a second language learners into a mainstream classroom, as long as it is organized so as to operate along the same principles. Unlike the Bullock Report (1975) which had to accept a very different teaching strategy for 'ESL' based on the different language learning theories for mother tongue and second language acquisition current at that time, Swann (1985) was able to return English language learners to the mainstream classroom.

However, it must be recognized that many classrooms were not already operating on the lines suggested by Swann (Galton, et al., 1980; Delamont, et al., 1986; Mortimore, et al., 1986; 'Better Schools', 1985.) It is here that a new role for the English language support teacher, no longer required in the 'ESL' class, was perceived by some LEAs. This emphasizes classroom organization strategies and a role in helping to support whole school change.

The ready availability of Section 11 funding for English language support posts and the already existing pool of English language support teachers have tended to lead to an expectation that English language support in the mainstream will centrally include extra staffing, rather than require expenditure on inservice for mainstream teachers, materials development, or research into classroom management strategies. By far the greatest emphasis has been laid on the development of roles for the English language support teachers, extra to staffing in mainstream schools.

Definitions of mainstream English and bilingual support teaching

In order to clarify the description of provision and practice which follows it is necessary to distinguish between two models of in-class support teaching as it has developed in practice. These models apply equally to bilingual support teaching in the mainstream.

The first is focused on the individual child, the second focuses on the whole curriculum (Hart, 1986). In taking the first, individual-oriented approach, language support teachers confine themselves to making changes in the presentation of the mainstream curriculum and in the tasks required on an individual basis. Their aim is to make sure that the bilingual children they are working with are able to gain access to the curriculum by receiving teaching and support appropriate to their particular needs. In this approach, in consultation with the class teacher, the language support teacher provides whatever additional or adapted materials or arrangements may be needed by each bilingual child, e.g. simplified worksheets, 'pre-teaching' in withdrawal periods, 'post-teaching' periods for consolidation work, or special homework.

In the second, whole curriculum-focused, approach, the language support teacher takes part in planning for and teaching the whole class, helping the classroom teachers to adapt their classroom practices to take account of the diversity of language and learning needs in the class, for example through the appraisal of the accessibility of worksheets, through setting up opportunities for flexible groupings for learning through talk and discussion (in English or other shared languages), through the provision of problem solving activities, and by the provision of models of written language, so that all children in the class can participate fully. This method of enquiry based learning and group work is, in fact, that which is recommended for all pupils by the Hargreaves and Thomas Reports (ILEA, 1984, 1985).

'Mainstream' language support teaching could then, refer to either of the two very different approaches referred to above, focusing only on identified individuals, or on the whole class. This will be seen more clearly in the descriptions of practice.

Having very briefly sketched the policy for English language support in the period 1985–87, the next section will examine provision as revealed in the study during the same period, and go on to look at how far in-service training provision has been made to support policy.

Staffing and organization

English language support staff in schools

In analysing the survey, the term 'English language support' teacher is taken to be a general term to cover all teachers 'extra' to normal staffing in schools or centres in posts which were aimed at teaching English and/or supporting the learning through English of bilingual pupils, regardless of the location or particular way in which these teachers worked.

The 1987 NFER survey identified 2551 English language support teachers working in schools in England across the 72 English LEAs responding to the survey. *English language support teachers formed 86 per cent of all language support staff made available for bilingual pupils (including both bilingual support staff and community languages teachers).* Just 10 LEAs had no English language support staff.

Four out of five Welsh LEAs which responded to the survey also made provision for English language support staff, employing a total of 27 teachers in such posts.

There was a wide distribution of numbers of English support teachers across LEAs in England. The biggest teams were based in Greater London and the metropolitan areas, with smaller numbers found in the shires. The majority of LEAs (55) had under 50 teachers for English language support, with just eight London LEAs, six metropolitan LEAs and one shire having over 50 teachers.

Since English language support staff made up 86 per cent of language support staff, and language support staff were found to be largely Home Office funded under Section 11, most of the results of the analysis in Chapter 3 on the location of Section 11 staff is also applicable to English language support staff.

Fifty-five per cent of English support staff were deployed in primary schools, 31 per cent in secondary schools; while 14 per cent of those identified taught unspecified ages or worked in cross-phase teams. These included small peripatetic teams and centre-based staff and also peripatetic 'ESL' support in LEAs with low numbers of bilingual pupils – often with only one or two 'ESL' teachers.

The ILEA employed around a quarter of all the primary and cross-age phase teachers identified, and almost a third of all the secondary teachers. While at the primary level Outer London boroughs tended to have on average similar numbers of teachers to the metropolitan areas, at secondary level Outer London appeared to employ more staff. When the comparative average size of the two categories is considered, this implies a heavier commitment to secondary English language support from the Outer London boroughs. This difference may have some influence on the way in which English support is organized in schools in the different types of LEAs, as suggested later in this section.

Cross-phase teams appeared to be more common in the non-metropolitan LEAs (15), but 41 LEAs altogether referred to combined teams, some in addition to teachers located in primary or secondary schools.

The organization of English language support

Through the NFER survey, it was possible to build up a picture of policy across the country towards English support provision, based on LEA respondents' descriptions of organizational strategies, policies, training and future plans. LEAs were asked to identify the types of organizational strategies they adopted for English language provision from seven categories provided on the questionnaire. These were: (a) No special arrangements; (b) full-time language centres not located in schools; (c) part-time language centres not located in schools; (d) full-time language classes in pupils' own schools; (e) part-time language classes in pupils' own schools; (f) language support within mainstream curriculum areas; (g) other arrangements.

The forms of organization listed were drawn from past research (Townsend, 1971; Little and Willey, 1981; Young and Connelly, 1981) and checked by visits to a number of LEAs, with discussions there of current practice. There was space offered for LEAs to add other types of provision, but few made use of this. There were also open ended questions on changes in policy and provision over the past five years, and on future plans, which offered LEAs space to give more detail on the forms of provision made. These will be summarized in this chapter.

Townsend's (1971) survey took place before local authority boundaries were reorganized, and therefore data in that survey is not directly comparable to the 1987 survey, there being 146 English LEAs in 1970 compared to 97 LEAs in 1987. The results of the 1970 survey show, however, that the most common form of provision at that time was part-time classes in pupils' own schools (105 LEAs [primary]; 61 LEAs [secondary]). Full-time language centre provision was less often found (18 LEAs [primary]; 17 LEAs [secondary]). More LEAs provided full-time English language classes in pupils' own schools or part-time centres (around 30 LEAs claimed each form of provision).

Although extra staffing for mainstream support for English is a comparatively new category and was not included in Townsend's survey, it should be noted that making no special arrangements at all for bilingual pupils is not new. Sixteen LEAs in 1970 made no arrangements for primary aged children, some commenting that young children 'pick up' a second language without any support (Townsend, 1971: p. 38), although providing for older children. It was also customary, as Townsend showed, prior to the changes in Section 11 criteria, to employ staff additional to normal school establishment in order to lower teacher-pupil ratios in mainstream classrooms. *It is important to note this possible continuity with provision in 1987, and to be cautious about assuming that all LEAs and schools which claim to provide mainstream classroom support mean any form of reorganized provision* (such as co-operative teaching, collaborative group learning strategies, 'specialist' linguistic input into curriculum development). It is possible that they might simply mean an 'extra pair of hands', to provide a lower teacher–pupil ratio. There are no clearly agreed definitions of practice, although later in this chapter material from the six more in-depth studies of LEAs will attempt to reach a clearer picture of what is entailed in the categories.

Table 3.1 shows the findings of the survey. 'Other arrangements' mentioned were the use of a small number of peripatetic teachers (three LEAs); the use of home tutors (one LEA); and in one London LEA, a main thrust towards advisory support and INSET for the whole school, rather than in-class support.

The survey found that 80 per cent of respondents making some provision for English support for pupils at a 'first' stage of learning English provided support within the mainstream primary curriculum. However, 51 per cent of respondents still provided part-time language classes, with many offering both forms of provision even at primary level.

Compared to the primary sector, the results indicate that the secondary sector is moving more slowly towards language support in the mainstream.

Townsend (1971) noted concern over provision for those pupils requiring 'second stage' English support; that is, those with enough English to 'get by', but who were perceived as underachieving academically. Little and Willey (1981) noted in their survey that pupils at 'more advanced stages' of learning English were still 'receiving less than their due share of attention'. Little and Willey commented of headteachers' responses: 'Priority was repeatedly given...to the need for new initiatives in the more advanced stages of 'E2L' provision' (p. 18). In the 1987 Survey, then, LEAs were asked what organizational strategies were being made for the support of bilingual pupils at a 'first', 'second' and 'third' stage of learning English.

Three LEAs queried the absence of any definition of these 'stages' in the 1987 questionnaire; however the majority of LEAs felt able to work with them.

The fact is that there are no precise definitions of the 'stages' although they have had a general currency as form of a 'folk' assessment. The ILEA defined 'second stage' and 'third stage' proficiency as follows in 1985:

> Second Stage Learners: These pupils have become quite fluent in spoken English but still make non-native errors. Their command of vocabulary and syntax is uneven and this makes many areas of school learning much harder for them than for their English speaking peers.

Table 3.1: *Organizational arrangements for supporting pupils learning English as a second language in 1987*

	Primary (5–11 years) learner level			Secondary (11–16 years) learner level		
	1st stage	2nd stage	3rd stage	1st stage	2nd stage	3rd stage
(a) Full-time Language Centres not located in schools	3	–	–	10	2	–
(b) Part-time Language Centres not located in schools	5	–	–	7	2	1
(c) Full-time language classes in pupils' own schools	5	5	2	8	3	1
(d) Part-time language classes in pupils' own schools	33	22	13	42	27	13
(e) Language support within mainstream curriculum	52	48	40	42	42	34
(f) Other arrangements	5	1	1	3	3	3

(Total Responses: 65 LEAs)

Third Stage Learners: Their spoken and written English shows few signs of non-native use, but pupils lack the full language range of native speakers of English of the same age and ability. 3rd Stage learners tend to achieve below their potential in subjects like English and History where language experience is important (ILEA, 1985 Language Census: p. 2).

According to the ILEA 1985 Census, 'second' and 'third stage' learners accounted for 23 per cent each of all bilingual pupils in Inner London, compared to just 17 per cent of '1st stage' learners. The remainder were fluent English speakers.

While a few other LEAs include questions about English proficiency in their language surveys, the use of such data is problematic: first because the categorizations are very subjective (Rampton, 1987); and secondly because where the data collected is used to direct resources to schools, there may be a tendency to exaggerate pupil difficulties, rather than focusing positively on their achievements. It is clear that few LEAs were in a position to respond with any clarity on the English language needs of bilingual pupils. Without adequate assessment procedures it would be hard to justify separate provision for English as a second language learners (CRE, 1986).

If Swann's position is taken, all teachers would be required to take much more responsibility for language needs within their own classes. It was therefore of interest to see if extra English provision was seen by LEAs in 1987 to be involved with greater numbers of pupils now than initial 'ESL' had been. This would seem to have implications either for staffing levels (if the focus was on 'individual support') or for specialist training programmes (if the focus was on providing advisory support and INSET for school staffs through extra staffing).

Space on the 1987 questionnaire was left for respondents to comment on the form itself. The majority of respondents seemed able to use it as it stood. However, one commented that 'we seem to have moved quite a long way away from what seem to be the main assumptions of your questionnaire'. This LEA wrote:

The main focus of support is for the school and class (or subject) teacher, to enable the better development of the notion of teaching and learning in a multilingual school. Initiatives drawn from an underlying antiracist analysis form a foundation for support to become an essential part of mainstream teaching.

While not stated elsewhere explicitly, it seems likely that there were other LEAs who used their language service in this advisory and mainstream in-service role as well (Harper, 1987). However, few services, including that of the respondent quoted, confined themselves only to a non-teaching advisory role.

Table 3.2: *Distribution of strategies for English language support*

	f/t centres		p/t centres		f/t classes		p/t classes		main-stream	
	Pri	Sec	Pri	Sec	Pri	Sec	Pri	Sec	Pri	Sec
'1st Stage' Organizational Strategies										
London	–	3	1	3	–	–	12	14	17	16
Metropolitan	3	5	3	1	4	6	9	13	19	13
Non-Metropolitan	–	1	1	3	1	–	11	14	14	11
Wales	–	–	–	–	–	–	1	1	2	2
'3rd Stage' Organizational Strategies										
London	–	–	–	–	–	–	2	4	13	15
Metropolitan	–	1	–	1	1	1	5	4	15	9
Non-Metropolitan	–	–	–	–	1	–	5	4	10	8
Wales	–	–	–	–	–	–	1	1	2	2

From Table 3.2 it seems clear that mainstream working has created a new 'client group', the '3rd stage learner', in all categories of LEAs. As far as support for '3rd stage' learners of English is concerned, responses from both secondary and primary sectors appear to indicate that not all LEAs feel they are able to provide any form of extra support. This seems to suggest that 'in-class support' for some LEAs is still seen to mainly consist of 'ESL' teachers working with *individual* pupils in classes, with a consequent limit on the number of pupils they are able to offer support to. LEAs developing whole class and curriculum support would be more confident in saying that they did also support '3rd stage' learners.

Only six English LEAs (four metropolitan, two shires) carried out *no* mainstream work in English language support. One of these based all its eight 'ESL' staff (Section 11 funded) in a language centre for primary and secondary aged pupils. No other English support provision was made. Another had 13 ESL teachers working on a withdrawal basis in schools. Apart from these two exceptions to the general trend towards the mainstream, the other four LEAs seemed constrained less by pedagogic policy than by the need to have a very few peripatetic teachers (less than five each) working across a number of scattered schools. However, other LEAs in a comparable situation indicated strong commitment to mainstream support despite the difficult conditions.

Over all, the strategy of the majority of LEAs at the time of the survey was a reliance on a mixture of withdrawal classes and in-class support. Comments made in the questionnaire section on provision and future plans (see below) made it clear that most LEAs wished to substitute more provision of in-class support in place of withdrawal.

However, it is important for those planning training programmes to note how varied provision in the field remained. This leaves teacher trainers with the question of how far it is possible to train 'change agents' in initial training (Bourne, 1987).

Just one London LEA claimed to provide full-time language classes within schools. Overall, the London boroughs had moved more consistently towards providing mainstream support right across the spectrum. This might be reflected in the fact already identified, that the London boroughs also tended to make more English support teachers available at secondary level than other areas.

However, with 42 LEAs claiming to provide language support within the mainstream at secondary level, together with the same number providing some 'withdrawal' at the early stages of English language learning, we now have a clear pattern of contemporary practice. It will be interesting to compare the pattern in three to five years time to see if the trend away from 'withdrawal' will continue.

While some LEAs aim to provide whole class support for the teacher and curriculum, and others aim to provide in-class language support for individual bilingual pupils, it is unlikely that any LEA (as opposed to any teacher) could claim to provide either one or the other. Although their policy may indicate a preference, there are likely to be wide variations in practice between teachers, even within the same school. By drawing on the in-depth studies in the next chapter, a more detailed picture of the ways in which LEAs may be providing training for and deploying staff to develop whole class strategies will be built up.

English language centres

Withdrawal of pupils to English language centres, although never widespread, has decreased rapidly during the 1980s. DES statistics (GB. DES, 1988d) reveal a steady drop in the number of centres in operation, from 28 centres (243 teachers) in 1980, to 19 centres (189 teachers) in 1984, and 10 centres (99 teachers) in 1987.

The trend towards closure of centres existed well before the CRE Report (1986) on Calderdale. However, the CRE findings in 1986 had had considerable impact on the three LEAs studied by the NFER which still had language centres; but like Calderdale LEA itself, the LEAs appeared to find difficulty in making changes.

In one LEA studied in-depth, the decision had already been

made to phase out language centres, and a whole school programme of in-service was underway across the first school provision, but with little enhanced inservice budget for the exercise. Administrative and financial obstacles had slowed progress. The main problem seemed to be that the school building programme had not kept up with the increasing school population, and there were few schools with vacant places able to accept pupils from the language centres. To continue to place pupils in the centres for this reason, however, would be clearly discriminatory, and unsatisfactory temporary measures had had to be taken, such as turning one centre into an infant school, the change in the first instance being more in name than in altered intake, other than in the Reception Class. It is likely that the Calderdale ruling will lead to the exposure of any inadequacies and failings of the educational system as a whole, both in its local and national levels, as much as of any deficiencies within the centres themselves. The issue cannot be compartmentalized as one that simply concerns pupils learning English as a second language, or just about the closure of a centre, but one that involves reappraisal of staff allocation, staff training, building programmes, and pupil allocation systems, which cut across a variety of LEA departments.

In the other two LEAs studied which had language centre provision in the secondary years only, the closure of centres was under active consideration following the Calderdale ruling, but no decision had yet been made. There was concern expressed that many schools were unprepared to support pupils at the early stages of learning English; however, in only one case had this concern been accompanied by restructuring the inspectorate and advisory teams in order to make more impact on whole school organization and curriculum delivery, to provide a more favourable context for the closing of the centres.

The remaining language centre provision appeared to be distributed across the country in 1987, with five centres in Greater London; six in the Metropolitan areas; and three in non-metropolitan LEAs. Eight LEAs included primary pupils in this form of provision.

DES statistics on centres for English language teaching are based only on those Centres where pupils are registered as full-time pupils. However, in a few LEAs, pupils were placed on the register of one of the local schools, but withdrawn full-time to the language centre. Thus the NFER 1987 survey revealed rather more use of language centres than was revealed in DES (1988d) statistics.

In addition, 12 LEAs had language 'units' attached to schools, six of these accepting primary school-aged pupils. The majority of these were in metropolitan areas, with one in Wales. The 'in-depth' studies of six LEAs found that there were in addition unofficial full-time 'language classes' in schools in one LEA, as in 'Ayton' School (see next chapter).

Two LEAs studied maintained both language centres and language units attached to schools, and it was reported in one LEA that pupils might pass though both before reaching the mainstream classroom, in which, again, they might be 'grouped' at a separate table. *Without monitoring arrangements it is not possible to say how far and how frequently pupils might have a school 'career' within ESL structures.* A longitudinal study of bilingual pupils' experience of extra provision would be necessary to examine this.

The continuing existence of language centres in some areas, although few in number, indicates that the move to the mainstream nationally, although strong, has been partial, and in some areas contested. There has been no consistent central lead given by the DES to the development of appropriate forms of provision for English language support. The HMI (GB. DES, 1988e) report on six LEAs was ambivalent but appeared to endorse provision in the mainstream 'providing adequate support is available to schools'.

Team or school-based support structures

The need for extra staffing in the form of English language support teachers appeared to be seen as an essential feature of provision in most authorities. In the majority of LEAs this provision was not seen as the responsibility of the school itself in meeting the needs of its pupils, but as part of a 'special' LEA service.

As part of the 1987 survey, LEAs were asked how English language support provision was organized. All English language support teachers were organised into a team based structure, answerable to a Head of Service, in 53 per cent of LEAs responding. Only 11 per cent of LEAs permanently based all their English support teachers in schools. In 32 per cent of LEAs teachers were found both in central teams and with others based in schools. The remaining authorities had just one or two peripatetic teachers.

It is likely that the 1986 'Section 11' criteria will emphasize the need for a team based structure, since Section 11 post holders have duties of accountability outside the school itself. At least one LEA was due to reorganize into a team structure in order to 'carry out Section 11 training more effectively'.

In some LEAs with mainly school-based English support, the 'team' was the old language centre staff now in an advisory role; in others, the team was peripatetic.

Of the six LEAs studied in more depth (see Appendix, Table A), three LEAs had strong central team structures, with primary and secondary teaching 'teams' led by a head of service. In addition, two of these LEAs ('Ayton' and 'Fordham') both maintained language centres where an average of 21 teachers were deployed. Both these LEAs had 'appreciable' (15–24 per cent) numbers of residents of NCWP origin (OPCS, Census, 1981) and followed a trend identified in this category of LEAs in emphasizing a need for 'special' and extra provision. Both had few advisory teachers, with just two full-time 'heads of service', plus some part-time staff based at the language resource centre, providing administrative and advisory support largely to the language support teams themselves.

In both these LEAs, the Heads of Service appeared to have a high degree of independence, with primary and secondary team heads operating independently of each other. They also operated independently of the heads of language centres, even within the same LEA, developing their own distinctive policies and pedagogies.

Lines of senior management of these large teams were unclear. While the Head of Service retained direct responsibility for the work of their teams, they generally did not hold the status of advisers, nor of Head teachers, and consequently were not involved in either advisers' meetings or heads' conferences. This may have tended to marginalize and isolate them from continuing curriculum developments.

The remaining LEA operating a team structure ('Seabury') was based in an area of 'high' (25 per cent plus) numbers of residents of NCWP origin (OPCS, Census, 1981). This LEA also followed the trend identified within this category of a commitment to mainstream responsibility for English language support, with a number of mainstream curriculum area advisers and advisory services adopting a multilingual perspective in their inservice work. The English language team appeared to be struggling to find a role and identity for itself which would enable it to operate in the changing mainstream context. The challenge appeared to be to help teachers, some of whom were first appointed to the old language centre as 'ESL' teachers, adapt to mainstream curriculum support models.

The remaining three LEAs without strong central team-based structures were all in areas with lower percentages of residents of NCWP origin overall (5–14 per cent), although in one LEA as many as 23 per cent of its pupil population was bilingual. The LEA (Deeshire) with the fewest English language support staff had placed all these posts in schools under the direction of the heads, with two advisory teachers based in an integrated in-service team with multicultural education curriculum development teachers, involved in whole school curriculum change. Beedon and Edham both allocated English support teachers to schools from a central 'service'; however, the team structure was largely a formality; there was little further contact between English support staff and the administration of the 'service'.

In all three of these LEAs without strong team structures, the classroom teaching roles of language support and mainstream class teachers were ideally seen to be interchangeable, with both taking on responsibility for the whole class. Since the 1986 regulations came into force the Section 11 status of the teachers provided an opening for advisers for multicultural education to involve themselves in curriculum development in the schools. Basing the support teachers directly under the school head appeared to have freed the central advisory teachers in all these three LEAs to carry out mainstream in-service and advisory roles, with the administration of the Section 11 service itself left to advisers and officers.

In contrast, the first three team-based LEAs retained a distinctive image as 'specialist' language services, with internal career structures, albeit limited, and internal in-service programmes. However, in day-to-day practice the team-based staff were also placed in schools, fulfilling similar functions to those in 'school-based' LEAs. The advisory teachers in those 'specialist' services had considerable administrative functions regarding the deployment, in-service and support of their teams, and were consequently less involved in mainstream in-service.

From evidence in the survey, this basic split in approaches to developing structures for English language support, as seen in the in-depth studies, seems to be mirrored more widely across England, as the next section will indicate.

Changes in provision and practice

Changes in provision

LEAs were asked what the main changes had been over the last five years in provision for English language support. The responses confirm the position reported by HMI (GB. DES, 1988e): 'In all LEAs the roles and functions of 'ESL' teachers are in transition as changes of policy and personnel, amalgamations and reorganizations affect the service.' Yet, although there were differences in types of organization and structure across the country, the responses show certain clear trends. Three broad categories of LEA response can be discerned.

(a)   There are a small number of LEAs who appear to have made no changes in provision since 1982. These consist of eight English LEAs (three Outer London, three metropolitan and two shire counties); two Welsh LEAs and two Islands.

(b) There is a large group of LEAs (46 per cent of respondents) who are expanding and consolidating their English language support services, often alongside reorganization of the service, by further recruitment of English language support teachers. The reason for the expansion most commonly given was a need to meet the demands of the changing role of English support within the mainstream. Mainstream support was seen to require more staff. However, a few authorities also mentioned an increase in the numbers of pupils requiring support. Three LEAs noted that the expansion was particularly related to support in the 'early years'; one LEA mentioned an expansion of language classes at tertiary level.

It was noticeable that 60 per cent of those LEAs with small numbers of residents of NCWP origin (OPCS, Census, 1981) had expanded their provision, while only 22 per cent of those with 'high' numbers had done so. This suggests that, following Little and Willey (1981) there has been an attempt in LEAs with few bilingual pupils to provide extra support for pupils learning English.

(c) The third category of LEAs (43 per cent of respondents) were reorganizing their support service without any notable increases in staffing levels. These LEAs fell into the following two sub-categories.

1. The first was those *consolidating the support service, with an increase in advisory posts.* Ten LEAs reported new advisers, heads of service, advisory teachers, co-ordinators and higher scale posts.

Often a new title had been given to the service; in many cases suggesting it had taken on a 'multicultural' curriculum development role, but without apparently a radically changed structure or staffing.

In at least three cases, reorganization was clearly linked to meeting the demands of the 1986 Section 11 criteria. Reference was made to 'More careful direction of Section 11 teachers through identification, monitoring, inservice'; 'more formalized allocation of staff, review and assessment'.

This sub-group's responses overall indicated a service growing in status (in terms of pay scales and career structure), increasingly being required to see its work within a wider curriculum context, in some cases advising on multicultural curriculum approaches, or monitoring curriculum delivery. Within the sub-group, five LEAs perceived developments hampered by a lack of increased staffing: 'attempts made to increase support and resources without extra staff or capitation'; 'staff numbers have remained the same although the number of schools requiring the service has increased'. It would appear that many of these LEAs saw increased staffing as a concomitant of the move towards mainstream English support but had budgetary constraints on expansion.

2.   The second, very much smaller, sub-category of reorganizing LEAs (three) were those who were clearly *seeking to change the nature of the support service more radically*. These included LEAs who were attempting to merge a number of different support services in order to share expertise and offer a unified service to schools.One LEA described its reorganization as follows: 'The merger of several detached services (Language, Literacy and Numeracy Support Service; Multicultural Development Service; Ethnic Minority Service, etc.) into the Education Development Service', with three local area centres at each of which a total staff of around 30 teachers included about eight 'ESL' teachers. The reorganization here also meant an amalgamation of resources and 'common training' to share expertise.

Another LEA spelt out its reorganizational aims as follows: 'The language resource centre has developed closer collaborative links with other curriculum development centres, to emphasise the need for a cross-curricular response to the multilingual nature of schools in the authority. Thus over the past five years the gradual dismantling of ESL as a discrete entity is being achieved.'

This move away from 'ESL' as an institutional entity was indicated in other LEA responses. In one, the adviser noted that posts had been 'changed from "ESL" to "needs analysis and monitoring posts"'. Two other LEAs stressed that 'a joint approach to language issues' was being developed within the authority. It may well be that this was the beginning of a new movement to remove bilingual language issues from the sphere of 'multicultural curriculum development' to a more specific language orientated but mainstream position. A clear example of this would be the ILEA (1988) Primary Language Profile, developed by the Centre for Language in Primary Education (CLPE).

In two cases at least, the number of 'ESL' staff in LEAs had actually decreased, as staff were moved into other curriculum development teams. An Inspector commented, 'However, these various teams are nevertheless involved in the children's language development albeit through new and innovative approaches'.

Contrasting this comment with one from a director of education in another LEA gives some indication of *the variety of the nature of the ethos in which English support teachers may work*: in this LEA reorganization meant the 'adjustment in the number of 'ESL' tutors proportional to the numbers of ethnic minority pupils with English language deficit'. Such widely different responses co-existed at LEA level across the country, and were mirrored in teachers' own varied attitudes within as well as between each LEA.

Across the three categories of LEAs sketched out above there were a number of widespread and interesting trends. A number of LEAs mentioned that a 'resource centre', 'multicultural centre' or 'language support centre' had been set up, sometimes using old language centre premises. (Recent ESG grants have been made to a number of LEAs to set up such resource centres for Section 11 funded teachers to draw on.)

The recruitment of bilingual support teachers was reported by nine LEAs. Just two of these were LEAs who were involved in expanding their 'ESL' services. In some LEAs, new community language teaching teams were being developed alongside existing 'ESL' teams, and the responses to the questionnaire on English language support indicated that it was hoped that these would provide bilingual support, that is, support for English and curriculum support as well as for the maintenance of other languages. Twenty per cent of responding LEAs reported attempts to employ more bilingual English language support staff. There was also mention of the recruitment of bilingual aides and NNEBs.

Some LEAs reported a shift of English support staff from the secondary to the primary sector as a significant change in provision. While this apparent shift in focus from secondary to primary is supported in the total numbers of teachers identified in the survey (792 secondary to 1407 primary), it needs to be seen within the wider current trend of expanding primary numbers. However, the comparatively low numbers of English support teachers at secondary level becomes significant in the discussion of changes in practice, below, especially when 'mainstream' support is perceived to require more support teachers than 'withdrawal' by LEAs generally.

Changes in practice over the past five years

While in detail there was a wide variety of practice between, and one suspects within, LEAs, the response to the 1987 survey identified one clearly perceived change. The majority of LEAs specifically reported the increased encouragement of mainstream in-class support over the past few years, rather than the withdrawal of bilingual pupils for English language classes.

However, many respondents also recognised that the policy was yet to be fully implemented in practice; for example, advisers wrote: 'All primary support is now in mainstream classes. Secondary support is moving towards all mainstream support as quickly as possible'; 'move from isolated learner provision (some still takes place as needed) to enhancing the skills of all teachers involved in TESOL'; 'while withdrawal still takes place in certain circumstances, gradually teaching methodology is changing'; 'we are encouraging an increasingly integrated classroom support approach'; 'major development: language support within mainstream curriculum areas and co-operative teaching, especially in primary schools (less so in secondary)'; 'more support in the mainstream, withdrawal on a restricted basis for first stage pupils only'; 'trend towards team teaching in ordinary classroom from withdrawal'; 'moving into the mainstream and into collaborative relationships'.

Thus while the picture is of a strong trend towards the implementation of a policy of mainstream classroom support, it is clear that the process of change is not yet complete nor secure, and that the realization of policy is still being worked out in practice within schools. While one response stated that a major change was 'in perception, so that class teachers are now taking responsibility for ESL', another commented: 'There is still some discrepancy between the expectations of head teachers and teachers, and the recommended training and practice of 'ESL' teachers. This conflict is slowly being resolved, although recent increases in numbers of first stage pupils have made some schools regress to language classes for logistical reasons.'

Of course, it was not only mainstream teachers who needed to be convinced of the viability of a mainstream support strategy. Much in-service work was devoted to helping English support staff develop strategies for co-operative teaching and for organizing classrooms in such a way as to encourage the language development of bilinguals – through small group problem solving, for example. While some respondents saw the move to mainstream support as being 'hampered' by lack of enough 'ESL' teachers, only one respondent explicitly expressed reservations about the trend to the mainstream. This adviser saw changes in practice in his LEA in terms of a move from earlier 'structural/situational' teaching programmes towards 'functional language programmes'. He was concerned that mainstream support strategies meant that 'children, especially beginners, do not get regular intensive daily direct tuition'. It is clear that this respondent was operating with a very different model of language, language learning and teaching than that which underlies the mainstream support strategy.

Changes in the support teacher's role mentioned by other advisers included: 'Development of whole school policies, a classroom support model of helping bilingual children and a recognition of the role of the first language'; 'less exclusive interest in "English" and more involvement across the mainstream curriculum'; 'developing language support as a cross-curricular service'; 'identification of children's needs and meeting those needs'; 'developing more learner autonomy in methods'.

A clear distinction appeared to be developing between the support teachers' Section 11 role and their class teaching role. The section 11 role seemed to be developing with a focus on the monitoring of achievement and the progress of pupils of NCWP origin across the school curriculum, rather than on individual interventions at the classroom level. Few structures seemed in place within schools for dissemination of these findings. The teaching role appeared to be committed to the development of co-operative teaching strategies and joint responsibility for the English language support of the whole class.

Just one LEA reported a change in 'greater community involvement in educational provision'.

While some urban LEAs with relatively high numbers of Black and bilingual pupils were emphasizing 'the professional development of mainstream teachers as urban language specialists' and 'the dismantling of "ESL" structures', an increased number of the so called 'all white' authorities had just begun to employ a small number of specialist English language teachers, often working on a peripatetic basis; e.g. 'For the last two years we have engaged the services of a qualified "ESL" teacher to teach the few children with identified problems'. A Shire county with a low percentage of its population of NCWP origin had expanded its specialist team over two years through Section 11 funding to nine full-time and some part-time teachers, and was looking to increasing provision further in the next few years.

Thus, concurrently, across the country contrasting strategies were being worked out, with some LEAs attempting to devolve responsibility for bilingual pupils' language development from 'specialists' back to the classroom teacher, breaking up or restructuring existing language 'teams', while in others, embryonic 'specialist' structures were being introduced for the first time.

These two very different emphases, one on expanding an 'ESL' service and the other focusing on mainstream and whole school awareness of and expertise in meeting developing bilingual's English language and learning needs, are revealed even more sharply by LEA respondents in commenting on their future plans.

Future changes expected in provision and practice

While the greatest emphasis remained on developing mainstream support strategies (13 LEAs), a 'more sophisticated approach' than currently often realized in practice was hoped to be achieved by a number of LEAs.

Responses by LEAs orientated towards school-based and mainstream teacher responsibility for English support appeared to be moving towards the development of a more comprehensive language policy in which to place English language support: 'to ensure schools develop a language policy that will take on board the needs of ethnic minority pupils'; to achieve a 'rationalization of "language provision" which embraces not only 'ESL' from a bilingual perspective, but also the importance and relevance of the first language in pupils' learning processes'; 'immediately, a consciousness raising exercise for schools on language'. Six more LEAs reported plans to develop bilingual approaches, or expand the numbers of bilingual support teachers; others reported a bid for a bilingual psychologist, and for more bilingual ancillary staff and classroom assistants.

Alongside a shift in interest in these authorities from English language support towards bilingual approaches, three LEAs stressed that for them the 'key issue is developing the expertise of *all* teachers' in supporting English language development. One LEA planned more school-based INSET through GRIST funding, with 'increased indirect advice/support/materials service for schools with lesser need'.

The majority of responses, however, were orientated towards the development of specialist English language support structures. Five LEAs were planning further expansions of support teacher numbers: 'we hope to allocate at least one language development teacher to every school which has bilingual pupils on its rolls'; 'the ultimate aim is to have a teacher in each school who is able to give immediate support'. Small authorities hoped to give part-time peripatetic teachers full-time posts.

Reorganizations of 'Section 11 services' were planned by at least three LEAs, with improved career structures available. INSET aimed at improving collaboration between support and class teachers was planned by three LEAs. One LEA hoped to develop resource based learning in the upper secondary years, another to use computers 'for effective distribution of resources'. Just one LEA said it hoped to develop more home–school partnership approaches.

For a number of LEAs, plans often depended on Section 11 bids and applications for ESG grants. One adviser commented: 'Much depends on the financial constraints of the effects of Government legislation – including rate-capping'.

Since INSET was likely to remain limited, another adviser responded: 'It would help greatly if teacher training institutions made this field mandatory in initial training courses. So many probationers arrive without any idea of how to deal with a multilingual class'.

In this context, the role of the English language support teacher was hoped by another adviser to be 'a catalyst for change within schools, ensuring that teachers are more sensitive to the wider special educational needs of ethnic minority children'.

In a number of LEAs, English support teachers seemed likely to be positioned within a 'Section 11 service' structure in the future; being school based, but deployed in schools as a team, allowing both for LEA control over their role and deployment in schools but also for their ongoing in-service to support such a 'catalyst' role. As members of a 'Section 11 service', rather than 'ESL team', a future possibility seems to be 'a diversification of the uses of Section 11 teachers' in response to changing circumstances and needs; for example in curriculum development, home–school liaison posts, and other roles which might tend to down-play the importance of the 'language specialist' side of their current role.

Resources and in-service training

LEAs were asked whether there were any Resource Centres maintained by the LEA 'for supporting teachers on language issues in multilingual schools'. Twenty- two reported that resources were held in multicultural education centres. A number of LEAs (14) said that all such resources were lodged with the English language support service itself. Ten further LEAs gave the names of local mainstream teachers' centres. Two LEAs kept resources in 'special needs' or 'remedial' centres (sic). Only three LEAs mentioned a range of resource centres, including reading centres, and a primary language centre for example. A few LEAs said that resources were also available from the library service. Materials, then, appear still to be seen as 'specialized' in most LEAs.

Forty-nine LEAs (82 per cent of those responding to the 1987 survey) claimed to provide in-service training for their English Language support teachers, 32 providing 'regular' sessions, 17 more 'occasional' in-service.

Those LEAs which did not provide any in-service for English language support teachers were found to be in areas with a low percentage of residents of NCWP origin (Census, 1981), with few English Language support teachers on their staff. There is clearly a need to encourage some secondments of support teachers from such areas to courses which would put them in contact with current thinking and help them to develop support strategies, particularly since, as is indicated below, English language support teachers appear to carry much of the responsibility for the in-service of mainstream colleagues in this field.

LEAs were also asked in the survey whether in-service for mainstream teachers had been undertaken since 1985 (post-Swann) on either linguistic diversity or on supporting bilingual pupils within the mainstream.

One of the first things to note about the responses is that where in-service was not provided in LEAs for the few English support teachers in post, neither was it provided for mainstream teachers on these issues. While these were areas with few bilingual pupils, there appeared to be little LEA support for teachers to develop strategies to meet the needs of those few present. Nor did there appear to be any support for teachers in these areas to respond to the Swann recommendation for all pupils to be encouraged to develop an understanding and appreciation of linguistic diversity appropriate to living in a multilingual society.

Thirty LEAs (50 per cent of the respondents) claimed to provide courses on linguistic diversity for mainstream teachers. Slightly more, 34 LEAs, provided courses for mainstream teachers on supporting bilingual pupils in the mainstream.

However, only 21 per cent of responding LEAs reported an increase in in-service provision as a significant change in their provision over the past five years. It is clear that extra staffing rather than in-service has monopolized LEA attention.

In-service for mainstream staff appeared to be of four main types: courses run by outside institutions; LEA resource centre-based courses; school-based in-service sessions; and informal school-based 'in-service' carried out as part of language support teams' work alongside teachers in schools. Each of these types will be briefly discussed below.

Only two LEAs mentioned secondments to colleges or teacher training institutions as part of their in-service programme for mainstream teachers. Another two LEAs mentioned attendance at DES Regional Courses on 'Education in and for a Multicultural Society'.

RSA Diploma courses in the teaching of English as a second language in multilingual schools were organized by eight LEAs; these included both English language support teachers and mainstream teachers in most cases. Other more formal courses run in multicultural centres and teachers' centres included: courses for 'language co-ordinators'; residential courses; a 'two day course to enable class and subject teachers to identify ways of providing "ESL" support within the curricular framework of the school'; 'yearly day conferences'; termly meetings for Heads of English; a 12 session 'Language Awareness' course for Head teachers; the opening of modules on 'language awareness' within the RSA Diploma to other teachers; short courses in the teachers' centre (six LEAs) and day and evening courses at the language support service centre.

Only one LEA had set up 'a rolling programme of in-service training for mainstream teachers' post-Swann. Few LEAs mentioned any focus on bilingual language issues in their probationary teachers' induction programmes.

Ten LEAs mentioned school-based in-service, carried out mainly at the school's own request, under school GRIST funding programmes. Whole school staff days appeared to have a wide focus covering, for example, 'the multicultural curriculum' or 'Language and Culture', with 'slots' for, or working groups on, language support or linguistic diversity included. This seemed to indicate that in-service in this area could be very limited even where it did take place.

'Informal school based INSET' appeared to be carried out in the course of the English language support teacher's usual work in the school, 'through a team teaching approach'; 'through advice, support, resources, etc., provided by the "ESL" team'. This was sometimes backed by whole school in-service sessions, either full day as part of GRIST, or taking place over a period of weeks 'in school assembly time'.

Much of the in-service work for mainstream teachers seemed to rely on the English language support service to staff and organize sessions, both formally and informally within the school, and often also at the centres. The effectiveness of this approach must depend on the qualifications and experience of English language support teachers if they are to be able to lead mainstream colleagues in school change.

In-service, often for mainstream as well as English support teachers, was carried out by advisory teachers appointed under Section 11. However, training opportunities for these advisory teachers them-selves appear not to be covered by Section 11. Under the new criteria, Section 11 is not to be paid for teachers while undertaking courses of training, nor are posts for RSA course tutors apparently any longer acceptable for Section 11 funding. The training of these key advisory teachers will in future then, seem to be a direct cost to the LEAs; yet it is upon the quality of their work and understanding of language that most in-service provision for sup-port teachers and whole school GRIST programmes will depend. Provision of in-service at advisory level, probably through second-ments, would seem a necessary feature of current provision, but was not mentioned in the responses to our survey.

Most whole school in-service work appeared to take place at the school's own request. This suggests that some schools may have little contact with developments in English support strategies where there is a lack of commitment from the head, or interest from the staff, or where the English support teacher is not strong enough to take a lead in negotiating whole school strategies.

One LEA commented that although it had provided courses for mainstream teachers: 'there has been very limited take up... as in many schools it is not perceived of as having a high enough priority for releasing teachers when compared to, for example, GCSE or TVEI training.'

This comment indicates that LEAs need to examine ways of ensuring that all in-service courses take up the issues of linguistic diversity, of supporting the English development of bilinguals, and of ensuring access to the curriculum for all students within the context of their own particular focus.

In addition, it seems necessary for LEAs to find ways of identifying, encouraging, and monitoring courses related to linguistic diversity and English support strategies for mainstream teachers, now that many schools are organizing their own GRIST programmes, if *all* teachers are to have access to such training. In-service for primary 'language co-ordinators' and secondary Heads of Departments outside school may be necessary as well as whole staff school based courses, to ensure continuity.

It seems important that the ESG-funded programmes on English following the Kingman Report also take on the issue of linguistic diversity and language support, areas unfortunately not developed in the Report itself.

The long running teachers' dispute over pay and conditions which took place over the period of our study undoubtedly affected the provision of in-service for mainstream teachers during this time. In most LEAs cover was difficult to provide for teachers attending courses during the school day, and after school courses were severely cut back. A number of language resource centres reported cancelled courses. The teachers' action, however, rarely affected English language support teachers' in-service sessions, since most support staff were Section 11 funded. As Section 11 teachers are supposed to be 'extra to staffing needs', there could be no excuse from Heads for not releasing them because of problems of 'cover'.

Indeed, during the period of the NFER study, the circulation of the changes in the criteria for Section 11 funding in 1986 appeared to have had a positive affect on in-service provision for Section 11 staff, who were in many cases called in from schools, sometimes for the first time, to discuss the implications of the changes for their roles in school. Some LEAs preceded this by sessions for Heads on the deployment of Section 11 staff, which also raised awareness of the issues involved.

In a number of LEAs, the 'Section 11 service' began to be brought together on a regular basis for training. These arrangements brought about more awareness of the existence of Section 11 staffing in the schools, and had potential for developing an overall LEA strategy by training each Section 11 teacher to intervene positively in the work of their particular institutions. A number of LEAs' responses indicated that all the English language support teachers' in-service courses they ran had been for 'Section 11 staff only'. However, if the main strategy for English language support is to be the development of team teaching, the failure to provide in-service on co-operative strategies for their mainstream partners is likely to seriously affect their success.

Summary

An examination of survey data in this chapter indicated that while most LEAs had accepted a policy of supporting bilingual pupils in the mainstream class, backed by the provision of withdrawal classes, there were very different co-existing perceptions of what mainstream support meant. There was, however, a fairly general agreement that mainstream support for bilinguals would require more, rather than less, extra staffing. This understanding was reflected in figures indicating that less mainstream support was provided in secondary schools where there were also less extra English teachers than in primary schools.

However, while the emphasis was on developing practice in the mainstream, Section 11 criteria were strengthening special structures for English language provision outside the schools. The English language support teachers appeared to have the dual role of jointly team teaching all pupils, and of monitoring the progress of curriculum delivery for pupils of Commonwealth origin. With most in-service training directed to the Section 11 teachers, their status within the LEA as advisory teachers appeared to be enhanced. Yet it was not clear how and whether schools had been prepared for, or had accepted, this change in role.

The next chapter will look at the organization of English language support in more detail, by drawing illustrations from studies of six junior or middle schools.

4 English Language Support: The Whole School Studies

This chapter will address the ways in which five junior schools and one middle school were adapting in response to the policy for bilingual pupils' language needs to be met within the mainstream (GB. DES, 1985). Changing perceptions of bilingual pupils' educational needs have implications for school structures, staffing, teaching strategies and routines. Bringing about change in any one of these factors is not easy. There is a considerable body of research on the imperviousness of schools to demands for change, and on the informal, trial and error, approach to dealing with new circumstances (e.g. Taylor, 1986).

At the time of the NFER study, although widely agreed in principle, the process of change to mainstream structures of support for bilingual learners was still in the early stages of implementation in most of the schools studied. This chapter will attempt not only to describe how mainstream support was being put into practice, but also what features of structure and management appeared to enable its effective development.

Multicultural education/antiracist/equal opportunities policies

One of the key factors identified in the school studies was the way in which whole school language provision policies for bilingual pupils had evolved out of the reappraisal of school provision from equal opportunities and antiracist perspectives. Across the six schools visited, English language support teachers worked within very different contexts depending on whether the rest of the staff had accepted responsibility for all the pupils' language and literacy needs, or whether this was still considered to require additional 'specialist' input. Teachers had to negotiate their roles and duties according to the context they were in, as well as according to their own experience and training.

Although all six LEAs visited had multicultural education, antiracist or equal opportunities policies approved by council, only three of the six schools visited had developed their own policy. Only in these three schools with developed policies was it formally accepted that *all* teachers in the school had equal responsibility for language development, and that in-class support strategies were to be preferred to withdrawal of pupils for extra English language work.

However, interestingly, although these schools stressed the need to 'value' languages other than English, they were not all committed to developing bilingual work in schools. Their uncertainty on this issue appeared to be related to a concern for the academic achievement of their pupils, and a fear that bilingual work, if not given proper staffing and continuity in provision throughout the school system, could be tokenistic and trivialized.

Nevertheless, two of the three schools with policies were beginning to introduce bilingual support into the schools, drawing on unqualified staff in one instance and on staff without DES recognized status in the other, in recognition of the need for a more multilingual ethos within classrooms, at the very least. This change in attitude appeared to be linked to increasing LEA commitment in terms of staffing for community languages maintenance at infant and at secondary levels.

The remaining three schools had no plans for developing their own policies, and therefore had no framework in which to assess their language policies. English language support in all these three schools remained essentially the province of specialist support staff, with whom the responsibility for the introduction of bilingual approaches and approaches to linguistic diversity also seemed to rest.

Staffing and deployment

Overall staffing levels

As a main strategy for developing English language education in a multilingual society, Swann recommended enhanced staffing to allow space for teachers to develop expertise. However, few schools visited had been provided with extra staffing other than Section 11 staff, who should not be used for enhanced staffing. One middle school visited was well staffed to cover the necessary subject specialisms. It was able to support a regular pattern of team teaching by maintaining large 'base group' classes of up to 30 pupils, allowing staff time free for planning. One junior school had managed to employ two teachers extra to establishment other than the Section 11 teachers, one for music and the other floating, both providing cover across the school for preparation, planning and in-service. In most schools, however, the only staffing other than class teachers were heads, occasionally also a 'floating' deputy head, and the Section 11 language support teachers.

Special needs provision overall was very low, averaging 0.2 provision per week across the six schools, with one school having no regular special needs provision at all. In this context, the pressure that was observed on Section 11 support staff to become involved in special needs provision becomes understandable. This limited their work within classrooms.

Pupil–teacher ratios across the six schools averaged 21:1, with the lowest being 17:1, and the highest reaching 25:1, including all support teachers. The school with the highest pupil–teacher ratio was also the school with the highest percentage of bilingual pupils on roll. In one school it was clear that Section 11 provided not only for extra support staff posts, but even for one class teacher's post, a clear abuse of the provision.

The schools adopting whole school strategies for English language support, where the extra Section 11 teachers were deployed in team teaching, had the lowest pupil–teacher ratios and also (in 3 out of 4 cases) the lowest ratio of bilingual pupils to extra language support posts. (In the fourth school, the majority of pupils were fluent bilinguals.)

The two schools which gave more emphasis to 'withdrawal' strategies (see below) both had higher overall pupil–teacher ratios and higher numbers of bilingual pupils to language support teachers. The school with separate 'Special Needs' classes where early stage learners of English were placed had the largest pupil–teacher ratio overall (25:1) and the lowest proportion of extra support teachers (260 bilinguals to 1 support teacher).

In no school were there more than 2.1 designated English support teachers (f.t.e.), nor less than 0.5 (f.t.e) However, in one school four extra staff were employed as 'Team Leaders' rather than 'English support' teachers, and two schools employed a bilingual assistant or instructor in addition to English support staff.

These figures, although based on just six schools, appear to suggest that whole school strategies were more easily developed in schools with generous staffing. However, care must be taken in drawing this conclusion. It seems possible that schools where the head was committed and vigorous in developing whole school change might also have benefitted in staffing levels by the head's ability to argue for and win extra staffing. Nevertheless, the planning time required for teachers to work together co-operatively does suggest that proper use of English language support staff would require enhanced staffing to provide more cover.

Deployment of English language support teachers

It was clear that most teachers in the six schools visited were aware that there was a long way to go before the sort of team teaching strategies and organization described at the beginning of Chapter 3 could be said to be in place.

Although there was mainstream support going on in all the schools visited, in at least half of them it would not be true to say that the language support teacher had equal responsibility for the learning in the classroom with the class teacher. In some cases both teachers appeared unsure of the English support teacher's role. In at least two schools, English support teachers did not have automatic access to all classrooms, but needed to be 'invited' to work within them.

However, the English language support teacher was rarely the only person to work alongside teachers in the classroom. It appeared to be becoming more and more customary for advisory teachers, teachers for hearing impaired pupils and other special needs teachers to work within the mainstream classroom. *If schools are to make best use of the variety of support services available to them in their pupils' interests, team teaching strategies need to be developed as a matter of professional routine, starting in initial training and extended through INSET. This would enable co-operative teaching strategies to be more effective in English language support.*

The focus of most English support seen was on individual early stage English learners, pupils with learning difficulties, and those perceived to be 'underachieving'. However, some of the teachers appeared to be attempting to develop strategies for more oral, interactive group work in the classroom, where this did not already take place.

Thus, two English support teachers were developing drama activities as part of their whole class teaching work. In some classrooms, English support teachers had planned whole class lessons involving group and pair problem-solving, which they taught collaboratively with class teachers. For example, in one class observed, pupils used questionnaire data to complete a variety of guided pictorial representations of results in different small groups.

However, in-class support appeared to focus more often on individual pupils, or small selected groups, with the English support teacher working alongside them to help them to carry out the tasks set by the class teachers. Their role in these situations appeared to be to explain the tasks more clearly; to provide help with vocabulary; to talk through work before pupils began writing; to provide models for writing and spelling, and help in sequencing sentences. Occasionally English support teachers brought work which they had prepared and planned into class to support individual pupils, but more often they were observed to respond to the ongoing class activities, often on an *ad hoc* basis, where teachers had had no planning time together.

In contrast, in a school where the floating teacher had higher status, having been made year curriculum co-ordinator or 'team leader', the focus was on the preparation of a range of materials for different levels of activity and for English language support integrated to the curriculum topic area. Regular team planning meetings were routine (out of school hours). In many of the classes in this school, a variety of activities took place at any one time, allowing either the team teacher or the class teacher to bring together different groups of pupils for specific purposes.

In one lesson in this school, first-year junior pupils (91 per cent bilinguals) were working on the theme 'Growth and Change'. As part of the theme a tank of caterpillars had been brought into the classroom. On one day, different groups of pupils were involved in a variety of small group and individual tasks. The team teacher organized activities, giving time for the class teacher to bring a small group of 'early stage' English learners together around the tank with magnifying glasses. After careful observation and free discussion, the class teacher began to structure the discussion, sensitively questioning the children about their observations. Later, the children were helped to use a Language Master to record words and sentences about the caterpillars that they might want to use in writing, recording on soundtrack the words in both English and Panjabi, their first language. The following day, when the team teacher was not present and the class teacher had less time to spend with them, the group was able to use the language master cards and machine independently to prompt their memory of the discussion, as a talking dictionary, and to provide models of spelling; to enable them to write about the current appearance, size and movement of the caterpillars in their diaries of 'growth and change'.

The variety of materials provided for groupwork in this class were transferred, often adapted after trial, to the second class in the year group, so that the burden of materials development for a variety of pupil needs was shared across three teachers. In the final stage of the project, the children presented some of their work in a bilingual assembly to school and parents. The pupils were also able to draw on the help of a bilingual assistant where they needed it – for example in checking whether the word for a caterpillar's egg remained the same as the word for a chicken's egg in Panjabi as well as English (an issue that caused great discussion).

In their report on English as a second language teaching (GB. DES, 1988e), HMI suggest that joint working by support and class teachers was most often seen in 'topic' areas of the curriculum, where it was possible to integrate a variety of activities and levels of support, and a variety of flexible and changing groupings. The observations in the NFER project fully support this. The most successful team teaching was seen in a school where the full curriculum was organized by year group teams into integrated topic areas.

However, it should also be stressed that this way of working was supported by whole school curriculum development workshops. Full documentation of termly plans were presented to the head teacher after team discussions.

Effective 'topic' work in the primary school is not easy to achieve, and is not as often established in practice as the rhetoric of primary pedagogy suggests. A major issue is 'how to ensure that topic work does in fact secure progression, continuity and coherence' (Eric Bolton, TES, 28/10/88, p. 18). Progression, continuity and coherence are, of course, central issues also for the language development of bilingual pupils. The development of mainstream strategies for language support is integrally involved in wider curriculum development issues, as part of the process of whole school improvement.

When the curriculum was organized into a pattern of 'language', maths and integrated topic work, as it was in other schools, a clear pattern of individual or small group 'streamed' support in the basic skills areas emerged, with team teaching only discernible in the topic areas. In these schools, pupils were 'streamed' or 'set' right across the school for English language, maths and reading.

This arrangement raises some questions. It was not at all clear how staff currently distinguished between English language needs and learning needs in their 'setting' arrangements. There appeared to be no generally accepted procedures for assessing pupils' English language skills in the schools visited. One language support service was working on the development of a 'profiling' system for pupils, but this was not being put into practice in the school visited. Overall, there appeared to be a concern among advisers to switch the earlier 'ESL' focus on individual pupils' language use in in-service courses to an evaluation and analysis of the language environment provided by the classroom. This meant that profiling arrangements for individuals were less often dealt with.

However, where 'setting' arrangements were common in schools, there was clearly a need for some kind of explicit assessment procedure. Despite an English support teacher being available, the five 'early stage' English learners in one school were found to be in the lowest 'sets' both for English and Maths. The support teacher worked alongside them, helping them in these groups. However, their need might not have been for the less cognitively complex tasks suitable for 'slow learners', but rather for linguistically simpler tasks with a higher cognitive content (see Cummins and Swain, 1986, p. 153). In such streamed situations different 'sets' for early stage English as a second language learners would seem necessary to avoid their placement with lower 'ability' groupings.

The introduction of standardized assessments in the future may not be helpful in avoiding the conflation of the two quite different concepts of 'ability' and 'English language skills'. Indeed, the presence of English as a second language learners raises awkward questions about the way 'ability' is both defined and monitored for all pupils. It may be necessary to question critically the whole notion of 'ability', and to work from the position that children come to school with very different experiences, for example, of print, of literacy activities, and of child–adult interactions. For while assessments may inform teachers of what children could or could not do in the particular context of the testing situation itself, it will remain up to teachers to work out what sorts of experiences children need in order to develop the concepts required by the education system, and to organize classrooms in order to provide an environment and activities within which such concepts and skills can be developed.

From this perspective, heterogeneous groups could be formed bringing together pupils who might benefit most from the particular activity or task to be undertaken, or experience offered; rather than groups arranged according to notions of 'ability'. In this context, second language learners might over the weeks be placed with a variety of other pupils. The automatic placing of early stage learners in groups with learning difficulties should raise questions; however, this did not appear to be under discussion in the schools visited.

Overall, occasions of genuine team teaching, with both teachers taking responsibility for planning, preparation and organization of the whole class, were rarely observed in most of the schools visited. Equally, there were few occasions when genuinely collaborative mixed ability group tasks were seen in operation. Where such activities took place, they were seen as often in classes where teachers were working *alone* in linguistically aware schools, as when teachers were seen working together.

It would seem that there are severe constraints on co-operative team teaching and the regular organization of interactive group work, even at junior school level. It seems essential to recognize this as a fact, and to seriously consider the most effective means of supporting change in schools; otherwise English language support for bilinguals through co-operative teaching is likely to remain at the level of rhetoric rather than reality in many places.

If co-operative strategies are to be adopted, it is a matter of priority to develop programmes of curriculum development which involve both language support teachers and their mainstream partners. The conclusion is *not* that co-operative teaching strategies are not an effective way of supporting pupils, but that they appeared to be rarely undertaken.

'Withdrawal'

In three schools out of the six junior schools visited, withdrawal of pupils from the mainstream classroom was a regular feature of work by the English support teacher. However, one school was phasing out the practice, policy discouraging it unless 'deemed necessary'. In one school, English support teachers claimed to spend about one-third of their time each in working with individual pupils, withdrawal groups and mainstream class support teaching.

Where withdrawal work was being carried out, it was explicitly stated by staff that the arrangement was made as much for what were believed to be 'pastoral' benefits as for language development. Withdrawal groups and special classes were described as offering more 'secure' environments, places where children could relax, or 'unwind'.Underlying these statements was the apparent assumption that the normal classroom cannot or does not offer a secure environment for language learners; yet in neither of these schools was it apparent that serious attempts were being made at policy level or in INSET provision to reorganize the mainstream so as to be more responsive to early stage learners.

Another reason for withdrawal work given was that in some cases support teachers had not been given access to pupils' classrooms by some class teachers, and thus they felt they had to withdraw certain pupils to ensure some specialist support. In these cases, there appeared to be no liaison at all between 'ESL' and class teacher, who operated quite independently from each other, leaving the English support work in total isolation for the curriculum.

Examples of activities reported as observed in 'withdrawal' sessions in the schools visited were the 'hearing' of individual children reading; group reading; reading and writing based on 'Breakthrough' sentence makers; class worksheets completed with the help of the support teacher; the elicitation of vocabulary prior to a topic task, with the modelling of written sentences on the blackboard; and topic-based work carried on with a small group independently of the class teacher where the support teacher had no access to the classroom.

The variety of the realities of organizational structures noted by Townsend (1971) continued to exist in 1987, even within LEAs. In-service providers need to be aware of the very different contexts English support teachers come from when they are designing courses for them. In one school, all pupils newly arrived from overseas were placed in two vertically grouped 'special needs' classes, alongside children with 'general learning difficulties' and 'behavioural difficulties'. Children were selected for these classes by the head, in consultation with the 'special needs' class teachers, the home–school liaison teachers, 'ESL' teachers and class teachers. No diagnostic assessment procedures were used. In 1987/8, out of 19 children in one of these classes, five children had been in the 'special needs' class for over a year, while eight were newly admitted. While it was intended to 'integrate' most pupils into the mainstream by the fourth year, some pupils had in the past been transferred into the secondary language centre, or one of the LEA secondary schools' language units. In this LEA, it was possible for junior pupils to be referred into 'Language (English) Development' streams in some secondary schools, with little likelihood of pupils then ever being admitted to the mainstream.

Within the 'special needs' class itself, in the junior school studied, there was no formal monitoring system for pupil progress or for assessing when pupils were 'ready' for the mainstream. Neither of the 'special needs' class teachers were English language specialists, and the aim of the classes was not English language teaching but provision of a 'normal' primary curriculum, within a smaller, more 'sheltered' and supportive atmosphere. One of the class teachers was bilingual, sharing the language other than English of most of the pupils. However, it had not been her policy to use this language in the classroom, and the class had not been planned in order to provide bilingual support, but support in English.

Most 'ESL' teacher time in the school was allocated to these two classes, from which two teachers from the LEA English support team withdrew small groups of pupils, as well as spending some time working alongside the class teachers in the 'special needs' classes. Although the head firmly supported these classes as targeting extra provision, the HMI report (GB. DES, 1988e) on 'ESL' found that 'linking "ESL" with special needs or remedial education' was 'unhelpful'. One 'special needs' class at the school had already been phased out due to 'falling rolls' by 1988.

This example gives some idea of the variety of approaches in reality to supporting bilingual pupils in schools in the mid-1980s, in contrast to the mainstreaming emphasis of most LEA respondents; and indicates the variation that exists within authorities despite official policies on practice.

Just one teacher in the NFER studies was observed to use some 'withdrawal' sessions for formal language teaching. This teacher was based in the school just described above, and withdrew pupils from across the school but mainly from the 'Special Needs' classes. This teacher was involved in an in-service project to implement a language teaching methodology developed in Wales (Dodson, 1985), aiming to draw on pupils' stronger languages in order to develop English. The methodology included short periods with an explicit focus on language forms, as well as the more usual use of the second language as the classroom medium.

These sessions as observed in practice were teacher directed, and mainly consisted of short dialogues based on familiar classroom language repeated in both English and the children's other language, followed by substitution practice based on the dialogues. An 'interpreter' worked alongside the monolingual teacher, acting on cue from her. The teacher had managed to arrange for bilingual teachers, a parent and some older pupils to act as interpreters in the appropriate languages in these sessions.

It is likely that withdrawal would be necessary for sessions in the form adopted by this teacher to take place, since they required homogeneous bilingual groups at approximately the same stage of learning English; appeared to be based on teaching material not directly related to the ongoing curriculum; and involved some group oral repetition, which would be inappropriate in most primary classrooms when peers were engaged on other tasks. Moreover, in the context of this particular school, where pupils reported being 'shy' to use their first languages in the mainstream, the teacher-directed use of first languages might be unacceptable in the mainstream class to the pupils involved.

It would not be appropriate here to attempt to evaluate the methodology as very little of this teacher's work was systematically observed. It would be fair to say, however, that the use of a teacher-directed bilingual methodology focusing on linguistic forms by a monolingual teacher relying on volunteer interpreters or 'informants' seemed problematic if the work was to be of real value, rather than simply a tokenistic use of other languages. Furthermore, the involvement of monolingual teachers in in-service to develop bilingual methodologies from schools where there are a number of bilingual teachers on the staff does not seem conducive either to the most effective teaching or to good staff relations. (Similarly, the use of Welsh to develop English in schools in Wales by English monolingual teachers would also be likely to be contested within a Welsh LEA.)

Apart from this single example, no activities appeared to be taking place in the withdrawal groups observed in the junior schools visited which could not have been organized within a mainstream classroom. Most of the work consisted of support for mainstream curriculum activities, in some cases with identical worksheets being carried out concurrently by peers in the mainstream and withdrawal classrooms. There seemed little to be gained by removing pupils from the classroom for these particular activities; and indeed, the ongoing in-service at the LEA language services in most of the LEAs concerned was focusing on the development of more in-class support, rather than on language teaching strategies for withdrawal situations.

Just as there were no clear assessment procedures for including pupils in 'withdrawal' groupings, so there appeared to be no assessment procedures for deciding when pupils no longer needed withdrawal support. In one school at least, support was seen as ongoing, rather than as a temporary measure, with one teacher reported as saying: 'Almost all Asian children have a narrow range of syntax and vocabulary and should qualify for support.' Withdrawal only seemed to cease if there were too many pupils needing attention. There were indications that at secondary transfer one of the main criteria for receiving special 'ESL' provision at secondary school was a referral from the primary service, suggesting that pupils, once selected for 'special attention' may have difficulties in extricating themselves from a school 'career' in English language support, which, when involving withdrawal, may deny full access to the mainstream curriculum.

From the observations undertaken as part of this study, limited although they were to six junior/middle schools but spread across six LEAs, the crucial debate clearly was not about withdrawal or mainstream support as alternatives. The question rather appeared to be about how to get whole schools working to develop strategies for supporting the English language development and access to the curriculum of bilingual pupils, using all the resources at their command. These resources included extra English language support teachers, often with an additional Section 11 responsibility, but were not limited to them. The development of the skills of mainstream teachers and of classrooms as interactive problem solving environments remained a priority; and alongside this, the development *of whole school in-service through a range of advisory services, all of them needing to base their approach on an understanding of multilingualism and with the intention of providing access to the curriculum for all pupils.*

The remainder of this chapter will examine approaches being made towards whole school change in the schools studied. The next chapter will go on to examine provision for bilingual pupils which requires extra linguistic skills which it might not be possible for schools to acquire simply through whole school reappraisal and in-service, but which would also need a reappraisal of staffing and recruitment priorities.

Developing mainstream responsibility

The HMI (GB. DES, 1988e) report found that 52 per cent of English support time in the schools they observed was spent in withdrawal teaching. In contrast, in the six schools NFER studied, which were mainly selected by LEA advisers to represent aspects of what they considered to be good practice, very little time overall was spent in withdrawal.

However, in adopting mainstream strategies for English language support, it was not the role of the English language support teacher which appeared to be crucial in effective support for bilingual pupils, but rather how this was fitted into, and was drawn on, to support whole school responsibility for the language needs of pupils.

The background to the approach to English support which most LEA advisers indicated through their choice of schools for observation seems best presented in Swann (1985, para. 2.12, p. 393): 'We would see the E2L needs of pupils in primary school being met within the normal classroom situation by class teachers.' To enable this to become the normal practice, Swann recommended school-based in-service provision; enhanced school staffing to free teachers to develop skills in English language support through courses and work alongside LEA advisory services; and the development of team teaching to pass on skills to colleagues, so enabling more teachers to develop ways of supporting language across the curriculum.

The emphasis, in other words, was on whole school change and development, not simply the transference of the English support teacher from a withdrawal class into the mainstream classroom.

The first observation on strategies of LEA support must be that while all LEAs provided enhanced staffing to the primary schools visited in order to develop English language support, few had provided time for whole school INSET to develop a cross-curricular language policy, and a plan for implementing it. This emphasis on extra English support staff rather than cover time for INSET has already been suggested to be an effect of government funding policy (Section 11).

Most whole school in-service work which was observed took place in teachers' own time, at lunchtimes and in after school meetings. As such, in some schools in-service was normally non-existent at the time of the NFER study, constrained by teachers' industrial action. In at least four schools, however, head teachers had organized a little time for in-service by taking whole school assemblies, providing music lessons, and in one case by employing a floating teacher to cover staff. In three schools, attached English support staff had a regular half-day free for in-service and preparation. However, other teachers were not freed for in-service to develop their complementary role in team teaching. In two of these cases, this had meant that withdrawal work and limited in-class support remained major features of the provision.

In the school (Deeshire) where the most effective team teaching seen had been developed, each year team had initially spent a full day together with advisory teachers from the multicultural education centre to develop a policy for team teaching and discuss constraints, problems and possibilities. Each team had a weekly timetabled half-day non-contact time, where one member was freed to visit the multicultural resource centre for advice and preparation of materials. In addition, cover had been provided for each teacher over a year to spend one half-day visiting another school in the LEA to observe practice, and one half-day visiting other classes in their own school, to develop continuity in practice across the school. This ongoing in-service was made possible by developing a team structure (described below).

In another school (Seabury), a variety of LEA advisory services had been called upon by the head to support teachers' working groups and to work alongside teachers in class, in order to develop new knowledge, skills and perspectives. Over about a term, staff (including the English support teacher) had been working with a multicultural and antiracist education curriculum development team, and another term the LEA learning support advisory team had provided a teacher to work part-time alongside teachers on helping children to write and produce their own, often bilingual, books.

In order to develop expertise in English language development, this LEA's English adviser had encouraged schools to form small consortium groups, drawing on the appropriate advisory services. At the time of the NFER study, the school staff were working with two other local schools and the LEA learning support service to reappraise ways of approaching reading in multilingual classrooms. They had reassessed and ordered new reading material, reorganized spaces in their classrooms for reading; provided visual support and audio equipment; shared ideas on supporting different kinds of reading for different purposes, and were working on developing ways of record-keeping and monitoring progress through their new 'core books' scheme, in each case taking multilingual classrooms and linguistic diversity as the baseline for organizing mainstream provision.

Both the head and the LEA's emphasis here was on classroom based in-service, led by teachers who had identified their own needs, with the support of advisory services, but within the framework of a strong school and LEA multicultural education and antiracist policy, which introduced minority community perspectives on provision. An important aspect of the in-service work was the meticulous record keeping, which enabled the advisory services to disseminate strategies for change developed in one school for discussion across further schools.

The linguistic awareness of advisory support staff in all curriculum areas seems crucial to making sure that linguistic diversity and differing needs for English language and literacy support are taken account of and built into all curriculum planning. Liaison between the various support teams was not always in evidence. In one Teachers' Centre for example, an exhibition by a community languages teaching team offered rich examples of bilingual language use in learning, while in just the next room an exhibition of maths curriculum materials offered no evidence of the existence of bilingualism in this multilingual authority.

At the national level, it was interesting to observe the influence of the National Writing Project, which has taken a multilingual perspective in its work, on developing an interest in bilingual language use in the schools where teachers were involved, reinforcing local LEA in-service from multicultural education centres. Equally, there was evidence of projects on parental support for reading having an influence on schools, often extended to include literacy in other languages.

Staff organization

In bringing about whole school responsibility for English language support, a number of features of school organization seemed important: first, the head's awareness of and commitment to a whole school response to linguistic diversity; secondly, school structures for joint curriculum planning; and thirdly, opportunities for team teaching in classrooms.

Most crucial was the commitment of the head teacher to bringing about change in the school, both to enable all teachers to take responsibility for language needs, and to enable co-operative teaching strategies to develop. Not all the heads visited were convinced of the value of bilingual work in schools, and where this was the case, evidence of bilingual activities in school, for example in multilingual assemblies and bilingual displays, and the pressure to recruit bilingual staff, was signally absent (despite authority policy in at least one instance). Even where bilingual teachers were on the staff, without head teacher support bilingual work could appear low status, or marginal, and bilingual teachers were sometimes therefore reluctant to develop a bilingual role for themselves.

Two LEAs at the time of the visit had begun to provide in-service for head teachers on the rationale for, and ways of supporting co-operative teaching strategies. Gaining the support of heads appeared to be a priority for effective provision to be developed.

The degree of existing autonomy or of co-operation among teachers in a school was a feature which could support or constrain the development of team teaching. Only one school visited had no structures for joint curriculum planning among staff, leaving class teachers a high degree of autonomy. In such an organizational structure, an English language support teacher remains very isolated, an anomaly on the staff, having no class within a class-based structure.

Curriculum working groups, which involved English and bilingual support teachers, offered structures in which issues relating to the language demands of the curriculum and the language needs of all pupils could be raised. In addition, some schools had also set up year curriculum planning groups, to co-ordinate work across the year, to share specialist skills, and to share resources. Where these groups existed, teachers were able to draw on a wider range of specialisms in planning the curriculum; English support and bilingual support teachers were involved at the planning stage; and a far larger range of materials could be produced by sharing materials with common objectives. However, in some cases, team work was confined to out-of-class planning sessions, with language support teachers being denied access to some mainstream classes, it not being 'to every teacher's taste to work collaboratively' (one head).

In one school (Deeshire), with a high percentage of bilingual pupils, the year group organization had been institutionalized by adopting a full team teaching structure, despite the physical constraints of an old school building. Year groups were split into two classes, each with a class teacher. A third teacher had been appointed as a team leader, to lead curriculum development and to team teach alongside the class teachers. The team teachers were to work within the classroom, 'being equally responsible for supporting the class teacher and developing all children across the curriculum at all levels'. The job description read:

the class teacher and the team teacher should, depending on the perceived needs of the children and activities planned, have interchangeable roles and flexibility of groupings...to provide more group work, more opportunities for children to learn through investigation and talk, more practical work and more activity based lessons.

This structure appeared to have been effective in helping teachers to reorganize classrooms and to reflect on practice.

Just one middle school was visited, chosen by the LEA adviser as offering an example of one way in which structures might be adapted to enable a variety of support teachers to be involved in work in classrooms in the older age range where specialist subject lessons became part of the curriculum. In this school, with around 60 per cent bilingual pupils, each year group of three classes had five teachers attached to it, led by a year co-ordinator. Within each year group, three teachers each took responsibility for one class or 'base group', while the two other attached teachers had responsibilities across the school (for example, Deputy Head, English language support, art).

Although a middle school with specialist subject teachers, each teacher was required to spend 50 per cent of their time outside their own specialist area in general class teaching and in supporting other teachers. All teachers, therefore, knew what it was like to work in a 'support' capacity. Within year groups, pupils worked mainly in mixed ability groupings, but individual children and small groups often worked with different teachers on different areas of the curriculum in flexible and shifting groups.

The two English language support teachers attached to the school spent up to a third of their timetable 'leading' a class in the year group to which they were attached, the rest of the time being spent in English support across the curriculum. Other teachers working within the teams were a special needs teacher and teachers from an attached partially hearing unit. Generous LEA staffing provision enabled this form of organization to be developed, with timetabled time for planning, preparation and record keeping. Within this type of structure, it would be possible also to attach advisory teachers for temporary in-service development, as well as more permanent bilingual support staff.

The issue in many of the structural and organizational developments in schools may be to get classrooms working in such a way as to provide the sort of environment necessary to both stimulate and support pupils learning English as a second language, while at the same time providing a context in which specialist teachers from one of the advisory services could operate temporarily alongside the class teacher. In this way skills could be passed on to the class teacher at the same time as providing specialist support within the classroom. *The 'enabling' rather than 'supporting' role of the specialist teacher seems vital*, since the numbers of specialists available is very small, and no school can expect very much specialist support.

For reflective co-operative teaching to take place, some joint time for curriculum planning appeared essential. Although most advisers would agree that in order for team teaching to work, some timetabled joint planning time is a non-negotiable factor, in fact planning time was not easily arranged. Most of the six schools studied had some joint curriculum planning time, most usually short periods during assembly, or music sessions taken by another teacher. In three of the schools, postholders had timetabled non-contact time, when it might be possible for English support teachers to negotiate some time for co-operative planning. Otherwise, all planning sessions, by year teams, curriculum groups or paired English support/class teachers, had to take place outside school hours, voluntarily.

The HMI report (GB. DES, 1988e) stressed:

> The presence of the E2L teacher working alongside the class
> teacher does not of itself ensure an effective response to the
> needs of E2L learners. Effective co-operative working requires
> the class teacher and the E2L teacher to share responsibility
> for the development of the pupils' language, and to plan
> and implement the work accordingly.

Liaison is just as important, although not as salient, where pupils are taught in withdrawal situations. But *the studies suggest that if co-operative teaching is to work, such consultation must be seen not only as the responsibility of the support teacher, but as a normal part of the mainstream teacher's professional role. Furthermore, the provision of directed time for planning should be seen as an essential part of the strategy. One clear conclusion suggested by the study is that if mainstream strategies are to work, schools need to be prepared for the deployment of support teachers.* Even where support teachers have had a formal course of specialist training, they may have neither the status nor the confidence to intervene to develop school structures and organizational strategies. For heads merely to limit the amount of 'withdrawal' provision made by support teachers may be to waste a more fruitful opportunity to change structures, leaving support teachers demoralized and uncertain in 'other people's lessons'.

Qualifications and roles

Qualifications

It is necessary to question how far one has ever been able to speak of 'ESL' or English language *'specialists'*, when discussing English language support provision in LEAs. In Townsend (1971), it is interesting to note that although there are frequent references to 'specialist language treatment', the research showed that there were extremely few trained 'specialist' language teachers employed in the language centres. Indeed, out of two LEAs, only one teacher trained in TESL was identified out of 41 staff (p. 93). Moreover, language centre and support posts at that time appeared to have low status, attracting large numbers of probationers, unqualified teachers and part-timers. Townsend and Brittan (1972) showed by survey data that only four out of 66 probationers had any training in TESL; and only 15 per cent of primary and three per cent of secondary teachers had attended any course on working with 'immigrant pupils'. Both 'specialist' and mainstream training were lacking.

While in 1987, the NFER survey identified over 2000 English support posts across the LEAs responding, in their report on English language support, HMI (GB. DES, 1988e) indicated that many 'ESL' teachers were still without any relevant specialist qualification. On the other hand, they indicated the presence of other teachers with a range of specialist qualifications, including relevant Master degrees and degrees in language and linguistics. HMI note, however, 'although increasing, the reservoir of appropriately qualified or experienced teachers is small' (p. 5). Only half of the six authorities they had studied 'had made concerted efforts to recruit teachers already qualified in 'ESL' and to train those already in post' (p. 4). Of the six LEAs we visited during the course of the NFER Project, only two were able to claim that almost all their language support team had appropriate specialist qualifications. However, Bourne (1987) in a study of initial training, has queried the appropriacy and relevance at that time of some of the initial training then being offered by institutions in view of the changing roles of English support teachers.

This variety of existing qualifications as well as experience needs to be taken into account by LEAs in planning how they might most effectively deploy existing English support teachers. It would be facile to suggest all 'ESL' teachers are equipped to become advisory teachers responsible for in-service development in their schools.

LEAs need to be careful not to assume that English language support teachers have the training to be able to provide 'specialist' help, either in class or in withdrawal. This is not necessarily to be taken as implying a criticism of staffing. Indeed some advisers strongly stress the necessity of substantial experience of mainstream teaching on which to develop sensitive linguistic awareness and strategies for intervention for specific needs as they emerge. It is rather a question about roles.

Secondly, where English language support teachers are considered to be essentially experienced primary class teachers, or secondary subject specialists rather than language specialists, one needs to ask what additional support and training they need to acquire to be able to *add* to mainstream classes when working as team teachers. Or should one instead of seeing teachers as sharing different 'specialisms', see teachers in partnership developing classroom strategies to support the learning of all pupils?

One also needs to ask what part an explicit knowledge about language and language acquisition plays within this partnership, and, if it has a part to play, what sort of knowledge, and where it might be developed, both in initial and in-service training. (The Kingman Report (GB. DES, 1988) recommends that every school should have a specialist English language co-ordinator as part of its mainstream structure.This would seem potentially fruitful in developing language policies.)

Roles of English language support teachers

This chapter has observed the distance most schools still need to travel to approximate the model of English language support provision for bilingual pupils in the mainstream which was laid out at the beginning of Chapter 3. Although the ideal model for the English language support teacher involved developing strategies through informal in-service for whole school change, in reality, the roles and status of the support teachers were often very different.

On the basis of the survey and the LEA studies, a number of different roles for English support staff can be discerned. These include:

(a)   The 'remedial' role: Here the English support teacher is perceived to be offering individual attention to pupils to help them to complete their school work, either compensating for a perceived English language 'deficit' in certain children, or providing extra support for learning in response to perceived underachievement. In some cases this role is also a response to a perceived 'social deficit' in pupils, where they are seen to need special provision for 'security'. This role may be played either in the mainstream or in withdrawal.

(b)   The 'specialist' role: Here the English language support teacher is assumed to have an understanding of second language development as well as of classroom language use and of strategies to intervene directly in pupils' language development, or in the language and learning environment, in order to enhance pupil performance. Again, this role might be played in the mainstream or in withdrawal.

(c)   *The 'catalyst' role*: Here the English language support teach-
      er is perceived to be an 'agent for change' in schools –
      sharing knowledge and experience gained through extra
      in-service with school staff both within the classroom and
      in curriculum planning; being able to reappraise practice
      from equal opportunities and antiracist perspectives, and to
      work co-operatively with colleagues to develop new strat-
      egies, while continually monitoring or evaluating progress.
      This role is essentially in the mainstream.

(d)   *The 'good teacher' role*: From this perspective, the English language
      support teacher is simply a good mainstream class or subject
      teacher, working co-operatively in a team structure with
      colleagues to respond to the language needs of all pupils
      as they emerge in the classroom in the context of a whole
      school equal opportunities and antiracist policy. Mainstream
      and support roles may be temporary and interchangeable,
      and the role is essentially mainstream based.

All these roles were described by LEA advisers and language
service staff in discussing practice in LEAs in 1986/7. While two
LEAs visited appeared to stress role (d), the 'good teacher', the fact
that all the English support teachers observed in the study were
employed in Home Office Section 11 funded posts may constrain such
developments. For example, where teachers carried out mainstream
subject teaching for part of their timetable, it might be hard to
justify full Section 11 funding. Similarly, where teachers are seen as
interchangeable, and regularly change roles, officially the Home Office
would need to be notified of the changed Section 11 postholders'
names. Section 11 posts by definition are to be specifically targeted
to meeting specific needs; the 'good teacher' role, while attractive to
many teachers, and most closely compatible with many of the Swann
recommendations for primary schools (GB.DES, 1985, p. 393), may
require mainstream or a different form of extra funding.

Role (a) still seemed to be the role most of the extra English
language support teachers we observed had adopted in practice,
whether in mainstream or withdrawal situations. Few of the English
support teachers in schools visited had any specialist language
training; and only one saw herself in an advisory and in-service
role in the school. However, where teachers have found themselves operating solely in this 'remedial' role, usually on an *ad hoc*
basis because of lack of joint planning time, they have sometimes
expressed a lack of job satisfaction and frustration at not being
able to develop the curriculum. Such a role would not always
seem the most effective use of a trained teacher's time.

Role (b) 'the specialist teacher' is an interesting one. If there is any consensus on the knowledge and skills such a teacher should have in the mainstream context, it would appear to be most explicitly set out in the RSA Diploma 'Teaching English as a Second Language in Multicultural Schools', which at the time of the study seemed valued in most LEAs as a relevant qualification. However, the RSA Diploma itself was explicitly directed to attracting mainstream teachers as much as English support teachers, and indeed had recently changed its title to become the 'Diploma in English across the Curriculum in Multilingual Schools'. It would, then, appear to be essentially not a 'specialist' qualification, but an in-service development for any teacher in multilingual schools – role (d). The emphasis on more linguistic input in training for all teachers expressed in the Kingman Report (GB. DES, 1988) would also support this.

However, there would still seem to be an urgent need for language specialists at the advisory teacher level, to work in schools and alongside teachers on a temporary basis, to enable change to take place in curriculum delivery, to initiate school-based in-service and to develop mainstream practice and curriculum materials. Such teachers should not only be familiar with ways of developing classroom teaching strategies for effective learning, but also have had time to develop a sensitive awareness of the language demands of different learning tasks, and ways to intervene in pupils' English language development. Secondments at MA and MEd level would probably be necessary to enable such expertise to be developed.

Role (c), the 'catalyst' role, appeared to be becoming a popular way within LEAs of looking at the English language support teacher, especially in their Section 11 role. However, where staffing has remained unchanged, from our observations it was clear that in many cases the expectation that 'ESL' teams could take on this role effectively was unrealistic. Uncertainty about future roles, and defensiveness about criticism of past practice make some support teams unlikely 'agents for change'. LEAs need to decide whether long-term in-service for 'ESL' teams alone is really likely to be more effective than focusing in-service resources on a programme of whole school development. Riley and Bleach (in Brumfit et al, 1985: p. 78) noted the difficulties faced by single teachers returning to 'an unchanged institutional setting' after retraining. The 'catalyst' role needs strong support and backing from the local authority if it is to be successful.

Creating whole school change

Riley and Bleach (ibid.) identified four main factors which made for successful change in the secondary school, in leading to whole school responsibility for language development. These were:

(a)   staff awareness of existing linguistic diversity and of the effects of racism in society upon the school;

(b)   the existence of curriculum working groups as a focus for discussion;

(c)   familiarity with team teaching;

(d)   a mixed ability teaching structure.

Despite the very different structural organization of a secondary school, Bleach and Riley's paper points to close similarities between secondary schools and junior schools when it comes to identifying the crucial factors for change.

Richardson (1985, see diagram below) describes the process of change within schools as cyclical.

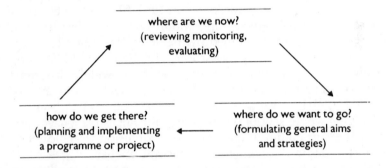

where are we now?
(reviewing monitoring, evaluating)

how do we get there?
(planning and implementing a programme or project)

where do we want to go?
(formulating general aims and strategies)

Often, too, the three stages operate concurrently on different issues within a school, progress in one area feeding into the others. If the language development of bilinguals is to be seen as a central educational issue in multilingual schools, then it has to be part of school planning in all areas of the curriculum and organizational decision making.

From the school studies, it was clear that some schools were working to create an environment which would enhance the language development of all pupils, carefully reorganizing in order to prepare mainstream classrooms and teachers for co-operative teaching to support interactive learning. It was also clear that LEA advisory services had played an important role in the more successful initiatives, providing expertise, advice, resources and, when needed, extra staffing. It must be remembered too that all the developments described had taken place during a difficult period of the teachers' and employers' dispute in the mid-1980s.

The evidence from the school studies suggests that when the whole school takes responsibility for the language development of all its pupils and sets up structures which *will support the review and reorganization of its provision, class teachers and English support teachers are enabled to begin to find ways of working together to support the learning of all pupils and provide suitable opportunities to meet any particular needs.*

However, there are strong constraints in traditional ways of organizing schools which need to be identified and altered if co-operative teaching in the mainstream is to develop. With the majority of LEAs in England claiming that their policy is to meet the needs of developing bilingual pupils in the mainstream, priority should be given to helping schools to reappraise their organization.

In our study the commitment of the heads was seen to be crucial, as was whole staff involvement in change, the support of a variety of advisory services, and some extra resourcing.

It is clear that while the movement of English language support into mainstream classes was widespread in 1985–87, it was interpreted in very different ways between and within LEAs. The detailed models of language support developed by the Schools Council Language in the Multicultural Primary Classroom (1982–83) and ILEA projects already referred to were unfortunately not as widely disseminated as the very much vaguer notion that pupils 'ought' to be supported within the mainstream. While some schools did appear to be developing whole school responsibility for English language support across the curriculum, there was some confusion over how best to support pupils learning English as a second language.

Probably because of the availability of Section 11 funding, more resources appeared to be being put into providing extra staff, even where their duties and function were unclear, than into in-service development for schools. *This appeared to be reinforcing the limited 'remedial' role of English language support teachers in many LEAs and schools, rather than the development of more effective use of extra staffing to enhance whole school curriculum delivery.*

Where extra English language support staff were employed, there was clearly a need for more thought to be given by school management to their role in the context of whole school responsibility for English development.

5 Community Languages, Bilingual Support, Linguistic Diversity

This chapter will begin by looking at the context of responses to linguistic diversity in which the introduction of community languages into schools has taken place. It will go on to examine the provision of staffing, training and management structures for developing community languages teaching and bilingual support within schools. Survey data will be used to identify the languages being provided within schools, and the numbers of teachers and schools involved in community languages work. Finally, we will examine the nature of the support given by LEAs to language classes run by linguistic minority organizations themselves. The next chapter will go on to look at policy and practice across and within LEAs, drawing on the questionnaire survey and more in-depth studies of the six LEAs.

While, as the Swann report (GB. DES, 1985) points out, 'in many respects ethnic minority children's language needs serve to highlight the need for positive action to be taken to enhance the quality of the language education provided for all pupils', meeting the full linguistic needs of bilingual pupils in schools in England may require a reappraisal of extra and mainstream staffing in many areas, in order to provide a wider range of linguistic skills among the teaching force.

Although Swann refers to educational provision for the 'mother tongues' spoken by pupils, a distinction does need to be drawn for the purposes of educational language planning between individual bilingualism, and situations of societal bilingualism. We have chosen here to call 'community languages' those languages which children not only bring with them to school but which are spoken and shared within the local area; that is, which have a local presence outside as well as inside the home, and for which, consequently, making extra provision could be justified both in terms of numbers of speakers and in *terms of their language's functionality and importance within local society.*

There are two aspects to considering provision for the languages other than English of bilingual pupils. The first is a response which attempts to make schools receptive to the 'mother tongues' (whether called languages or dialects) that children bring to school with them. The second aspect is to appraise the practicalities of making provision for the 'community languages' shared within the local and school community.

It seems useful to distinguish three basic forms of emerging provision for supporting the languages other than English of bilingual pupils found in LEAs in England. These forms are not contradictory nor exclusive, but could all be found within one school, in different permutations, or alone. They are: (a) supporting language development in multilingual classrooms; (b) bilingual support for curriculum learning; and (c) community language teaching.

The last two forms of provision, bilingual curriculum support and community languages teaching, differ from the first in requiring staff with special languages skills; the first, while enhanced by the knowledge and skills of bilingual teachers, aims to develop strategies for all teachers to support bilingual pupils' learning across the curriculum.

Language development in multilingual classrooms

This aspect of LEA provision fits easily into school responses to multicultural education by 'valuing' all the languages pupils bring with them to school, as part of their culture and identity. The Swann Report (GB. DES, 1985) echoed the child-centred approach of the Bullock Report of 10 years earlier, but with Swann extending the dialect continuum to other languages. Bilingual language use in the early years is then seen as part of a pupil's language 'repertoire', on which schools should build and extend pupils' language use into the range of ways of speaking and writing which are currently valued in society and considered important for academic achievement. Thus 'linguistic diversity' was seen by the Swann Committee to be 'a positive asset': 'all schools having a role in imparting a broader understanding of our multilingual society to all pupils' (para. 3.15).

Recognizing that teachers are 'unlikely to be able to bring about significant change unless they receive considerable structural support from the education system' (Houlton and Willey, 1983), a number of curriculum development programmes during the 1980s have attempted to make classroom teachers more aware of pupils' other languages, and of the ways in which pupils might be encouraged to draw on them to support their own learning and to support linguistic awareness among all pupils in the classroom. The most notable projects in this field have been the Schools Council Mother Tongue Project 1981–85; and its EC funded successor 'Linguistic Diversity in the Primary School' 1986–89, which aimed to explore the teacher training implications of linguistic diversity.

However, apart from these projects, linguistic diversity has become an issue taken up as part of many multicultural education courses, and its incorporation into educational thinking at national level is seen within the School Curriculum Development Committee (SCDC) National Writing and Oracy Projects, where projects developing bilingual work in multilingual classrooms were a feature of some local projects (e.g. SCDC Newsletter on the National Writing Project 9/1988). In some authorities the main purpose of school language surveys were said to be to raise awareness of pupils' other language use among teachers, in order to develop informal approaches to valuing linguistic diversity in schools, rather than to assess the practicalities of more formal provision.

In-service for, and practice in, supporting linguistic diversity in multilingual classrooms may often be co-existent with and indeed sometimes scarcely distinguishable from the mainstream English language support strategies discussed in the last section. However, the distinction needs to be made since in some LEAs and schools, as the NFER study showed, language support was in practice limited to English, with no overt encouragement or evidence of the existence of other languages within the school, other than perhaps a reference in school policy to the effect than other languages should be 'valued'.

For example, one of the schools visited, 'Edham', had a multicultural education policy which endorsed the principle of English language support within the mainstream, and whole school responsibility for English language development, but did not encourage the use of 'mother tongues' in the school. While the school placed some emphasis on its multicultural education policy, linguistic diversity was given a very low profile, with little evidence of any spoken or written use of languages other than English observed within the school.

However, the creation of a climate in schools which celebrates linguistic diversity, and which attempts to leave space for bilingual pupils to draw on their skills in languages other than English in approaching their learning has substantial support in current educational policy. One of its main advantages in being readily accepted as policy is in its ability to fit in with mainstream policy towards language development in schools. The famous quotation from Bullock: 'No child should be expected to cast off the language and culture of the home as he crosses the school threshold, and the curriculum should reflect those aspects of his life' (DES, 1975, p. 543) can be applied as easily to developing bilingual pupils as to developing bi-dialectal pupils.

For English ('mother tongue') teachers, the English language development of bilingual pupils has, in consequence of this tradition, perhaps been easier to accept as part of a continuum of language use from standard to a variety of non-standard forms, than it has sometimes been for 'specialist' 'ESL' teachers, who have worked with a 'two separate systems' conception of first and second language learning.

So far, the 'multilingual classroom' approach has wide support, in theory at least. The Kingman Report (GB. DES, 1988a) commends an example of primary school pupils drawing on their knowledge of Urdu to contribute to a class discussion (in English) on the nature and use of certain words in English (p. 44), and appears to accept a repertoire approach to language development (p. 14), provided the priority consideration is the acquisition of written 'standard English'.

Similarly, the National Curriculum English Working Group (GB. DES, 1988f) reported that bilingual pupils'

> knowledge and experience can be put to good use in the classroom to the benefit of all pupils to provide examples of the structure and syntax of different languages, to provide a focus for discussion about language forms and for contrast and comparison with the structure of the English language (p. 58).

The concept of supporting linguistic diversity in classrooms does not challenge the priority of English as the medium of education nor the existing skills and expertise of monolingual teachers. It is, therefore, still the most acceptable form of acknowledging bilingualism for most monolingual teachers and policy makers.

However, within the framework of a common curriculum, a number of educationalists have begun to explore the possibility of extending provision to reflect more centrally the linguistic and educational needs of a multilingual society.

Bilingual support and community languages teaching

Having established a framework of linguistic diversity as the norm in classrooms, rather than the exception, at least in theory, from which to begin planning educational provision, there was less consensus at the time of the NFER study on how far to go in making diverse curriculum opportunities available.

Alongside the development of support for monolingual teachers or teachers not sharing the same languages as many of their pupils, the Schools Council and EC funded projects already mentioned above had also examined the sort of provision that might be possible in the primary school both to provide bilingual support within mainstream schools for pupils' learning, and to develop literacy in community languages. Another EC funded Project 'Community Languages in the Secondary Curriculum' (Broadbent, 1987) explored the possibilities of bilingual work on both these fronts in the secondary school.

Agreement at policy level on bilingual approaches to learning was not as strong as for 'linguistic diversity' approaches. The Swann committee (GB. DES, 1985: p. 406) found that it could not accept bilingual teaching in mainstream schools. However, its objection was based on a belief that bilingual support would essentially mean segregation of bilingual pupils. This was at least partly due to its perception of languages as 'mother tongues' rather than as shared community languages:

> It is clear that both bilingual education and mother tongue
> maintenance can only be of relevance to mother tongue speakers
> of languages other than English...Where such provision has been
> made therefore it has inevitably meant that ethnic minority
> pupils have had to be separated from their peers for 'spe-
> cial' teaching. As we have stressed throughout this report,
> we are opposed in principal to the withdrawal of ethnic
> minority pupils as an identifiable group and to the concept
> of 'separate' provision' (GB. DES, 1985: p. 406).

In the climate of personal and institutional racism which the Swann report recognized as existing in England, such separate provision, whatever the intention, was feared as likely to be discriminatory and racist in *effect* in this context (GB. DES, 1985: p. 28). The issue must be, however, whether the way to tackle racism is most effectively met by denying a curriculum which meets the specific needs of bilingual pupils.

In any case, the models for bilingual support developed both in the Schools Council and EC funded projects were essentially grounded in mainstream provision and mainstream classroom settings, and hence appear anyway not to warrant the Swann objection, although the overall social context in which educational policy is implemented needs continual appraisal (and intervention) for its effects. Even Swann (p. 427) recommended the provision of 'a bilingual resource' person on the staff in primary schools; and the provision of minority community languages in the school curriculum as part of the modern language options system, open to all pupils. This statement was the nearest we had to a national policy statement on community languages at the time of the survey, and gave a lead to local authorities not already involved in providing for community languages.

In the 1987 NFER questionnaire survey, LEAs were asked to give details of teachers and instructors for (a) community languages in class during school hours; and (b) supporting curriculum learning in school through the use of community languages. The results of the survey are examined in the next section.

Community languages in English schools

The survey carried out by NFER showed that in 1987, at least 36 LEAs in England (55 per cent of LEAs responding) were involved in making some provision either for community languages teaching or for bilingual curriculum support within schools. Twenty-six LEAs were providing for community languages teaching during school hours, and 25 LEAs providing staff to support curriculum learning through the use of community languages.

All the Welsh LEAs responding (five), provided both community languages teaching and bilingual support. While one Welsh LEA claimed that 'most' staff teach Welsh and provide bilingual support, the others had from 842 to 147 Welsh teachers each. All the Welsh staff involved in teaching Welsh were qualified teachers, as were most of those involved in curriculum support, but two Welsh LEAs provided 130 and 22 bilingual classroom assistants in addition. (The details of the Welsh response are to be found in Chapter 7.) None of the Channel Isles responding to the survey made such staffing arrangements.

Table 5.1: *Number of English LEAs employing community languages/bilingual support teachers across the age range*

	Number of LEAs
Primary community language teachers	9
Secondary community language teachers	20
Primary bilingual support teachers	18
Secondary bilingual support teachers	4
Total no. LEAs	40

Table 5.1 shows that in 1987 provision was made largely for bilingual support in primary schools and more formal community

language teaching in secondary schools. In addition, five LEAs had community languages teachers working across the age range, and two LEAs had cross phase bilingual support.

The findings suggest a growth in community languages provision. Townsend (1971) found just 3 per cent of LEAs making some provision for the teaching of community languages, including French and Italian where these were spoken by pupils as first languages. Townsend and Brittan (1972) in a survey of 230 schools found that no primary and only four secondary schools provided some teaching of the languages of pupils' 'countries of origin', and although Townsend (1971) suggested that some bilingual support work did take place, this appeared to be confined to language centres on the individual initiatives of certain teachers (see also Goldman, 1967). Townsend (ibid.: p. 41) wrote:

the use of languages of immigrants' countries of origin by teachers or pupils is, however, generally discouraged, the emphasis being on direct method teaching and the constant use of English within the school.

By 1979, however, there seems to have been a growth in community languages provision (although it is difficult to compare data drawn from a variety of LEAs, as each survey had a different base). In a national survey, Little and Willey (1983) identified 13 LEAs (out of 94 respondents) reporting the teaching of minority group languages. Tsow (1983) identified 15 LEAs providing for community languages work in schools. Finally, Tansley and Craft (1984) in a survey of primary schools alone, identified 20 English LEAs providing some form of 'mother tongue teaching' in 165 English schools.

It would appear, from the 1987 survey, that post-Swann there has been a significant increase in interest in LEAs, both in community language teaching and bilingual curriculum support.

The 1987 survey identified a total of 646 schools providing either community languages teaching or bilingual support, 287 primary schools, 246 secondary schools, and a further 113 schools with age phase unspecified by LEAs. These schools were not just in the Greater London or metropolitan areas, but included 72 schools in the non-metropolitan LEAs. Nor were the schools making community languages provision limited to areas with 'high' or appreciable numbers of bilingual pupils, but distributed across areas of 'low' and 'moderate' numbers of bilingual pupil populations as well.

The findings, then, show that community languages teaching/bilingual support is not limited to areas of relatively high numbers of linguistic minority groups, but that there is a commitment to bilingual support also in non-metropolitan areas. Table 5.2 identifies the number of teachers involved in this area.

Table 5.2:   *Numbers of teachers involved in community languages teaching and bilingual support*

	Teachers of community languages		Bilingual support teachers
(a) Primary	72	(f.t.e.)	133
(b) Secondary	129		12
(c) Unspecified age-range	64		7
Total no. LEAs 69			

In 1987, 64 per cent of staff were involved in community languages teaching, and only 36 per cent in bilingual support across the curriculum. This proportion may well change in the future since Section 11 funding has become less easily available for community languages teaching, but seems to be still available for bilingual curricular support.

Provision appeared to be made fairly evenly across the age range, with just over half the staff (59 per cent) being identified as working solely in the primary sector. Again, the withdrawal of Section 11 funding from teachers working on modern languages option courses may change the trend, possibly switching new posts to the primary level, but perhaps increasing bilingual support for new arrivals at the secondary level.

Comparing the results with the survey of extra English support teachers, across all LEAs there was an overall ratio of one community language or bilingual support teacher to six English support teachers. In areas of 'moderate' (5–14 per cent) concentrations of people of NCWP family origin (1981 Census) 'ESL' staff still outnumbered community language/ bilingual support teachers on average by 17 to one at primary level and 14 to one at the secondary level.

The survey found that there were also 211 unqualified staff or 'instructors' involved in community languages teaching or bilingual support in LEAs responding to the survey mainly based in primary schools and largely funded under Section 11 or Manpower Services Commission (MSC) schemes.

Only four LEAs commented on the use of MSC funded schemes to employ bilingual instructors, but these four LEAs were employing as many as 73 instructors altogether under this scheme. In the main, it appears that LEAs were aware of the problems associated with building up teams of unqualified bilingual instructors, in terms of status, career prospects, lower payscales, and of perceptions of the creation of a 'second class bilingual service'. LEAs appeared to keep fewer records of the languages supported by the unqualified staff.

Languages taught and supported within schools

Figure 2: *Number of qualified teachers and unqualified instructors for community languages or bilingual support with number of employing LEAS (In addition there were 50 qualified teachers and 67 unqualified instructors of unspecified languages.)*

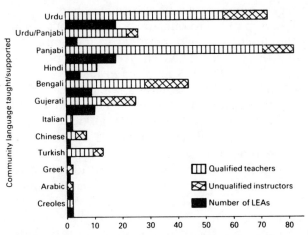

At least 11 languages were taught or used in bilingual support for the curriculum, according to responses from 73 LEAs. In addition, there were 50 qualified teachers and 67 unqualified teachers teaching a combination of different languages which were not specified separately by eight LEAs responding.

Figure 2 shows the numbers of qualified and unqualified teachers of each language who were identified, and beside each column, the number of LEAs employing these teachers. It does not distinguish between those teaching community languages as modern languages subjects, or as first languages ('mother tongues'), or those providing bilingual support for the curriculum, nor does it separate primary from secondary teachers.

Figure 2 does not indicate the numbers of teachers employed by overseas Embassies and Consulates to provide language education for pupils with family origins in their own countries, teaching, for example, Italian, Spanish, Greek and Arabic in schools by arrangement with LEAs. In some places these numbers are substantial. In one 'case study' LEA, for example, Italian consulate teachers were involved in teaching both collaboratively in class and by withdrawal of small groups in a number of primary schools.

Furthermore the chart shows only those teachers and instructors of whose work the LEA has been notified, or on whom the LEA keeps records.We are aware that a number of schools have made provision out of their own allocations both for teachers of community languages and for bilingual classroom assistants. To establish a comprehensive picture would need a national *school* rather than LEA survey. Our figures give an indication of current official provision. They are not, however, simply limited to the numbers in central teams. A number of LEAs also gave numbers of school-based teachers.

Not all LEAs responded to our survey. Broadbent's (1986) study of secondary Urdu teaching provides evidence, for example, that Urdu is being taught in three further LEAs which did not respond to the NFER Survey, with 19 further teachers involved in 1986.

'Urdu/Panjabi' teachers in Figure 2 we understand to refer to those aiming to teach and develop literacy in Urdu as well as to maintain Panjabi for Panjabi speaking children.

The majority of the staff were employed by LEAs to teach one of the first five most widely spoken languages in that LEA. Only 15 qualified and four unqualified staff were identified as teaching languages with smaller percentages of the pupil population, and most of these were employed by the ILEA, which provided for nine languages altogether. Discounting the ILEA provision, then, just nine teachers and three instructors of Panjabi, Hindi, Arabic and Creole were identified in LEAs where those were not one of the five most widely spoken languages. This represents just 3 per cent of all community languages teachers and 2 per cent of all instructors. Hindi and Arabic, of course, like Urdu, hold importance for some minority groups as markers of religious identity, as well as being national standard languages in their own right, although they might not be the 'mother tongues' of many pupils.

'Creoles' (details unspecified) were listed as among the five most widely spoken languages by four LEAs (see Chapter 1); but none of these claimed to provide teaching or bilingual support in Creoles. The two LEAs who claimed to provide teaching staff were one non-metropolitan and one metropolitan LEA; on further enquiry it was found that both were providing support for learning in the infant school only. Of the LEAs studied in depth, two LEAs had provided Afro-Caribbean support teachers. Although neither would have described these as teachers of Creoles, part of their role was likely to be a response to Creole use among pupils; the raising of awareness among teachers of the systematicity of Creole forms and of the richness of Creole oral traditions and literature. There is likely to be a number of such teachers across

LEAs who would not have been identified in the NFER survey as 'community languages' or 'bilingual support' teachers.

Overall, Creole usage appeared to be perceived within a contin-uum of dialects of Caribbean origin in England. The development of multilingual classroom approaches was seen as an appropriate response to dialects; with pupils being encouraged to move through a range of repertoires, while being helped to gain access to a wider range of styles of English.

Over a third of all LEAs were identified as involved in some way in teaching community languages or bilingual support. Those that were averaged three languages each. However, it is important not to overestimate involvement within LEAs. Taking the language, Panjabi, with the largest number of teachers/instructors, the results show that only four of the LEAs involved in teaching Panjabi (15 LEAs) had more than three Panjabi teachers. Numbers are generally very low. Again, for the next largest group of languages teachers/instructors, Urdu, two-thirds of those LEAs teaching the language (18 LEAs altogether) had no more than three Urdu teachers. Looking at Bengali, although nine LEAs offer some support in the language, one LEA had 34 Bengali teachers/instructors; two LEAs had two teachers, and the rest only one teacher/instructor.

Only six LEAs, in fact, had over eight teachers/instructors of any one language, these being Panjabi, Urdu, Bengali and Turkish, the last two being provided for within the same LEA.

Although Chinese was listed by a few LEAs as being the language of the largest linguistic minority group, it was not taught by any of these same LEAs. Chinese tended to be the largest linguistic group other than English in areas with very low bilingual pupil numbers overall, so that the largest group of Chinese speakers identified by any LEA in the survey (other than the ILEA), consisted of only 366 Chinese speaking pupils. No provision was made there.

Just three English LEAs out of those responding claimed to provide support for Chinese within the mainstream curriculum. Of these, only one reported efforts to teach Chinese as a language within the school timetable. (These findings are similar to those of Tsow, 1983, and Tansley and Craft, 1984, and appear to show no significant increase in provision over the past seven years.) The Home Affairs Committee (HAC) Report (1985) noted that only eight teaching posts approved for Section 11 funding were specifically designed to assist in supporting Chinese speaking children. The Home Office Circular 72/86 on the new regulations for Section 11 funding invited LEAs to consider employing staff to meet the needs of smaller linguistic groups by making joint bids for shared staff. No evidence was found of such

developments, other than for the employment of teacher-trainers for linguistic minority group teachers. Joint LEA staffing might be a way to respond to the needs of Chinese speaking pupils, who were frequently mentioned as present in neighbouring LEAs, but for whom (outside the ILEA) no teachers were provided by the LEAs responding to our survey. (However, Section 11 funding would not be granted for posts created to meet the needs of those of Vietnamese or Taiwanese origin, nor for those from mainland China.)

While the HAC report expressed concern that there might be an inadequate supply of teachers of Chinese, this does not appear to be the cause of the absence of Chinese teaching. Only one LEA (ILEA) reported having difficulties in recruiting sufficient teachers of Chinese. It seems likely that most LEAs have not tried to recruit in this area.

Chinese does appear, then, to have low priority even where LEAs are making community languages provision. In contrast to mainstream curriculum provision, however, Taylor (1987) notes that the Hong Kong Government Office listed 83 Chinese language schools operating in the UK in 1984. As for parental and community attitudes towards language maintenance, the HAC (1985) Report noted that mother tongue teaching was the subject most commonly mentioned by those interviewed in the course of their inquiry into the concerns of the Chinese community in Britian.

However, overall numbers of bilingual pupils within LEAs was not a final deciding factor for provision within the curriculum. For example, one of the so-called 'all White' counties had a population of less than 250 pupils speaking the most widely spoken local language other than English, Bengali. Yet it had employed a peripatetic Bengali support assistant to work across six schools in the LEA.

Supply and training of teachers

Of all the LEAs responding to the NFER survey who made some provision for bilingual pupils, 46 per cent (30 LEAs) claimed to have had difficulty in recruiting qualified teachers of community languages.The languages involved were Urdu (13 LEAs), Panjabi (10 LEAs), Gujerati (8 LEAs), Bengali (8 LEAs), 'all' (5 LEAs), and 'South Asian' (3 LEAs).

A recent survey of secondary schools (Rees, 1989) found very few teachers of other curriculum subjects who had a degree or teaching qualification in one of the languages identified in this project as being widely spoken by pupils in English schools, other than those who were already working as community languages teachers. If this survey is correct, it would suggest that there is not a large already existing source of teachers with recognized qualifications in the appropriate languages, currently teaching other subjects, to draw upon. There will be more qualified teachers who were not identified in Rees' survey who, although without formal qualifications in the languages concerned, are themselves fluent bilinguals. Without the identification of these teachers, however, the extent of this 'hidden resource' is unknown.

Some of these subject teachers, if willing, would need in-service support to adopt bilingual methods in class. Others might appreciate provision of the sort of intensive language classes available to teachers in Wales to become fully confident in teaching their languages. However, it is likely that many teachers of other subjects might be unwilling to become identified as 'bilingual teachers' if this involved the lack of a clear career structure.

To maintain minority languages and support pupils' learning needs in the short term, some LEAs have found it necessary to look for alternative sources of bilingual teaching staff. A number of LEAs have attempted to gain DES qualified teacher status (QTS) for bilingual teachers with overseas teaching qualifications not recognized in England. In many cases these teachers were already working as 'instructors' in LEA schools. But although 30 LEAs in the NFER survey had claimed to have had difficulty in recruiting staff, only 17 LEAs had made an attempt to gain QTS for a total of 48 minority ethnic group teachers with overseas qualifications over the past five years. Twelve of these LEAs had been successful in gaining QTS for a total of just 18 teachers, with a decision on a further eight teachers 'pending'.

However, four of these LEAs said the figures given above were specifically for applications for 'community languages teachers' and that 'many more bids' had been made for 'mainstream subject teachers'.

QTS may be granted by the DES if an overseas training course is 'approved as comparable' to a UK teacher training course, and if the teacher also has an accepted 'O' level equivalent in mathematics and English. Under Schedule 5, Section 2(e), Education (Teachers) Regulations 1982, recognition may also be gained if the applicant is specifically approved on recommendation of an LEA, with a number of years teaching experience, and maths and English 'O' level equivalent. The DES reported that the main reason for turning down LEA applications was the applicants' lack of 'O' level equivalents in maths and English (personal communication dated 20.5.88). This would seem to be an obstacle LEAs might consider overcoming by arranging tutorial classes.

In at least two LEAs visited, LEAs supported instructors' applications for QTS by regular advisers' supervision reports and courses in maths and English with recognition from the DES. These same LEAs had also been active in developing PGCE and access courses in teacher training institutions, providing financial support to trainees and seconding staff to tutor on courses. Three primary and one secondary PGCE courses specializing in bilingual support in the mainstream and community languages teaching were known to have been set up in cooperation with local authorities in the mid-1980s, at least one drawing on Section 11 funding to pay the course tutor.

A DES draft circular on 'Ethnically based statistics on school teachers' stated that the government will be encouraging 'more initial teacher training courses, specifically designed to attract students from ethnic minority communities' (GB. DES, 1987). However, concern was expressed by LEAs that DES changes in training college recruitment policy which limited the entry numbers of mature students were in fact acting against these recommendations. Such effects need monitoring.

In-service and curriculum development

In-service provision for community languages/bilingual support teachers did not appear to have high priority within all LEAs making some community languages/bilingual support provision. Of those making some provision (36 LEAs overall) 13 provided regular in-service, with nine LEAs specifying providing in-service sessions weekly, and four more monthly in-service sessions. Many LEAs left this question unanswered, but five admitted that no in-service at all was provided.

Fewer LEAs provided weekly in-service for instructors (six LEAs), but rather more provided occasional in-service (eight). Four LEAs admitted to making no in-service arrangements for instructors at all. Five LEAs, in addition to other in-service arrangements, provided support for staff to take the RSA Diploma in Community Languages Teaching. One LEA provided weekly in-service for teachers and instructors only during induction.

Bearing in mind the concern expressed by many LEA advisers that qualified teachers were hard to recruit and that overseas trained teachers were not getting qualified teacher status from the DES, it seems rather surprising that more support was not being given to staff without DES numbers within LEAs, in support of their applications at least for recognition within that authority.

Further, in view of the fact that materials, visual aids, tapes and other resources are rare in the field, it is again rather surprising that materials development was so rarely supported by in-service sessions and curriculum groups.

The HMI report (GB. DES, 1984) on mother tongue teaching in four LEAs expressed concern that there should be adequate provision of in-service for teachers working in this new and developing field. In one LEA visited, Education Support Grant (ESG) funds were provided for the formation of a regular working party of mainstream bilingual teachers (first and middle schools) to come together regularly to develop practice along the lines of previous Schools Council (SCDC) teachers' 'action research' projects.

The influence of the Schools Council Projects (SCDC) ('Language in the Multicultural Primary Classroom', 'The Mother Tongue Project') and the ILEA 'Bilingual Under Fives Project' was also observed in a number of other LEAs visited, in the ways in which they were approaching in-service through teachers' working groups at the primary level. Another LEA visited was involved in the three-year EC funded pilot project to develop community languages in the secondary curriculum (Broadbent, 1987) with three schools piloting new developments and teachers being involved both in LEA working parties and language specific meetings with teachers from the other two participating LEAs and the Ufficio Scolastico Italiano (organized by the Italian Embassy). The emphasis was on syllabus development, developing methodology through action research into learning in the classroom, and materials development.

The introduction of the GCSE had involved LEAs in developing suitable curricula and this also had an in-service spin-off. Broadbent (1987) reports that many LEAs were arranging special GCSE training sessions for community languages teachers. As the more in-depth studies in LEAs were already completed by 1986, it is not possible to comment on the effects of the introduction of GCSE on community languages secondary provision.

The community languages teachers at secondary level who were interviewed commented on the problem of scarcity of suitable materials for teaching community languages within the UK, and on the amount of time required of teachers to prepare their own appropriate materials.This was a particular problem where teachers were school based, rather than in a team structure with timetabled periods back in the teachers' centre. Although avoiding a separate language teaching force which might be seen as 'marginalizing', the school based policy in one LEA had meant that for the whole period of teachers' industrial action during the mid-1980s, no in-service had been possible for the secondary community languages teachers. Previously the teachers had formed working groups to share materials production, with each having the opportunity to spend one day at the centre about every six weeks. However, during the period of teacher industrial action, this opportunity ceased. Every teacher then had to be 'curriculum developer, writer, calligrapher, artist and teacher' within their own school, as the advisory teacher explained.

Nevertheless, by supporting secondments and with the help of supplementary training programme funds, this LEA had produced a complete course in Urdu, as well as textbooks, charts and flashcards, which were available on sale to schools within the LEA and outside it.

Although a central materials development agency, such as the Welsh Books Council, or a national community languages project, bringing together skilled seconded teachers with materials production experience, would seem to be essential in securing a firm place for community languages within the system, more use might perhaps also be made of ESG and GRIST funding schemes to finance local working groups with combined in-service and curriculum development objectives.

At the time of the NFER study, projects for the development of community languages appeared to fall between two stools. In one LEA visited, an ESG proposal for training community languages teachers had reportedly been turned down by the DES in 1986 on the grounds that the project should be eligible for Section 11 funding. Soon after this, Section 11 appeared to be withdrawn from secondary community languages teaching options by the Home Office. It would now appear that community languages teaching should be eligible for mainstream training funds. As part of the national curriculum development, LEAs could claim GRIST funding under a national priority area heading (offering 70 per cent funding).

Line management

Line management for community language/bilingual support teachers was often unclear according to studies of the six LEAs visited. Swann (1985, p. 409) recommended that at secondary level

> we would expect to see modern languages advisors having responsibility for the whole range of languages offered, including the languages of ethnic minority communities, rather than, as is usually the case at present, provision for the latter, if recognised at all, falling within the remit of the multicultural adviser or the E2L specialist.

The NFER survey did not inquire which officer was responsible for managing either community languages or bilingual support provision. However, although many questionnaires were signed by CEOs, AEOs, and other unidentifiable officers, of 26 clearly identifiable responses, questionnaires on community languages provision were returned by four modern languages advisers;

one humanities adviser; nine multicultural education advisers; two equal opportunities advisers; five special services AEOs; two 'ESL' advisory teachers; and three primary advisers (none of whom made any provision for bilingual support).

However, in most of the LEAs visited, efforts had been made to integrate community languages provision with modern languages at secondary level, while responsibility for bilingual support at primary level was shared in two authorities by groups of advisers, including primary advisers, early years advisers, multicultural advisers and in one LEA also the modern languages adviser. In one LEA primary bilingual support was seen as the responsibility of the multicultural education adviser alone. In this LEA the primary adviser stated that ways of working to develop linguistic diversity were not tackled in his own in-service work: 'Bilingualism is not a problem here. It's not a problem I'm addressing.' (The LEA had an ethnic minority population of over 5 per cent).

In three of the five LEAs that we visited which were developing community languages/bilingual support provision, community languages at secondary level were officially the responsibility of modern languages advisers. However, conflicts of interest were reported in two LEAs between maintaining the strength of traditional modern languages departments and pressure to introduce new languages into the system. In one LEA, for example, the modern languages adviser reported concern at the small uptake of modern languages at the 14+ option level among pupils, in the context of which the introduction of community languages would possibly have, he thought, serious effects on staffing numbers and maintaining curriculum options in French and German.

From the perspective of community languages teachers themselves, there was concern that foreign language teaching methodologies were inappropriate models for community languages teaching, where many pupils spoke the languages as mother tongues. There was a felt need to develop methodologies more appropriate to the pupils' experience of using both languages in daily life.

In another LEA, line management was very unclear. The modern languages adviser accepted responsibility for the teaching of one of the minority languages taught in secondary school, Italian, but Urdu teaching was in practice organized by the multicultural education adviser, and the modern languages adviser was unable to give details of provision or records of achievement in Urdu at GCE level, but referred the researcher to the multicultural education adviser.

In the largest LEA visited, the community languages service fell within the multicultural education service structure, under the multicultural education inspectorate. However, it was planned to restructure the LEA, placing community languages with modern languages, English and mathematics in a new 'Communications' department, but with a new post of adviser for Bilingualism to protect its interests and possibly to expand developments into bilingual curriculum support.

Some special attention does appear to be necessary to support the introduction of community languages within LEA structures if they are to develop in the curriculum, since community languages are consistently excluded from modern languages guidelines and research projects (GB. DES, 1986, 1988a; Rees, 1989). Consequently, unless modern languages advisers are highly committed, conflicts of interest or simply different priorities could lead to the neglect of community languages.

Once again, *the need for policy co-ordination across the advisory services seems important, as is the recruitment of advisers with knowledge and experience of bilingualism and bilingual language use.* Ideally, the introduction of community languages would require new skills at all levels of the education system which are linguistically based, not simply part of multicultural education.

Team or school-based structures

Although few LEAs had large numbers of community languages/bilingual support teachers, the majority of responding LEAs described their organization as 'team' based (18 LEAs). Overall, the picture was of growing recognition of the need for structural support within LEAs for their community languages staff while avoiding 'marginalizing' them into isolated services.

Two LEAs said that community languages/ bilingual support teachers were incorporated into a team along with 'ESL' teachers. While this might encourage the development of bilingual support strategies, there is a danger that unless it is common practice for the team to provide whole curriculum support, community languages work may be seen as 'compensatory' provision by pupils and staff, leading to deficit connotations.

Just six LEAs directly appointed staff to schools. One LEA had provided additional support through an Advisory teacher with a resources base.

Seven LEAs, some of the larger providers, had both a central team and staff on the permanent establishment of some schools. In one case the primary bilingual support staff were team based, the secondary community language teachers appointed directly to schools. Another LEA said that peripatetic staff were 'team' based, but that staff assigned for more than half of their time in the school were put on the establishment of that school. The one Welsh LEA which responded had both peripatetic and school-based teachers of Welsh.

While the benefits of a team structure are support, training and flexible deployment, disadvantages can be relative isolation from the rest of a school's staff, and possible lack of involvement in curriculum planning. However, the studies of English support teachers from teams in schools suggested these disadvantages need not be necessary. *The biggest problem for community languages teachers seems not that of being isolated by a team structure. Rather, it is the nature of peripatetic work, which makes it hard for any teacher to attend staff meetings, get involved in curriculum groups, and to become part of the school. This is especially so where teachers are working across more than two schools.*

Support for community languages outside the curriculum

After-school classes provided by LEAs

Resources for classes in community languages taking place in school after school hours were provided by 16 English LEAs (22 per cent of respondents). Forty-six LEAs said they did not provide any such classes (63 per cent). Eleven provided no information.

After-school 'clubs' for language, cultural and social activities were supported in Manx (Isle of Man) and Welsh (by two Welsh LEAs), usually at least partially staffed by bilingual school teachers. Further Education provision was also open to school pupils in two LEAs for GCSE in Cornish and Manx, the curricula for which were developed with the support of the LEAs concerned.

After-school classes provided LEAs with the opportunity of making provision for languages spoken by smaller numbers of pupils, who could come together for classes from a number of local schools. Of our respondents, at least two were providing classes in Cantonese, for example.

One LEA made funding available to schools wishing to provide after-school classes on the same basis as funding to voluntary organizations. However, only three schools in this large, multilingual authority appeared to have taken up this opportunity. It was not clear whether this was because of lack of interest on the part of the schools or lack of publicity by the LEA.

Classes in community languages may be run by school community languages teachers where there are timetabling problems which mean that a number of pupils miss the regular community languages classes during the school day, and sufficient numbers are prepared to stay after school. In other LEAs, after-school classes are the only regular feature of the LEA's commitment to languages maintenance. In these LEAs, members of the school staff who teach other subjects, but have skills in certain community languages, provide after-school classes, sometimes paid, sometimes in return for free periods during the day. (Of course, not included in our data are details of the many teachers we heard of who *voluntarily* provide community languages teaching to pupils in their own time. Our survey only looks at LEA supported provision.)

Three LEAs said they were resourcing 'twilight classes' in community languages, 'end on' to the school day. In one case, these were run by the LEA bilingual language service, but were not confined to community languages teaching, often covering other areas of the curriculum bilingually. In another LEA, at least four secondary and two community schools provided 'twilight' classes, staffed by school teachers alongside community organization teachers and parents.

A number of other LEAs opened classes at local FE colleges or Adult Education centres to school aged children, either in the evening or on Saturdays. In one LEA community languages classes for children were run by the Continuing Education Section 'back to back' with classes in English for the parents. In a few LEAs, all these different types of provision were in operation, twilight classes, Adult Education institute classes open to children, community languages classes on school timetables in some schools, as well as support for voluntary organizations to run their own classes. However, most initiatives were small scale; and seemed to be resourced piecemeal from a variety of budgets, or, in the case of the Adult Education/FE classes, from inappropriate budgets, with consequent insecurity in the long term.

Where other LEAs claimed to be making provision for after-school classes by paying teachers' fees (nine LEAs), the distinction becomes blurred between LEA provision of community languages teaching and LEA support for voluntary organizations through grant aid. It is not always clear whether the LEA provides the after-school teacher, or whether in fact it provides a grant plus free accommodation to an organization. In the majority of cases, the after-school classes do appear to be in fact organized by voluntary community organizations with support from the LEA, and these will be discussed in the next section. However, two LEAs make provision which is worth mentioning.

One LEA adviser 'pilots' new community languages classes after school prior to introducing them into the school timetable, both to gauge and develop interest, and to persuade the LEA of its viability.

Another LEA had established a Manpower Services Commission (MSC) funded community project with a full-time co-ordinator, covering 25 classes in 16 schools, each offering two hours tuition weekly. The LEA applied for Section 11 funding in 1986 to 'put the funding of this project on a firm foundation'. However, 'under the new criteria', Section 11 funding was not granted. Funding in this area seems problematic. It is interesting to note that the 1988/9 Education Support Grant Programme includes provision for an after-school study skills centre focusing on support for Afro-Caribbean pupils taking GCSE courses. Similar centres providing bilingual curriculum support might be possible through ESG funding, while staffing for after-school bilingual support for the curriculum would seem to fall within Section 11 criteria. As things now stand, there seems to be little secure source of funding for after-school classes; ESG funds are temporary; MSC funds do not offer instructors any security as only 12 month placements are offered. There would appear to be little real commitment from most local authorities to implementing Swann's recommendations for developing community languages maintenance through supporting community organization classes, in terms of regular provision within an earmarked budget.

Voluntary community-based classes

The extent of community organization involvement in the teaching of languages within England only began to be realized by educationalists outside the minority communities themselves when researchers began to take an interest in documenting 'mother tongue' provision. Despite a long history of provision in some languages such as Italian and Hebrew, it would appear that it was during the 1950s and 1960s that provision seemed to escalate among most of the minority community groups, according to reviews of research (Taylor with Hegarty, 1985; Taylor, 1987, 1988). This growth was often made with the support of religious or cultural organizations, sometimes with the support of overseas embassies.

Little and Willey (1983) reported that in a 1979 survey, 28 LEAs out of 40 supported community-based classes, but usually only by providing 'free' accommodation. Tansley and Craft (1984) in a survey of 92 LEAs in England and Wales found that 53 LEAs were aware of classes in community languages organized by local community groups in their areas, with 28 languages being provided for. Over 1981–82, the Linguistic Minorities Project identified classes in 18 languages providing for over 8500 pupils in just three LEAs (Bradford, Coventry and Haringey). However, LMP found that while all three

LEAs made provision for the support of some community-based classes, the majority of the classes identified received no support either for accommodation or for teachers' salaries.

While some linguistic minority communities receive support for language maintenance from overseas Embassies, subsidized in many cases by the European Communities Social Fund (for example the Italian and Spanish communities), other linguistic groups tend to be self-financing either through parental contributions or through funds from religious organizations, or both.

In 1985, the Swann Committee (GB. DES, 1985: para. 3.18, p. 408/9) recommended that LEAs should undertake the support of community languages classes which were contributing to the overall education of bilingual pupils in schools. It was suggested support could be given by: (a) offering free accommodation in schools; (b) making grants available for books and teaching materials; (c) providing in-service courses, and advice from LEA advisory services.

The NFER 1987 survey found that 48 out of 65 LEAs responding to the survey were anxious to show that they made some provision to encourage pupils' development of their community languages. Only seven LEAs of those who made any provision at all for bilingual pupils, including 'ESL', did not make some provision for community-based classes.

However, it is important to stress that, as LMP (1985) showed, LEA provision may not touch many of the classes in existence. Furthermore, few LEAs have researched into the numbers of community classes in their areas, and may know little of them, other than about those which have chosen to apply to the LEA for support or accommodation.

The majority of LEAs which claimed to provide support offered free accommodation to community-based classes; these were 31 English LEAs and three Welsh LEAs. An additional three English LEAs made accommodation available at 'reduced rates'. This was the main form of LEA support.

Resources (books and equipment) were made available to community classes by only 12 English LEAs. Only four LEAs specified a budget allocation for these resources, with figures given of £1700; £3000; £5000 and £10,084. A number of other LEAs bracketed resources allocations with grant allocation to community classes (see below).Other LEAs were unable to specify the figure allocated for resources.

Twenty-six English LEAs made grant payments to community-based classes. Grants ranged in size from £500 to over £346,000 across LEAs. Ten LEAs had grant allocations under £10,000. Four LEAs made grants over £30,000 each; taken together, these totalled well over £500,000.

It did not appear to be the case that LEAs made allocations to community-based classes instead of making mainstream provision. Three out of the four LEAs which made large grants (over £30,000) to voluntary classes also provided community languages classes within schools. Overall, 18 out of 24 LEAs which provided grants also provided for community languages within the school timetable.

The majority of LEAs making grant payments were in London and metropolitan authorities, with only four non-metropolitan LEAs claiming to make grants to community-based classes. It did not appear that these grants were tied to teachers' salaries. In some cases, as indicated above, they were also intended to cover resources. In most cases it appeared that grants were allocated to community organizations to deploy as they thought best.

Despite encouragement within the Home Office Circular 72/86, few LEAs appeared to have claimed Section 11 funding to support secondments to 'outreach' posts based within the community organized languages classes. Although specifically asked to mention Section 11 support in the NFER survey, only four LEAs reported Section 11 funding for posts connected to supporting community classes. Two of these were posts for LEA community class co-ordinators with a monitoring and administration as well as advisory function. A further three LEAs had bids for Section 11 posts 'pending', one of these being for '90 hours teaching'.

It would appear that very little Section 11 funding was, then, being channelled by LEAs into supporting community-based classes to meet the needs of pupils of Commonwealth family origin.

Four LEAs mentioned that some funding was still being distributed to a few community organizations through remaining Urban Aid programmes, and one LEA received funding for grant aid through an inner city partnership programme. One LEA visited where Urban Aid had been withdrawn, had continued to support classes so funded in the past from its Youth and Community budget, but this could not cover teachers' salaries. Few LEAs explained how funding was made available. One LEA noted that grants were made by 'the Council' not the education department. In many cases, it appeared classes were paid for out of FE budgets. Just two LEAs described a 'rule' for funding – one made a grant of £8 'per capita' of pupils, the second a grant of £200 per class of a minimum of eight pupils.

In the six LEAs studied in depth, five LEAs made some funding for community- based languages classes. In the sixth authority (Fordham) social services paid for classes run by an Asian Women's centre, and no other funding was made available; classes were even required to pay 50 per cent of the accommodation costs in school.

The contrast between provision in LEAs is instructive. In a second LEA, Ayton, most funding was by an inner city partnership fund, but direct funding was also made by the LEA to three organizations. In Edham, classes run by 25 organizations were supported by the Adult Education Institute. A bid for Section 11 funding for a co-ordinator to support, but also to monitor, classes had been made.

In Deeshire, the warden of the local teachers' multicultural education centre kept records of 24 local community-based classes providing for over 700 pupils, with a budget of £450 for providing stationery. Termly meetings were held for voluntary teachers, where the warden attempted to deal with accommodation problems, show new materials and suggest reading. However, the situation was not felt to be satisfactory: 'They leave feeling frustrated because I can't offer them salaries, and I leave feeling that because I can't 'deliver', I can't influence them.' The warden, in a Section 11 post, himself belonged to one of the local linguistic minority communities.

Another LEA (Beedon), had a long history of community based languages teaching, with a total of 71 organizations providing classes to over 8000 children in 1986, mainly in Asian languages, but also in Greek, Italian, Ukranian, Polish, and other languages. A supplementary schools officer had been in post since the early 1980s, to keep a register of these classes and to liaise between the organizations and council departments such as the planning department, education department, building and works. Although the LEA had offered free accommodation, there had been little uptake, with organizations preferring the flexibility and security of their own premises, some having in the past been made 'to feel uncomfortable' on school premises.

While registering with the LEA brought the advantages of funding and support, as with other LEAs visited, LEA support in Beedon also brought with it a control element. Once registered, voluntary classes were liable to be examined by the Council for planning permission, compliance with fire regulations, etc. Religious organizations which felt they had a duty to provide classes for their children had found difficulty in finding the large funds necessary to comply with statutory regulations. Some had raised money to buy buildings only to face closure on these grounds. Therefore, some classes were reluctant to publicise their existence, as costs could, they felt, outweigh benefits.

Beedon LEA had tended to make use of funding allocated to support community classes by providing training and materials for community class teachers. Out of a budget allowance of £30,000 for supplementary classes, £20,000 had been spent on the production of teaching materials by LEA-seconded mainstream community languages teachers. These materials were distributed free to local community classes. Only four community organizations had received funding for teachers, made through old Urban Aid programmes, which also in the past supported some building repair work.

It was LEA policy not to make payments to teachers, since the LEA 'accepts that the long term aim is to provide for the teaching of community languages in the mainstream system within the school curriculum'. However, there was growing recognition that even where languages were provided on the school timetable, some linguistic minorities would, for cultural and religious reasons, prefer also to provide some instruction.

Supporting supplementary schools cut across council departments, often raising issues of equal opportunities and racial discrimination. The support of these classes, one councillor said, required a re-thinking of departmentally based and fragmented council support services. There was a need to rethink whether administrative rules could not better fit the 'reality of the community'. The multicultural education consultative committee was in the process of reassessing provision, by 'going back to the communities and asking what they want the Council to provide and how they want it provided'. A bid for over 50 Section 11 funded posts for community tutors was one result of the consultations. However, it is understood that with a change in political control in the LEA, both the new posts and the consultative committee itself were no longer in existence at the time of writing.

In 'Seabury' LEA, although there was a policy of support for community languages within the mainstream school, provision for community classes had been around £66,000 in 1987 with over £28,000 given in direct grants to community classes to pay for tutors. LEA policy was that 'it is vital that the communities be enabled to retain control of language and language maintenance'. Community organizations ran after-school and weekend classes in over 80 per cent of LEA schools, some schools hosting classes in two or three languages. An LEA officer co-ordinated accommodation and liaised between LEA and community groups.

While the majority of classes were for Asian languages, there were organizations running classes in Greek, Irish Gaelic and in African languages. It was intended that direct grants would help establish new classes, with classes becoming self-supporting by the following year. A bid for Section 11 funded tutor posts was being considered. In addition, the Adult Education service ran a number of language classes which were open to school-aged children. It is understood, however, that soon after the NFER study, a rate-capping exercise led to substantial cuts in the LEA's provision.

Other support given to community-based classes reported by LEA respondents were co-ordinators and advisory staff (5 LEAs); surplus furniture and equipment (one LEA); teacher secondments to prepare materials for use in community classes; and in-service training and advice for voluntary class tutors.

The in-depth studies indicate a variety of responses, which reflect the findings of the national survey, while pointing up the need for LEAs to respond to local situations, demands, and perceptions of the wider social context.

Resource centres and in-service for voluntary tutors

The majority (26) of LEAs which had resource centres for supporting teachers of community languages (33 LEAs), replied that these centres were freely open to tutors working with voluntary community organizations. However, three metropolitan LEAs said their centres were not open to community tutors. Another LEA said the centre could be open 'where requested'. Three LEAs did not know if the centre was accessible, one writing: 'There is no firm policy on this. It probably needs to be better publicised.'

Following from the Swann recommendations that continuing in-service and advisory support should be made available to community class-based tutors, LEAs were asked whether they made in-service provision regularly, occasionally, or not at all.

Only four LEAs provided regular in-service. One LEA, in addition, provided a weekly in-service session alongside mainstream community languages teachers as an 'induction' during the first year of service. Seven LEAs provided occasional in-service, but 27 LEAs said no in-service at all was provided for community tutors. Four LEAs ran an RSA Diploma course in community languages for LEA teachers and voluntary class tutors. Just under half the LEAs did not respond to this question.

The survey questionnaire did not provide an opportunity for LEAs to give details of who was responsible for carrying out in-service where it was available. Where the authority employed community languages teachers, it seems surprising that more in-service for voluntary tutors could not be arranged, since LEAs could draw on their community languages teachers' experience to organize in-service sessions to share skills. Where no community languages work exists in the mainstream in an LEA, support for community based tutors to have the opportunity to appraise available materials, to meet together to discuss ways of working, and to liaise with local schools and class teachers appears to be even more important and worth subsidizing.

The Swann report recommended that LEAs should support linguistic minority communities in their efforts to maintain their languages by encouraging them to use school premises, as this would encourage liaison with mainstream teachers. As has been indicated, a number of LEAs (just half of those responding) did make free accommodation available. The in-depth studies of six LEAs indicated that this provision gave only limited help towards contact between the mainstream and voluntary sectors. Three out of the six schools studied had after-school classes on the premises. In one school, the voluntary classes had little impact on the school staff, although the head kept in contact over accommodation problems and administrative issues. Most teachers kept no register of pupils attending the after-school classes and appeared to have little knowledge of their activities. In a second school, voluntary classes were held on Saturdays, and although invited to school events and occasionally having given support in organizing special school assemblies, there was little contact.

In the third school, a 'community room' was established in school, where English classes for parents were held during the day, and where after-school classes took place, as well as other parents' meetings and events such as the school weekly 'bookshop'. A 'community teacher' post was established for organizing events and for liaison. Although the school did not organize the after-school classes (arranged by the local Sikh Temple), attendance at the classes was arranged through the school at the beginning of the year. Contact with the classes had led to the decision to base classes for first-year junior pupils within the school day, to avoid fatigue. However, teaching for these classes was provided by the LEA language service, not the voluntary organization, which continued, unfunded, in its work with older pupils. There was no record of liaison between teachers over pupil progress.

In many of the schools studied, few teachers had ever visited one of the community-based schools in operation. However, the few community-based classes visited by NFER researchers appeared to welcome visitors, and to be ready to explain their activities, expressing interest in closer contact with schools, on equal terms.

The need for links and liaison between community classes and mainstream classes has been repeatedly stressed in the past (Houlton and Willey, 1983; GB. DES, 1984; GB. DES, 1985). While the appointment of community class co-ordinators and advisory teachers does seem to have provided a level of communication between LEA and language class organizers, few LEAs appear to have set up structures to enable and encourage greater contact between school teachers and community tutors to take place.

The Swann Report suggested that after-school classes on school premises might lead to school teachers being better informed about 'their pupils overall education'. The studies indicate that physical presence might not be enough, and that other structures need to be set up to enable more sharing of experience. At the same time the studies reinforce the need for more information and contact between the sectors. Only in one of the schools studied in depth was there any register of pupils' attendance at after-school classes, but no record of progress was maintained. Information on the developing literacy of pupils could be extremely useful to schools attempting to support bilingualism and respond to multilingualism, as well as in raising teachers' awareness of what their pupils could achieve.

However, since many community classes are run voluntarily, schools would need to think how they might contribute to the classes and tutors in return for the useful perspective they could offer. This may require central government support for LEA funding for community classes.

For most teachers, the pupils themselves would be the first reference point in finding out about community provision. However, the National Council for Mother Tongue Teaching has been involved in a DES funded project to develop a 'mother tongue teaching directory', following on from the work of the Linguistic Minorities Project, which would aim to provide information to parents seeking language classes, and to community organizations about possible means of support.

Summary

The findings of the Bilingual Pupils Project examined in this chapter have shown that over a third of all LEAs in England were making some provision for community languages teaching or bilingual support within well over 600 schools. Most provision appeared to be focused on bilingual support in the primary school, and on community languages teaching in the secondary school. In almost all cases, the languages catered for in schools were those most widely spoken within each LEA. Little provision was made for the languages spoken by more scattered and less numerous linguistic groups.

LEAs committed to developing community languages tended to provide for more than one language other than English within schools, and also to provide financial support to linguistic minority organizations for voluntary language classes.

However, overall, numbers of community languages staff were low in comparison to numbers of English language support staff. Problems of recruitment were not helped by LEA difficulties in obtaining qualified teacher status for experienced and valued staff, nor by LEAs' inability to claim Section 11 funding for instructors undertaking training on secondment. Few LEAs appeared to be pressing for more support to develop training. Recent signs of central government support for increasing the numbers of teachers from minority ethnic groups were, however, encouraging (GB. DES, 1987); as was the evidence of increased structural support within LEAs following the appointment of some advisers for bilingualism.

Voluntary community language classes were shown to be thriving within the LEAs studied, and to be providing a complementary rather than alternative form of provision to mainstream community languages classes, where these were available (as, indeed, do the classes run by youth groups in Wales, outside the Welsh medium schools). However, funding for these classes differed greatly from LEA to LEA, and remained on a generally insecure basis.

Provision and practice within LEAs will be more closely examined in the next chapter.

6   Community Languages – Policy and Provision

This chapter will look at LEA responses to the 1987 survey on provision and practice in community languages teaching, and go on to examine in more detail the way community languages were being introduced into schools in the six English LEAs visited.

Changes in policy and provision in LEAs

LEAs were asked what the main changes had been since 1982 in both policy and provision of resources for pupils' other languages, and what future changes in policy, provision and practice they expected. There appears to have been a lot of activity, although possibly small scale, in this area. Seventy English LEAs responded to this question.

Apart from the 10 LEAs who made no provision for bilingual pupils at all, only 13 English LEAs responded that there had been no change in either policy or provision. Four of these were non-metropolitan areas in South and South-West England, all with under the national average number of residents of NCWP origin (1981), although one LEA included one town with 5 per cent of the population of NCWP origin. None of these currently made any provision for community languages either within school or as support for voluntary classes. The seven others reporting no change were metropolitan areas. Of these, three with 'low' numbers of NCWP origin, currently made no provision. Three offered free accommodation to voluntary classes, and another made grants totalling over £7000 to voluntary organizations. The seventh organised 21 hours of classes in three languages, Hindi, Greek and Chinese, outside school hours. The two final LEAs in this category were Outer London boroughs, one of which provided free accommodation to voluntary classes.

Despite the lack of activity to report, however, four of these LEAs indicated that the situation was being reviewed. One of the 13 LEAs discussed above commented that a new language survey was being carried out, and provision would be made if the survey showed it was 'warranted'; another expected more support to be made available to community organizations in future. Another commented: 'Issue constantly on the agenda now.' Yet another hoped that as its 'Section 11 Service' was developed, 'any serious need for community language teaching would be identified'.

Overall, the response to the questionnaire suggests that *the overwhelming majority of LEAs (all but seven of those responding) were anxious to be seen to be doing something positive for community languages in their area.* Many sent policy statements, working papers and committee reports. The influence of the Swann Committee report was evident both in many policies, and also in comments where there was no official LEA policy, e.g. (non-metropolitan LEA):

> Policy not formally promulgated but in practice along the lines of Swann. We have seven teachers working in nine secondary schools with a pilot project for infants covering four languages.

Provision for community tutors was planned. Another non-metropolitan LEA stated:

> The authority is seeking to enhance its provision for bilingual pupils in terms of access to the curriculum including through language support. It is also seeking to ensure that all children are prepared for life in a multiracial multicultural society.
> The Education Committee has endorsed the principles of the Swann Report.

This authority was providing bilingual subject support in three languages covering five secondary and two junior schools by employing five qualified teachers and one teaching assistant. In addition Urdu and Italian teaching were provided in one junior and two secondary schools.

Both the above examples do indicate a wide gulf between the intention and the resourcing which was current at the time of the survey, just two years after the publication of the Swann report, as LEAs moved towards curriculum expansion in this area. One London borough succinctly summarized its position: current policy was '*Recognition* of the fact that a child's home language has a role in the learning process; *recognition* of the importance of community languages.' Current provision, however, was limited to free accommodation for voluntary classes. Nevertheless, a school language survey had been carried out in 1987, and an adviser for multilingual education appointed. Future provision was planned to include 'the teaching of community languages in secondary schools and more in-service support for community schools'.

A number of other LEAs had moved on to take up much more clearly committed positions with respect to multilingualism. The minutes of one Education Committee meeting in 1987 noted that the DES (GB. DES, 1986) draft policy document on Foreign Languages, while welcome in its recognition of the need for the positive promotion of languages teaching, was

> inadequate for local purposes in the following key areas:
> the equality of consideration for classical, community and
> other languages; the need to include one language other
> than English in the curriculum core in years 4 and 5; the
> opportunity to study a second European or community language
> for all pupils in years 1–3.

The Committee was 'aware that policies have been developed to support community languages and that these have been expanded recently to include support of bilingualism from the nursery stage onwards'. To draw these initiatives together, an officer working party was established to consider the teaching of all languages, other than English, 'in the context of a framework which recognises bilingualism as a major and welcome development in our schools'. This move towards a unified languages policy, offering continuation across the years of schooling came from an outer London authority, already with 13 teachers covering two languages in 13 secondary schools, as well as providing tutor salaries, free accommodation and resources totalling around £3000 to community associations.

In this last example an officer Working Group had drawn up a report and recommendation on bilingualism and languages other than English, prior to releasing the draft for consultation with community organizations. Another LEA had proposed to review its languages provision by setting up area working parties chaired by an LEA inspector and composed of officers, heads, teachers and lecturers, parents and members of local communities. A central support group within the LEA was to be organized to service and co-ordinate the working groups. The aims of the working groups were:

(a)   to review existing provision for languages teaching and support and 'ESL' provision within each area;

(b)   to discuss issues arising in relation to existing provision and estimated need;

(c)   to extend the discussions among institutions, community groups and local cultural organizations;

(d)   to finally present a written submission to the co-ordinating group on the outcome of the discussions.

Such participatory policy making in education seems unusual in the UK, and it is not surprising that the organization of such a review should cause some controversy and some difficulties in organization. In the event the review did not materialize. Our NFER study has revealed no other attempts to widen participation in policy making in England to this extent as yet.

However, the influence of community pressure in bringing about policy formation and its implementation in staffing and resources should not be underestimated. In a number of LEAs studied there had been pressure on local politicians to account for provision. Yet unless communities are vocal in their demands, community participation in decisions regarding language education (community languages or methods of 'ESL' delivery) appears to be rarely sought (see Chapter 2). The following passage from the Council for the Welsh Language report (Welsh Office, 1978) 'A Future for the Welsh Language' suggests community participation should be a starting point:

> In our desire to arrive at a generally agreed view of what
> should be done to save and foster the Welsh language we
> needed to know and assess what the people of Wales think
> and feel about the language question, including their reaction
> to the task before us...We held consultative meetings all over
> Wales, to which we hoped that those committed, opposed or
> hitherto indifferent to the language would come (p. 45).

There is evidence from both the questionnaire responses and our case study data that where joint consultative committees had been set up, or minority group representatives included on Education sub-committees, there was a concentration on pragmatic issues. These included the recruitment and training of minority ethnic group teachers; the monitoring of achievement; career structures for minority group teachers in schools, especially Section 11 and community languages teachers; more liaison and communication with minority organizations.

In general, it also seems clear that provision had largely pre-ceded and often outstripped policy, indicating commitment from the grassroots, from teachers, schools and local communities, in many areas, and rather more reluctantly made explicit in LEA policy. Thus the officer of one LEA with 36 qualified teachers of community languages and four unqualified assistants, working in 17 junior/middle schools and 12 secondary schools, and covering five languages, commented that policy 'has not existed, therefore ad hoc growth. A working party has now been established to recommend a policy framework to the Education Committee'.

One LEA which has introduced a small amount of community languages teaching at secondary level (two teachers in three schools) and some bilingual support assistance in a few primary schools has adopted a 'doing good by stealth' (Kirp, 1979) approach. Considering the issue to be 'political dynamite', the officers had 'not judged it prudent or helpful to open a debate' until models of good practice had emerged on which a convincing case could be rested for the benefits of such provision. The annual report (mid-1980s) of another LEA with 1.5 f.t.e. teachers of community languages notes: 'Comprehensive policies towards community languages and mother tongue teaching continue to present the Committee with difficulties.'

Another non-metropolitan LEA where there are comparatively few bilingual pupils, has received a strong policy lead from council. While the LEA had so far only employed two bilingual support teachers covering three languages in two infant and one secondary school it had a 1987 policy stating that the LEA 'will support the use and learning of community languages within the curriculum where appropriate, or through grants to minority groups'. Future provision is expected to include the appointment of a co-ordinator of community languages, a language survey and additional appointments for bilingual provision in schools.

Again, a north-eastern metropolitan area, with just '246 bilingual pupils scattered across 57 schools' had a policy for mother tongue support 'wherever possible', and was working towards 'the development of individually prepared support packages on distance learning principles with bilingual consultant involvement and direction'.

Some LEAs which had substantial numbers of 'ESL' teachers indicated a wish to recruit more bilingual 'ESL' teachers, moving the service towards bilingual support over time with members of the team contributing 'as appropriate' to work in 'mother tongue' by having a timetable which included either all English support, or a mixed bilingual support timetable, or a full mother tongue teaching timetable, according to the teacher's skills and the needs of pupils and schools.

These LEAs were balanced by other LEAs commenting on the need to recruit more mainstream teachers with bilingual language skills, and indicating considerable commitment towards this by involvement in schemes for access courses, and teacher training initiatives such as those based in Leeds, Manchester and London which aim to increase the numbers of bilingual teachers in schools, mainly at primary level.

Examples of provision in schools

The following examples of provision are based on reports made on visits to the six LEAs studied in depth by NFER researchers and by bilingual teachers and advisory teachers on exchange visits to each other's LEAs.

Only a small number of schools and classes were visited during the project, and the examples are not necessarily representative of provision, merely illustrative of the variety of work observed.

Community languages teaching

Only in one LEA visited were withdrawal groups for 'mother-tongue' teaching at the primary level observed. This work was carried out by teachers who also regularly withdrew pupils for English language support, and often took place within the same 'language room' or area. In these classes the emphasis appeared to be on moving towards literacy in the pupils' languages other than English. In the early years, work seen consisted of songs and stories in Gujerati; a Bengali speaking group of children using a magnet board and cut-outs to recreate a story, and going on to draw and sequence pictures of the story, using 'Breakthrough' type cards in Bengali to help them write their own captions; pupils reading from Hindi/English dual text 'Terraced House' books; children reading 'Where is Spot?' in the Panjabi version, then filling in gapped task sheets with the missing words in Panjabi; a junior class of 9–10 year olds being taught how to form plurals and later completing written exercises using the forms, the exercises designed for three different levels of skill in Panjabi; a class book being made using photographs taken by the group.

It was not clear that most of the activities carried out in the withdrawal groups could not have taken place in the classroom. Given an environment in which children have come to operate bilingually quite freely, similar activities could be carried out in the mainstream. However, we recognize that such a multilingual ethos has to be deliberately built up and maintained.

If not 'withdrawn', the children would remain working in an environment where English was still the dominant language in their surroundings. While this may be a case for separate classes, it is unlikely that the very short periods of withdrawal for 'mother tongue' teaching which were observed would have been enough to counter pupils' experience of English as dominant in the school. The advantages in these short sessions seem unlikely to outweigh the disadvantages of withdrawal in excluding other languages work from the mainstream classroom and ongoing curriculum.

The NFER project has data from four LEAs on the organization of secondary school community languages classes. In all cases classes were either optional and open to all, or part of the mainstream curriculum for all pupils. None of those LEAs appeared to restrict secondary community languages teaching to the 14+ option slot, although some schools did. It seems clear that when this is done, it is unlikely that many pupils not already speaking the languages concerned would feel confident about undertaking an examination course within the two years left, especially where this involved learning another script.

In one LEA, community languages classes in one school began at 13+ as an option subject along with other second modern language options, with Urdu, Italian, Spanish or German options open to all pupils. In 1986 there were four English monolingual pupils taking Urdu in the school, with most of the pupils taking Urdu being Panjabi speakers, so that the classes contained a range of skills in the language. Graded Objectives in Urdu and Italian had been worked out, alongside those of the other languages. However, so far these were available in Urdu only to Level 1, the first basic oral level with few literacy requirements. Unless further levels were developed it would not be fair to say that Urdu was offered on the same basis as other language options. Exam entries were as follows: in 1985, eight 'O' level passes were obtained in Urdu and one at 'A' level. In 1986 13 children were entered for 'O' level, one for 'A' level in Urdu.

Continuity of staffing was a serious consideration for pupils undertaking an Urdu course in the LEA; with only two teachers of Urdu in the LEA and with a history of problems of recruitment, pupils had to rely on the teacher staying on to complete the course. In schools in other LEAs visited there were reports of courses folding when teachers changed jobs.

In a second LEA, four secondary schools offered regular timetabled classes in Gujerati or Urdu. In two schools Urdu could be taken only as a 14+ option; and in another school only in the fifth year and sixth forms. In one school provision was made throughout the age range, but there were problems of staffing at the time of the project visit.

Where community languages teachers are employed as members of another subject department (the science department in this case), but timetabled also to carry out language teaching, there are reasonable concerns that the school will be unable to replace both subject and language skills within one post if that member of staff leaves. Provision remains tentative, and unsatisfactory as a feasible option course for pupils. Some stability of staffing and LEA commitment to ensuring GCSE course completion seems essential.

A new initiative which was being developed in another secondary school in this LEA was a pilot first and second year course in 'language awareness'. This included a one year course in Gujerati for all pupils, taught in tandem by the modern languages teacher and a Gujerati language assistant, with support from the Gujerati advisory teacher, followed by two terms of French and one term of Spanish. It was hoped to be able to follow this up with the option of GCSE in Gujerati, but staffing was a serious problem again in this LEA.

In a third LEA with a strong community languages teaching commitment, and a large teaching team, the numbers of pupils taking Urdu and Panjabi had risen from 62 pupils to over 2000 pupils in 11 upper schools over a three-year period. Over 550 pupils were registered for the new GCSE in 1986. Syllabuses in Asian languages had been worked out with the local examination boards. Community languages teachers were part of the schools' permanent establishment. Since community languages teaching was generally available only in the upper schools, few monolingual English pupils were expected to undertake courses.However, just under 20 new community languages teaching posts had been agreed, with Section 11 funding, for the middle schools. Two middle schools had already introduced Urdu into the curriculum. In both cases, classes were open to all children and some children with monolingual English and Afro-Caribbean backgrounds were reported to have opted for the subject.

In one middle school, a bilingual English language support teacher taught Urdu on one afternoon weekly in a rolling programme to all third-year pupils. Pupils came to Urdu classes in groups of 25 for one term each, and had three sessions each afternoon, covering oral, written, and tutorial periods – to cater for the range of skills within the groups while including everybody. The majority of pupils were Panjabi speakers, but the groups included Gujerati/English bilinguals, and bi-dialectal and monolingual English speaking pupils, learning to share a local community language.

The EC Pilot Project (Broadbent, 1987) concluded that the secondary timetable framework which best suited the promotion of community languages was one which 'offered access to at least two languages in addition to English within a curricular core' extending across the 11–16 age phase. Such a timetable would allow for the development of local community languages teaching while still giving pupils access to the other 'community languages' of the European Community.

The attachment of community languages teachers to one school, rather than peripatetic working, would also allow for the development of bilingual curriculum support in secondary schools where there are pupils still developing the English language skills needed to participate fully in the curriculum. One effect of the new Section

11 regulations might be to encourage more bilingual team teaching, since this would attract Section 11 funding. The experience of bilingual team teaching in the early years suggests this could be to the benefit of the linguistic awareness of all pupils and also support the development of the community languages of bilinguals fluent in English in a wider range of domains across the curriculum.

However, while 'support' teaching is still seen as having low status and a poor career structure, bilingual teachers are unlikely to wish to develop this role. *Again, as with English language support, there is a need for a sustained programme of in-service to develop team teaching strategies, involving advisory services working alongside teachers in school on a much more regular basis to develop 'normal' tandem teaching structures across the school, into which bilingual support would also fit.*

The role of bilingual support teachers

Bilingual support in the LEAs visited, as in the national survey findings, was found to be in the primary age range rather than at secondary level.

The in-class bilingual support work seen in the LEAs visited appeared to fall into one of three main categories, with most teachers or 'assistants' undertaking all three at different times:

(a)   *Individual support for pupils in the class:* where unqualified assistants were deployed in schools there was sometimes a concentration on helping individual pupils newly arrived in England, or in other classes, on helping 'slow learners' with their work. It would seem important to think through the 'hidden curriculum' involved in this, in terms of pupils' perception of the status and value of other languages in the society and in learning.

(b)   *Translating work:* bilingual teachers and assistants undertook tasks such as labelling displays in two or more languages, making bilingual notices, preparing audio tapes in other languages, and working with pupils to translate their own work for dual language texts.

(c)   *Whole class work:*

(1)   leading the class – a number of lessons were observed which included bilingual story telling sessions; in one case a bilingual support teacher led a class developing work on spices, but added to her multicultural education objectives by including work on calligraphy, with all pupils writing the names of the spices in Panjabi;

(2)   in partnership – full tandem teaching of lessons which the bilingual support teacher or assistant had been

fully involved in preparing, involving the full class and linguistically mixed groups of pupils; with the bilingual teachers using both English and another language as they moved round the groups. The tasks sometimes involved written work in other languages, or sometimes it was left to pupils to choose how to record their work. This sort of partnership teaching was only observed in infant school classrooms in the schools visited.

It is important to note that in visiting the schools it was found that simply the presence of teachers and assistants who happened to be bilingual in schools was no guarantee of a multilingual ethos in the classroom or of bilingual support. In the same way as little use of the languages other than English was observed in some schools visited even where there was a high number of bilingual pupils sharing the same languages, so, too, where schools had no positive policy of bilingual support, bilingual teachers and assistants sometimes felt it was either inappropriate or 'uncomfortable' to use other languages with pupils in class.

In some cases, bilingual mainstream teachers clearly resisted efforts made to involve them in bilingual support or community language teaching roles which they felt might 'marginalize' them, and for which they themselves had not received a convincing rationale through in-service development.

Some bilingual assistants with no previous teaching experience had received no briefing or training on being appointed to schools, and both they and some teachers were very unclear of their role in comparison with the monolingual classroom assistants or 'helpers'. *Job descriptions need to be carefully and clearly negotiated.*

Some teachers, although already involved in regular and effective team teaching with colleagues, did not involve the bilingual assistants in lesson planning and preparation, or find time to explain the objectives of tasks to them, or even in some cases, the sort of outcomes expected. Consequently the assistants' interpretation of the activity naturally sometimes failed to match that of the teachers'. *Whole-school in-service would appear to be particularly important where unqualified bilingual assistants are to be employed, to prepare schools to receive them, and to negotiate their objectives, their roles and their status within the school, as recommended with regard to English language support as well.*

Although not part of LEA funded provision, it is useful to draw attention to features of one school's provision in particular. This primary school had in 1985 initiated a community languages programme of its own with a steering committee and regular external evaluation. Drawing initially on inner city partnership funding, it had later received funding from a private trust for over a year. It was hoped that external evaluation would lead to LEA support.

The school had employed six 'Education Workers', parents who were bilingual in English and either Panjabi, Bengali, Gujerati or Urdu. A deliberate decision had been taken by the Head (himself bilingual) and the steering group, to employ parents, because the school hoped to provide them with skills and confidence, perhaps leading to further training; as well as to develop links between the school and local community. The 'workers' were employed for four or five hours each. Special concern had been paid to salary levels and ensuring status within the school, and although hourly rates remained low, they had been more than doubled since the programme's initiation (to £7 per hour in 1987). The project included a training programme for 'workers' of a half day weekly throughout the programme.

The crucial feature of the project was the Head's determination to involve the whole school staff. All the 'workers' worked in class, alongside class teachers. A weekly lunchtime programme of 'liaison' meetings was set up for the whole school, including workers, to discuss and plan progress. The plan for one early meeting read: 'Checking viability of classroom placements. Discussing training programme for workers – any omissions or irrelevancies? The schedule of prompts for lesson planning. Don't send your partner to the corner!'

The 'schedule of prompts for lesson planning' stressed collaborative working and the issues that needed to be worked out together before joint work in the classroom, e.g. lesson content, grouping, and materials required. The prompt asked 'Should we try to demonstrate by talking to each other and to the class, as teaching partners, how important talk is?'

Workers reported that while some staff were 'not supportive' at the beginning of the project, they had largely been won over through the regular staff meetings. Once again, as in the more effective English support initiatives, an integrated topic based approach to the curriculum had been the vehicle through which issues of mixed ability teaching, language support and co-operative teaching had been approached.

While this example indicates the involvement of the whole school in developing bilingual practice, the question of the status and recognition of the bilingual 'workers' must be crucial in evaluating such projects. *LEA recognition and support for the further training and career development of workers seems basic if their work is to be recognized, especially where some had overseas qualifications and experience.*

In another LEA, the authority had organized the placement of extra qualified primary teachers, with good bilingual skills, in the reception classes of infant schools, to work in tandem and with equal status with the class teachers. In one school visited, the bilingual teacher worked alongside the class teachers in three reception classes, supporting the children's learning in English and in Urdu, where they were from Urdu speaking homes. Urdu was the language spoken by the majority of children from linguistic minority backgrounds within the school, and the whole school reflected the linguistic background of the pupils, with displays and books in other languages, mainly in Urdu, around the school. The work was supported by the framework of a strong school antiracist policy.

The reception classroom visited had displays of children's work labelled in two languages, English and Urdu. When giving instructions to the whole class, or talking to a small group, the teacher spoke in Urdu and English consecutively, and she did the same when speaking to individual children where they came from Urdu speaking families. The children worked for most of the time in small mixed groups, frequently 'code-switching' from one language to another as they talked to one another.

One table had a dual language text written and recorded in both languages on language master magnetic cards. Another table had a number game with numerals written in both English and Urdu, and mixed groups of children played the game, counting and adding in both or either language up to 20. Children from English speaking homes were heard asking children from Urdu backgrounds how to say a number in Urdu, and Urdu speaking children asking the meaning of English words.

Three other groups were involved in various other practical activities and during the morning the groups were rotated. The teachers circulated around the groups, the one operating bilingually, but both responsible for all the children. (In a similar class visited in the LEA, a dual script word processor programme was being operated by the children to make the texts for their 'own' books, in English, or Gujerati, or as a dual text.)

The head's aims in introducing bilingual work in this school were to enhance the cognitive and social development of linguistic minority pupils; to develop stronger home–school links between parents and teachers, as well as to give continuity for the pupils; to enable the children to adapt to an English medium curriculum in the later years; and to develop the language awareness of all children.

There was no further bilingual support in the school (although there was another bilingual mainstream class teacher), so the approach was essentially at this stage transitional, to 'assimilate' pupils into the English system without denying the value of their other language, or its use in learning. For this reason, more emphasis was placed on reading in English within school, although parents were strongly encouraged to read to and with their children in other languages as part of the school's drive for parental involvement in reading.

One 'spin-off' of the bilingual work in the reception classes was claimed to be a more general awareness and use of other languages across the school, with a few members of staff learning Urdu themselves after school. (In most of the six LEAs studied in depth, regular classes were available at teachers' centres for teachers to learn some locally spoken languages. If teachers are really to show they 'value' their pupils' languages, it seems necessary to learn them, especially where the majority of the class share that language.)

The LEA had experienced difficulty in recruiting qualified bilingual teachers for this 'tandem teaching' role, once again because of uncertainty about status and future career structures. Consequently, it had agreed to employ unqualified assistants with biliterate skills in future on the condition: (a) that they met the minimum requirements for entry to an initial teacher training course; (b) that through in-service and guided school experience they were given as much support as possible to gain access to such training; and (c) that the LEA would support them while training.

Organization of provision in six LEAS

It appears that the introduction of community languages teaching/ bilingual support in many places is preceding or going alongside policy development, rather than being policy driven. It is also apparent that the whole issue of the introduction of the languages spoken within local communities, even where they hold the status of national languages elsewhere in the world, into the curriculum either at primary and secondary level is becoming highly politicized. At the time of the study, however, central government responses were unclear and the nearest document to a national policy, the DES Swann Report, had given an ambivalent response. As already indicated, Swann appeared to have influenced decisions to make provision in the early years and at the 14+ option stage in many LEAs.

In 1986–7 local councils themselves were determining policy on community languages in schools, an issue which was controversial within both politically right wing and politically left wing groups. While in some LEAs, as already discussed, LEA advisers and certain schools adopted a small scale 'hidden' implementation, in other LEAs advisers set up action groups and working parties, to lay out the rationales for supporting bilingualism in schools and to attempt to provide evidence to local councils on its benefits.

It is often not possible to compartmentalize issues in looking at bilingual provision – making bilingual provision seems to have effects which cut across LEA administration and management, and those most concerned with developing provision do not limit their interests to the classroom. Indeed, where bilingual teachers are not employed in any numbers by the authority, LEA officers *cannot* limit their interests to classroom methodologies, but must become involved in first identifying constraints on employing bilingual staff, and then overcoming them, if a policy supporting bilingualism is to be implemented.

Illustrations from the LEAs studied in more depth give more idea of the complexity of the issue. Three of these LEAs had Black and bilingual representatives on the council, and Black and bilingual personnel in the advisory services, with evolving community consultative structures. In one of these (Seabury, bilingual pupil population 41 per cent) a formal policy statement on bilingualism had been made in 1983. This stated that because the authority

is committed to a policy of multicultural education, the prevailing notion of a monolingual society is anachronistic. The authority intends to help bilingual children develop systematically their full educational and cultural potential by supporting home and community languages.

The basic aims of community languages/bilingual support teaching across the age phases in this LEA were laid out as:

(a)   'The main aim of the supportive use of mother tongue in *Infant* schools is to aid pupils through a transitional period to a stage at which major concepts and skill acquisition can be achieved through the medium of English.'

(b)   At *Junior* school level: 'Whilst the main thrust at this level will be to achieve full competence in English, support of mother tongue remains important to enrich linguistic and personal development and to reach full bilingual ability.'

(c)   *Secondary*: 'Of central importance is the recognition of the equal value of both European and non-European languages in the school's language policy.'

However, there were fears expressed by some members of the linguistic minority communities that in a school system that was largely staffed by monolinguals, and still perceived as largely ethnocentric or even racist, community languages teaching or support could become a way of 'putting black children on one side' by withdrawing them from other subjects for language classes, thus impeding their school achievement, however well intentioned the teachers were. A senior LEA officer within the authority expressed a 'horror of seeing bilingualism caught in a racist mode' like this. While multilingualism was a necessary part of an equal opportunities programme, all language provision in the LEA had to be seen within the context of ongoing, mainstream full curriculum reappraisal and restructuring – not as an 'add-on'.

This LEA had therefore, initially, concentrated on mainstream recruitment of Black and bilingual teachers reflecting the multilingual, multiracial composition of the area. Financial support (over £28,000 in 1986) had been given to local voluntary organizations towards language maintenance. The provision of community languages teachers in secondary schools was seen to be the responsibility of the schools themselves. While the LEA recommended: 'every secondary school must include some language(s) of non-European countries in its option scheme', schools were 'expected to seek to employ staff with this ability as vacancies occur'. This position was taken not merely because of budgetary restrictions, but because it was felt that schools' own commitment to the languages was necessary. As the language options were for all pupils, Section 11 funding was considered inappropriate and no bid was forwarded to the Home Office by this LEA.

At primary level, there was agreement within the LEA to appoint a number of trained teachers who were themselves bilingual in the most widely spoken languages. These teachers would be extra to school staffing numbers, to work 'in tandem' with reception class teachers, to support bilingual pupils' learning and maintain and develop their first languages. There was to be no 'hidden curriculum' message of low status for certain languages and language speakers – the teachers were to be qualified, experienced and appointed at Scale 2, with equal responsibility for the full class.

In the event, three years later there were just two bilingual primary reception tandem teachers in post, and at secondary level just two part-time community languages teachers, each with a language assistant, in the LEA's secondary schools. The highly principled approach within this LEA seemed to have failed (for whatever reason) to increase provision for minority languages in schools. The LEA then decided that since it appeared unable to recruit enough qualified infant teachers to team teaching posts it would employ unqualified assistants, but with the guarantee that their training for qualified status would be supported if they could gain a place in a training institution following LEA training and support for English and Maths '0' level courses, if required. Provision at secondary level remained totally dependent on LEA funding, since Section 11 funding for these staff was rejected by community consultative committees even before new

Section 11 regulations withdrew support for secondary options. At the time of the study no extra funding had been allocated for secondary community languages teaching. It remained the responsibility of schools themselves to recruit staff as modern languages teachers.

This example illustrates the struggle within LEAs to define appropriate provision and its place within the educational system and structures from equal opportunities perspectives. *It is not simply a matter of resourcing and the availability of bilingual teachers, although both of these are crucial. It is also a question of preparing a place for supporting bilingualism within LEA management and school structures which have previously been premised on monolingual education and the unquestioned dominance of one or two European foreign languages.*

In a second LEA studied (Ayton), new policy and provision appeared to be a direct reaction to inner city conflicts, strong community pressure and a series of highly critical research reports on equal opportunities within the authority. It is indicative of the difference in approach in this LEA to date that no figures were available on either the numbers of bilingual pupils or the ethnic minority pupil population.(This was the only LEA studied in depth which could provide no figures.) According to the 1981 OPCS Census, 15 per cent of the total population was of NCWP family origin. It was the biggest LEA studied in depth, with consequently enlarged management problems in co-ordinating and implementing policy.

No explicit policy on bilingual language support existed at the time of the study. Since 1983, however, community languages had been introduced into the secondary curriculum, with 16 teachers working mainly peripatetically covering four languages as modern languages options. The teachers were based as one 'unit' of the LEA's large multicultural support service, managed by the multicultural inspectorate. In many ways, community languages teaching in this LEA at the time could be seen as an 'added-on' service, Section 11 funded just like its 'sister' units, including the 'ESL' service, an Afro-Caribbean unit and a Special Education Unit for minority ethnic group pupils. At the same time, an LEA survey and report (1984) had stressed the lack of impact that multicultural and antiracist perspectives had had on the awareness and practice of most schools in the authority.

In this context, local community pressure for the introduction of bilingual support in the primary schools was ambivalent. CRC pressure was for support for voluntary community classes in the first instance. A voluntary organization provided a small team of language assistants for LEA primary schools at heads' request, under an MSC funded scheme.This provided a service to some schools in introducing bilingual support, in the hope that schools would take on the trainees after their MSC year. However, local critics pointed out that the assistants received low pay with no security and that the service removed pressure on the LEA to make alternative provision of its own.

The LEA was supporting in-service training to develop a bilingual methodology for English language development. However, the teachers receiving this training were the largely monolingual 'ESL' teaching team rather than bilingual mainstream or community languages teachers. The methodology therefore mainly relied on volunteer bilingual help, raising once again issues of the LEA's commitment to improving the status of community languages and community language speakers in schools. Overall, then, LEA provision for community languages was 'added-on', rather than part of mainstream policy, in a context where, in the LEA's own terms, equal opportunities for minority groups were problematic.

At the time of the survey, wide ranging plans for the reorganization of the Section 11 service in this LEA were underway, with Black and bilingual Section 11 staff being appointed both within curriculum development, policy implementation and monitoring advisory teams. A new post had been created for an adviser in bilingualism. The emphasis, within the Section 11 service at least, appeared to be on intervening in mainstream structures both within LEA management and within schools, in the first instance. Schools advisers were discussing guidelines for schools to support pupils' bilingualism, including the development of comprehensive language policies, purchasing of bilingual materials, community involvement and bilingual school displays and notices. They also stressed:

> In writing job descriptions, advertisements and determining
> where to publicise vacancies, particular attention should
> be paid to attracting staff who understand and share the
> linguistic and cultural needs of pupils...The engagement of
> bilingual staff, teaching and non-teaching, is a priority issue
> for schools with a predominantly bilingual population.

While not official LEA policy, the recruitment of bilingual staff at all levels appeared to have become a central issue in moving community languages into the mainstream school.

In a third LEA (Beedon, bilingual pupil population 23 per cent) all political parties had joined together in 1982 to endorse a statement on race relations which among other pledges, committed itself: 'to build on and develop the strengths of cultural and linguistic diversity'; 'to respond sensitively to the special needs of minority groups'. Responding to these aims more specifically meant: 'developing a multi-ethnic and multilingual administrative structure', not simply the employment and deployment of bilingual teachers. This LEA has since that period undertaken a number of initiatives focused on recruitment and selection procedures to bring about an education service more representative of local communities. By 1985 the officers' working group to monitor equal opportunities policies was calling for direct support for the training of Black, bilingual teachers. It had also realized that job specifications themselves must be open to critical scrutiny: 'Until there are sufficient numbers of trained bilingual applicants, we may need to consider new kinds of job specification and a different grading structure for some posts in order to draw in the necessary linguistic and cultural skills in the immediate future.' With all party support and a committed advisory race relations working group, it has been possible for the LEA to move forward in recruitment and the implementation of bilingual support and community languages teaching programmes more rapidly.

The LEA has supported the development of access courses for teachers and NNEBs at the local college, employing 16 bilingual trainees (1986/7), to attend an access course leading to the NNEB, supported by an LEA-seconded tutor. While support for qualified status to match that of existing staff in schools was always the first goal, in view of the immediate needs of pupils up to 60 bilingual primary classroom assistant posts were planned, depending on Section 11 funding being granted.

This LEA and its consultative committees had accepted pragmatically the need for extra resourcing if it was to bring about change in schools.Its 1983 Race Relations Action Plan acknowledged: 'The energetic pursuit of Section 11 monies will underpin to a large degree the implications of the Equal Opportunities policy.' Structural changes in the service were thus an early focus, with two advisers for multicultural education and a number of extra officers being appointed through Section 11 funding to manage policy implementation, including policy for supporting bilingualism which was clearly framed within a context of whole school and LEA reorganization in order to provide equal opportunities for minority groups.

Although an 'add-on' in the sense of extra staff being provided through special funding, every attempt had been made to embed provision within reorganized mainstream structures. Bilingual teachers were not encouraged to join any special bilingual team, indeed no such team had been set up, but were placed on the permanent establishment of schools whether as mainstream primary class teachers, or secondary subject teachers, including secondary teachers of community languages (who are located within modern languages departments). There was one advisory teacher for community languages based in the Modern Languages section of the teachers' centre. At the time of the survey there were 23 teachers of 'Asian Languages' working in 11 upper schools, teaching four languages to well over 2000 pupils. There were plans to introduce a fifth Asian language into the schools. Five hundred and fifty pupils were registered for the first year of the GCSE in three Asian languages.

Allocation of language teachers to secondary schools was made partly on the basis of the Language Survey results. Most heads in 'likely' schools did their own surveys of parental and pupil attitudes towards taking up an Asian language option. Once assigned to a school, the Asian language teachers joined the permanent Modern Languages staff. It was considered important that the teachers should be seen as part of the mainstream school staffing, not as an 'outside' team.

All resources for Asian language teaching came from the school's own modern languages capitation, including the purchase of the LEA's own publications. The advisory teacher provided informal back up and support to teachers in schools, but mainly concentrated on materials development, with the aid of seconded teachers, producing text books for schools and supplementary classes.

As in Ayton, there were the beginnings of a developing career structure for the community languages teachers, for while 12 teachers were on Scale 1, five were on Scale 2 and two on Scale 3. New Section 11 bids had been made to increase the number of scale posts available.

Four teachers did not have qualified teacher status (QTS) and were employed as 'Instructors'. Two of these had overseas teaching qualifications. In the past the LEA had been able to get DES recognition for instructors, following two years of internal appraisal by the school and advisers. This indicated that with LEA support and commitment, QTS could be attainable for more 'instructors' in other LEAs.

Now that the upper school community languages teaching programme had been established, there were plans to introduce community languages formally into middle schools, with a Section 11 bid for just under 20 teachers. The aims for the middle years were threefold:
(a) community languages teaching; but also
(b) mother tongue maintenance (where a language other than a national standard language was involved);
(c) bilingual support for learning (drawing on English, mother tongue and community languages as appropriate).

At first school level the main emphasis was on bilingual support for learning, either by a bilingual mainstream class teacher or, more usually, by an NNEB or classroom assistant working alongside a class teacher. However, mother tongue maintenance was also on the agenda, with two experimental 'extended day schemes' funded by the LEA, and more planned.

These schemes operated by drawing together teachers and parents to share methods, topics and resources, so that children's experience of learning Asian languages was not divorced from their classroom learning experience. Stories and topics covered during the school day were extended into Gujerati, Panjabi or Urdu after school by bilingual instructors and class teachers working collaboratively, with 'extended day' classes open to all pupils.

A DES Educational Support Grant (ESG) had been obtained to develop a project in which bilingual mainstream classroom teachers from first and middle schools were brought together to develop ways of drawing on their own linguistic skills and bilingual experience in supporting bilingual pupils in their classrooms, whether they shared their languages or not. This was a continuing development from involvement in two Schools Council Projects ('Language in the Mainstream Primary Classroom' and the 'Mother Tongue' Projects). A co-ordinators' post and in-service supply cover were provided.

The key issue for this LEA, however, on which all its community languages initiatives rested, remained 'the need to recruit bilingual teachers' so that different strategies for supporting bilingualism could be developed, and to work to provide a mainstream context and ethos in which these strategies would have positive effects for pupils.

The school-based approach would seem to need to be backed by central co-ordination for support, advice and the development of materials. An interesting feature of the approach in this LEA was the 'action research' perspective taken in curriculum development, a continuation of involvement in earlier research programmes, so as to include evaluation and dissemination elements. The availability of extra funding for such developments, either through ESG or another form of research fund, seems crucial to allow such classroom based work to continue.

The work in this LEA contrasted strongly with other LEAs where a 'specialist' approach to bilingual support was being developed, with team structures for community languages teachers. Fordham, bilingual population 26 per cent, had responded to community pressure through the CRC for community languages teaching by carrying out a language survey in 1983. At about the same time, the LEA involvement in the Bilingual Under Fives project (Schools Council) provided what they saw as evidence of the benefits of using 'mother tongue' at Nursery level. The education committee drew up an outline of what a 'general policy for community language support would ideally include'. This recommended the recruitment of bilingual teachers; in-school community languages maintenance and development; dissemination of information about resources; in-service on linguistic diversity for all teachers; the involvement of community groups; and 'a clear statement of principle about the place of minority languages...linked with policies on equality of opportunity and antiracism' (the same themes as those centrally involved in the other LEAs, above).

However, this particular authority came under little political pressure from members, being politically stable. A large measure of autonomy was allowed to schools and support services. This had meant that while developments had been made in the primary language support team, these were not matched in the secondary age phase, which appeared less influenced by the council recommendations.

Community languages in the primary sector were supported by the LEA's language support team, which combined English language and community languages curriculum support and teaching. Of a team of 50 f.t.e.Scale 2 teachers, 38 per cent of the staff were bilingual by 1986, with no obvious difficulty in recruitment reported by the team heads.

The LEA offered Scale 2 posts to all language team members, so support teachers had enhanced pay and status. In-service courses leading to the RSA diploma in community languages and to the RSA in English as a Second Language in Multilingual Schools were offered to all bilingual team members, who had one half-day in-service session each month in addition to the monthly full language support team in-service session.This meant that bilingual teachers could come together to discuss issues relating both to supporting bilingualism and to their role in school.

Teachers were deployed in schools where they shared languages with the pupils as far as possible, and were expected to provide English and community languages support, as well as community languages classes within school timetables 'as appropriate', in negotiation with school heads and supported by their team heads (one of whom is herself bilingual). The bilingual teachers appeared to often work peripatetically, with the 19 bilingual teachers covering 27 schools. Community languages teaching, as opposed to curriculum support, took place in 10 schools (two infant schools and eight junior schools).

The primary team heads also organized some in-service for mainstream teachers and heads, to develop the linguistic awareness of the schools in which the community languages teachers worked, as well as to develop mainstream support for bilingual pupils with or without support.

However, whole school in-service provision was dependent upon the influence of team members within the schools themselves as 'change agents' – a role made difficult by the often peripatetic nature of their work.

One further problem appeared to be some ambivalence on the part of some of the bilingual teachers about taking on bilingual support, where they had trained and saw themselves as 'ESL' teachers, and were reluctant to move into what they saw as a different area of work, and one which was possibly less secure.

At secondary level, community languages teaching took place within the LEA language centre and as timetabled options within two schools by one part-time teacher. It was not the policy of the secondary language support team to function bilingually.

The danger of the combined 'ESL'–community languages teaching primary school approach seemed to be that community languages could be associated with compensatory provision. Even where offered to all, community languages classes could be perceived by pupils and even teachers as catering for those pupils experiencing difficulties in using English, and who were already in 'withdrawal' English classes. The encouragement of language support team members to work more within the mainstream, alongside class teachers should help to minimize this risk, as would a policy that ensured that pupils with fluent English also had the opportunity to participate in community languages teaching groups.

The question of whether community languages teaching groups should be confined to pupils already speaking the languages concerned is also raised by this form of rather specific provision. In this LEA there appeared to have been no clear guidelines drawn up and agreed on by all parties on policy for grouping for community languages teaching in schools, nor a clear statement of its purposes and objectives in relation to the rest of the curriculum. These decisions were taken by individual schools and teachers.

Perhaps, if provision is to develop in consultation with minority linguistic groups in the area, it was too early to expect such clear policy, but the issues are serious and need to be addressed. The LEA had announced its intention of drawing up an action plan for equal opportunities at the end of the period of the NFER study. It is possible that this might lead to wider changes in LEA structure, a comprehensive policy towards community languages, as well as a clearer place for bilingual support within the curriculum.

Although in this LEA, the issue of who should participate in formal community languages teaching in the curriculum arose in the primary phase, the same questions do arise in the secondary school. Broadbent (1987) pointed out that the assumption that community languages classes will consist only of pupils with previous knowledge of the languages concerned 'does contradict the principle of defending a right for each and every pupil in maintained schools to exercise choice with regard to the balance of culture that he or she will adopt and in the forms of language that he or she will use' (p. 12). (This principle is accepted for English in the National Curriculum English Working Group report, p. 14.)

Many LEA advisers have stressed in interviews the necessity of any *extra* community languages teaching groups being both optional to linguistic minority group-members (they should have the choice *not* to take part) and open to all the pupils. This is seen as essential to equal opportunities.

Future plans for community languages in LEAs

A number of LEAs saw the future development of bilingual support and community languages teaching as severely constrained. Some responses were ambiguous (e.g. one stated on future changes: 'None, if the present climate continues.'). It was not clear whether the problem referred to was lack of local council support or lack of central government support – although the two are likely to be connected.

One LEA officer noted that existing policy agreed in 1985 which was supportive to bilingualism had had to be referred back to a council working party. He feared that the policy would be dismantled and initiatives reversed. He noted a growing argument against in-school provision, although support for supplementary schools was likely to be continued. Temporary funding for part-time hours for community languages in secondary schools had been obtained through the use of funds earmarked as the LEA's 25 per cent contribution towards Section 11 bids for languages posts which had not gained approval. However, the Home Office decision not to fund languages options in secondary school seemed to have clearly had a contributory effect on attitudes towards provision for languages in this authority. It was hoped, however, that a Section 11 bid for bilingual support in primary schools would still be agreed.

Some LEAs responding made it clear that any future provision for bilingual support/community languages would be dependent on Section 11 funding. Clearly, a number felt that provision would not be made from LEA mainstream funding. Some LEAs were making 're-applications under the new Guidelines' for posts and 'pilot projects', and complained of 'delay' in gaining approval. Another LEA, noting Home Office funding uncertainty, wrote that 'some county money (£20,000) has been directed to develop pilot projects in 1987/8', e.g. in grants to voluntary organizations. The response continued: 'If Home Office support were available, the programme could develop at a much faster rate.' Yet another respondent wrote: 'the Authority would wish to amalgamate and extend these projects (a community languages teaching team in secondary schools and a project for after-school languages teaching). Failure to obtain Section 11 funding has delayed these plans'. The response continues:

> The Authority would wish to extend its policy and practice if resources are available from one where community languages are taught and where bilingual support is available where 'possible' to one where community languages are taught and bilingual support is available as required. However, this depends on availability of suitably qualified applicants and the necessary growth of expenditure to create these posts. It is hoped that secondary schools will appoint teachers of community languages to modern languages departments thereby freeing the peripatetic team to work in schools where there is a small minority of ethnic minority children.

This response neatly sums up many of the issues raised: *a general feeling of good will from most LEAs towards the development of community languages support, but an assumption that this requires enhanced if not special funding; a recognition that there may also be problems in staffing programmes; and a not unfamiliar devolvement of responsibility onto schools themselves to appoint community languages teachers as modern languages staff where schools think this appropriate.* It is only a minority of LEAs which have taken on these issues themselves in order to finance, staff and lead as well as support schools in responding to multilingualism within the community.

Even in these LEAs, there is recognition that gains have not been made easily, and are not fully secure. Thus one respondent in an LEA with a large proportion of bilingual pupils wrote: 'The LEA is committed to making mother tongue learning accessible to all children in its schools and colleges.' The LEA currently had 17 teachers working across the age range, covering three languages in 24 schools. However, on future developments the respondent could only comment: 'It is hoped that the Authority will maintain its current mother tongue provision in the foreseeable future.'

If this seems an ominous note on which to end this section, it seems appropriate to finish by quoting from one inspector's brief report on changes over the past five years, to reflect on some of the gains made and foundations to be consolidated:

> Policy and Provision: (1) Provision of in-school teaching in secondary schools; (2) Increased use of bilingual support instead

of monolingual 'E2L'; (3) Greater availability of bilingual staff; (4) Better training for all categories of Section 11 staff.

In none of the LEAs visited was there any interest expressed in, or even discussion of, the development of separate schools for bilingual education, or for bilingual 'units' attached to schools on the Welsh model. The emphasis throughout was on developing strategies for effective learning through the medium of English in a multilingual society. However, some LEAs were also experimenting with ways of providing openings for pupils to extend their language repertoires and to develop literacy skills in more than one language within the mainstream system.

The next chapter will look at the development of bilingual education in Wales.

7 Welsh Language Education

Policy

A clear statement of current central government policy for Welsh in Wales is contained within the National Curriculum 5–16 Consultation Document (GB. DES, 1987), which reiterates the 1981 policy document 'Welsh in Schools':

> In English-speaking areas all pupils should be given the opportunity of acquiring a sufficient command of Welsh to allow for communication in Welsh, while bilingual education should be available to pupils whose parents desire it for them.

In discussing policy for Welsh teaching in Wales, therefore, it is necessary to distinguish two elements of any approach, the place of Welsh for those already bilingual or wishing to become fully bilingual, and the place of Welsh for the English speaking majority in Wales who would continue to be educated through the medium of English.

The aims of educational policies for Welsh in Wales have been essentially political, responding to a desire to maintain a bilingual society where it existed in certain areas of Wales, and to create a shared societal bilingualism in the rest of Wales. Policy has not been centred on the individual personal needs of the child entering school, but on societal goals.

The average percentage of fluent Welsh speaking pupils in primary schools in Wales was known to have fallen to as low as 10.6 per cent by 1976 when the Secretary of State for Wales invited the Council for the Welsh Language to prepare a full report (1978) on which to base a policy for the Welsh language. The interest in Welsh medium education was obviously not inspired simply, or even primarily, by the need to make education accessible to pupils speaking Welsh at home.

In 1967 the Welsh Language Act was passed, giving Welsh 'equal validity' with English within the borders of Wales. This meant that either language could be used in administrative and legal proceedings, according to the choice of the participants. While this Act should have given impetus to the need for pupils to learn Welsh for employment purposes, in itself the Act made no specific provision for language in education.

In their 1978 report the Council for the Welsh language concluded that the Welsh Language Act of 1967 had not had the effect intended by legislators of 'raising the status of the Welsh language in Wales to one of equality with English' (Welsh Office, 1965). The Council for the Welsh Language affirmed

> To us, bilingualism means that throughout Wales every individual should be enabled and encouraged to achieve sufficient facility in both Welsh and English to choose which of the two languages to use on all occasions and for all purposes in Wales (1978, p. 49).

In other words, the aim was to develop societal bilingualism, 'to support and restore the Welsh language and its attendant culture' (Baker, 1985: p. 41).

The 1980 policy proposals by the Secretary of State for Wales (Welsh Office, 1980) suggested that Welsh should be 'supported and fostered' to prevent its decline, since 'Wales has a distinct identity recognised by the people of Wales themselves, by the United Kingdom at large and by others', and this identity was 'to a considerable extent associated with the existence of the Welsh language' (p. 3).

This being given, more educational arguments in support of its inclusion in the curriculum were asserted (p. 9). Supporters of bilingual education in England will be pleased to note the Secretary of State's recognition that 'there is reason to believe that the use of two languages can facilitate the understanding of concepts and that in a bilingual programme transfer of language skills can take place between English and Welsh'. Furthermore, the proposals claim that

> there is no evidence that the inclusion of Welsh as a subject has had a harmful effect on general educational progress, nor that it bears significantly on the attention given to English, mathematics and science. Nor is there any reason why its study should result in a denial of opportunity to study at least one foreign language (p. 9).

Indeed, 'many pupils may be attracted to take a foreign language in addition, particularly in view of the beneficial effects on language learning which a bilingual education may bring' (p. 9–10).

Finally, the Secretary of State reported that

> A wider use of Welsh across the curriculum and in the life of the school generally can help pupils to acquire literacy

in both English and Welsh and the ability to use the two
languages outside the classroom (p. 11).

There were, therefore, no educational reasons for not permitting
Welsh medium education for those who chose it. It should be
noted that it was only possible for the Secretary of State to make
these statements because Welsh medium education was already in
existence, and had been backed by a number of research projects
evaluating provision.

However, although the government appeared now to give full
support to the teaching of and through Welsh in Wales, including
some financial support, local authorities were urged to pay careful
attention to the views of parents and their wishes for their children's
education. The 1980 document suggested

> authorities should explain the rationale of their policies, in-
> dicating why the wishes of minorities cannot always be fully
> met and justifying compromises which may have to be adopted.
> Where there is relevant evidence about the educational effects
> of various kinds of provision, it should be made available. The
> individual school can seek to enlist the active co-operation
> of parents by explaining to them the provision offered and
> suggesting the kind of support they can give.

Explicit language policies were thus required of each school.

This position appears to have remained the basis of government
policy. Thus the 1987 National Curriculum Consultative Document
(GB. DES, 1987) recognized variation in provision for Welsh within
Wales and stated that it 'would not at present be appropriate to
require the study of Welsh throughout the period of compulsory
education for pupils who study through the medium of English'.
Attainment targets were to be provided for Welsh 'wherever it is
taught'. In Welsh medium education it was suggested that Welsh
could be an additional 'foundation' subject on the curriculum.

The implementation of policy for Welsh was seen to require
sensitive local responses to parental and community feeling. The 1980
proposals (Welsh Office, 1980) in recognizing linguistic variation within all areas of Wales, suggested that the balance between Welsh and
English within the curriculum might need to be delicately adjusted,
especially in the primary phase, to 'strengthen the weaker language'
(p. 6). At secondary level the proposals also recognized that there
might be difficulties in providing full Welsh medium education, where
there were insufficient bilingual teachers or low numbers of pupils
wanting Welsh medium education in some subjects. In such cases it
was suggested the continuing work of after-school Welsh provision
through societies and youth groups would need to be supported.

In mixed language areas, the proposals were that both English and Welsh should appear within the curriculum 'both as subjects and as media through which other areas of the curriculum are taught' (Welsh Office, 1980).

In mainly English speaking areas, the authorities were encouraged to provide 'where possible' a full bilingual education in order to cater for the Welsh speaking minorities and any others who chose Welsh medium education. The Secretary of State for Wales also considered it 'a reasonable objective' for most pupils to have acquired enough Welsh to be able to communicate with Welsh speakers and some ability to read and write Welsh through second language lessons in the primary and early secondary years.

The development of Welsh medium education

Although strong supporters of Welsh medium education continue to feel disappointed that the government has not taken a firmer stand on the place of Welsh in the curriculum for all pupils (Baker, 1985), the position of Welsh medium education appears stronger today than at any time this century. The first designated bilingual primary school appears to have been established in Wales only as recently as 1939 (Baker, 1985). However, the movement towards Welsh medium education both within and outside mainly Welsh speaking areas has grown rapidly since then. By 1960, even before the Welsh Language Act (1967) came into force, there were already 28 designated bilingual primary schools and one bilingual secondary school in Wales, quite apart from the more numerous but less easily identified schools in Welsh speaking areas which taught through the medium of Welsh.

Although called 'bilingual schools', the 'Ysgolion Gymraeg' appear to teach almost entirely through the medium of Welsh. They provide for the Welsh medium education of pupils largely from English speaking backgrounds in mainly English speaking areas.

Apart from the designated bilingual schools, other initiatives have taken place to develop Welsh medium education in schools. From 1968 to 1977 a Schools Council Project was set up to foster experimental bilingual primary schools. The aim (Price and Dodson, 1978) was to enable 'initially monoglot English speaking children in anglicized areas to achieve a high standard of proficiency in Welsh' by 11 years. It was therefore essentially a second language teaching project. It appeared to differ from the Ysgolion Gymraeg or designated bilingual primary schools, in that the school day was divided up so that both English and Welsh were used for part of the school day.

It was similar to the Ysgolion Gymraeg schools, however, in that the programme seemed intended to be begun early in the reception class and continued throughout primary school, discouraging pupils from opting in and out during that period. By 1980, 187 schools were reported to be using the 'bilingual approach' devised by the project.

As well as the 'designated bilingual schools' and schools taking part in the bilingual project, a number of local schools in Welsh speaking areas of Wales also taught all or part of the curriculum through the medium of Welsh. These schools are sometimes called 'natural' Welsh schools. Despite the terminology, then, one is likely to find as many or more pupils from bilingual home backgrounds in schools not designated 'bilingual', but which teach through the medium of Welsh, as in those that are called 'bilingual' schools.

There seems little doubt that the encouragement of more pupils in Wales to learn through Welsh apart from those already fluent in the language has helped in emphasizing the need for the development of curriculum materials for Welsh medium education. Again, it may not always be appreciated by people outside Wales just how recent the move is towards the development of curriculum materials in Welsh. It was only in 1968 that the Welsh Joint Education Committee established the Welsh National Language Unit. Throughout the 1970s this unit produced primary Welsh medium materials, together with a reading programme in Welsh. From 1969–75 a Schools Council secondary materials development project was carried out. In 1978, another Welsh Office secondary project was set up to develop materials for secondary schools in geography, history, RE, and later biology, CDT and rural sciences. In 1983, a new Welsh Office project was set up to develop materials for fourth and fifth year curriculum areas. In 1986 a new SCDC project was begun (Ehangu Gorwelion) to develop GCSE materials. What seems substantial and established current provision from an English 'community languages' perspective has in fact had a very short history as institutionalized provision.

Local authority provision

Welsh Office Circular 185/77 (see Welsh Office, HMI Wales, 1983) noted that all local education authorities in Wales had some provision for the teaching of Welsh either as a first or second language by 1980. However, there was variation in the response between different Welsh LEAs. While all the Welsh LEAs appeared to offer at least Welsh medium primary schooling in certain districts for parents who chose it, not all offered Welsh medium secondary schooling. The most recent Welsh Office report (1988), 'Statistics of Education in Wales: Schools No. 1.', offered a similar picture of variation between the Welsh LEAs in the quantity of Welsh medium provision. However, by 1988 with the opening of a Welsh medium secondary school in Gwent, Welsh medium education throughout the statutory years of schooling was available in all Welsh LEAs, although not in all areas within them.

In addition to full Welsh medium education, however, Welsh LEAs continued to offer a variety of provision for the teaching of Welsh either as a first language or as a second language at primary and at secondary levels. In some cases this was offered as a compulsory subject for all pupils; in other cases, especially in the last two years of secondary school, as an option subject, and in some LEAs only in limited numbers of schools (see Welsh Office, 1983; Baker, 1985).

Welsh language surveys

A short series of questions on Welsh/English language use is included in the OPCS Census. The 1981 Census results suggested that 19 per cent (503,549) of the total population of Wales were Welsh speakers. Baker (1985) discussed problems within the survey form, (p. 2–6), which, as in the language surveys carried out in England, may lead either to over- or under-estimation. However, the existence of a language question, however simple, has permitted some detailed analysis of the distribution of Welsh speakers (however defined) within the borders of Wales, and comparison of this distribution with LEA educational provision (see Baker, 1985). This sort of comparison has led some theorists to suggest the possibility of 'language zoning', planning school language provision to match the demographic features of different areas (Williams, 1981); again an approach which it might be possible to apply to English LEA provision for local languages. However, at the present time, in the absence of any central language planning policy, language provision in Wales appears to rest mainly on parental demand, LEA policy, and available finance and staffing.

The Welsh Office (1988) reports the result of a 1986 survey in which primary head teachers were asked to assess the numbers of pupils fluent in Welsh in their schools. The results of this survey are shown in Table 7.1.

The Welsh Office report also showed that 72 per cent of primary schools in Wales had under 20 per cent of fluent Welsh speakers. Only 9 per cent of Welsh Primary schools had over 80 per cent of fluent Welsh speakers.

Table 7.1:   *Primary school pupils in Wales (5 years and over)*
by ability to speak Welsh

	%
(a) Speak Welsh at home	7
(b) Speak Welsh fluently although not at home	6
(c) Speak Welsh, but not fluently	11
(d) Cannot speak Welsh at all	76

Source: Welsh Office, 1988 Table 5.02

However, Welsh-medium provision in Wales is not made only for pupils who are already Welsh speaking, but also to develop the ability of children from monolingual English backgrounds to use Welsh. Pupils in bilingual schools have a variety of backgrounds. They might have two Welsh speaking parents, one Welsh speaking parent, or parents who do not themselves speak Welsh. They might come from an English speaking family with a Welsh cultural ethos, or from a home with a more English cultural 'atmosphere'. Again, the community in which they live may be more or less Welsh speaking. Children from any of these backgrounds may be found within Welsh medium education.

It seems clear that much Welsh medium education in Wales at the present time is provided for political reasons, to develop and maintain societal bilingualism in Wales, rather than primarily to give access to the curriculum for Welsh first language speakers, since Welsh is the home language of comparatively few pupils in Welsh primary schools.

Indeed, 'designated bilingual schools' (Ysgolion Gymraeg) were set up specifically in predominately English speaking areas in order to encourage the spread of societal bilingualism. This form of provision has steadily increased from 28 primary schools and one secondary school in Wales in 1960 to 67 primaries and 16 secondary schools in 1987 (Welsh Office, 1988).

Apart from the specially 'designated' Welsh medium schools, a number of other schools make some provision for Welsh medium education for those pupils who choose to be educated through Welsh.

Primary schools

In 1987, 358 primary schools were teaching at least some streamed classes using Welsh as the sole or main language of education, with another 227 schools having some teaching through the medium of

Table 7.2: *Primary schools teaching through the medium of Welsh, 1986/7*

	% schools	% pupils
(a) Schools having classes where Welsh is the sole or main medium of instruction of first and second language pupils.	20	12
(b) Schools having classes of first and second language pupils where some of the teaching is through the medium of Welsh.	6	3
(c) Schools with classes of second language pupils where some of the teaching is Welsh medium.	7	6
(d) Schools where Welsh is taught as a second language but not used as the medium of teaching.	46	46
(e) Schools where no Welsh is taught.	21	34

(Total no. of schools: 1762; total no. of pupils: 254,051)

Source: Table based on Welsh Office Report 1988. (The Welsh Office report notes that in fact schools may have classes in more than one category, although they appear in this table under just one appropriate heading.)

Welsh. Where Welsh was not used as the medium of education, 806 schools taught their primary pupils Welsh as a second language.

Secondary schools

Although there were only 16 'designated' Welsh medium Secondary schools in Wales in 1986/7, this figure does not include a large number of schools in mainly Welsh speaking areas where one medium of instruction was Welsh (Welsh Office, 1988). A total of 53 secondary schools in Wales offered classes taught through the medium of Welsh to pupils aged from 11 to 16 years old. Thirty-four schools offered Welsh medium classes in over 11 curriculum subjects, with a further 19 schools offering from one to 10 subjects taught through Welsh.

Subjects taught through Welsh ranged from Religious Knowledge and History (51 schools, with 7.4 per cent of the pupil form total involved) to Chemistry and Drama (20 schools, with 1.3 per cent and 2 per cent of pupil form total involved). As many as 25 schools claimed to teach French through the medium of Welsh

(3.3 per cent of pupil form total). In 1987, subject entries through the medium of Welsh in WJEC examinations represented 2.3 per cent of all CSE entries, 2.8 per cent of all 'O' Level entries, and 2.3 per cent of all entries at 'A' Level (Welsh Office, 1988).

Alongside Welsh medium education, however, the majority of secondary schools in Wales made some provision for the teaching of Welsh either as a first or a second language (86 per cent). Each school appeared to have made a decision on whether to approach Welsh teaching as a first or second language, based on the linguistic background of pupils within its particular area. While only 4 per cent of the 234 secondary schools taught Welsh as a first language only, 51 per cent taught Welsh as a second language, and Welsh was taught as a first and second language in 31 per cent of secondary schools (Welsh Office, 1988).

However, not all pupils learnt Welsh throughout their schooling. Forty-eight per cent of secondary pupils were still not taught Welsh at all in 1986/7. Eleven per cent were taught Welsh as a first language and 41 per cent were taught Welsh as a second language. Regional variation was important. Over 75 per cent of those taught Welsh as a first language were in schools in just two Welsh LEAs, Gwynedd and Dyfed. In Gwent, 92 per cent of pupils were not taught Welsh at all.

Finance

Some extra funding for supporting LEAs in Wales to develop Welsh language policies has been made available by central government through the Welsh Office. In 1988/9, over £3m was allocated altogether to support the Welsh language. This sum included just over £1m to LEAs, £1.3m to other bodies promoting Welsh such as the Welsh Books Council, Yr Urdd, the National Eisteddfod, and Welsh Sunday schools. Other grants were made to Higher Education and to the Welsh examinations board (WJEC), for example. No further funding for extra staff to maintain Welsh in schools was made.

From figures given in the Welsh Office Report (1988), it would not appear that provision of more Welsh medium schools or classes was necessarily more costly than English medium education for all. Table 7.3 (overleaf) compares the two Welsh LEAs making the least bilingual provision and the two LEAs making the most Welsh medium provision.

The figures suggest that LEAs have not found it necessary to recruit substantial numbers of extra teachers to provide bilingual programmes alongside English speaking staff, but have responded by recruiting Welsh speaking teachers as mainstream class teachers

Table 7.3:   *Comparison of expenditure in LEAs with 'high' and 'low' Welsh medium provision*

Gross Pupil Unit Costs	Primary	Secondary
	(£ outturn prices)	
Low Welsh medium provision		
Gwent	793	1,206
Powys	982	1,259
High Welsh medium provision		
Gwynedd	805	1,126
Dyfed	838	1,129

(At January 1986; Welsh Office 1988, from tables 11.05/6.)

(Unit costs include teacher's salaries, books and equipment, as well as other recurrent expenditure.)

for the primary years; and bilingual subject teachers in the secondary years, who are able to teach both in English or Welsh in schools with different language streams. Pragmatically, where a bilingual subject specialist was not available, figures for Welsh medium teaching in different subject areas suggest (Welsh Office, 1988) that the subject is taught through English medium even to otherwise Welsh-medium streams.

Rather than extra funding being used for staff costs (as in England), extra funds in Wales have been used to provide institutional support for Welsh language work, through the organizations referred to above, and through curriculum development projects.

Organization of provision in schools

A Welsh Office survey of 232 secondary schools undertaken in 1978–80 (Welsh Office, 1983) found that in mixed language areas of Wales, streaming or setting arrangements seemed to be in existence in most schools, grouping pupils according to fluency in Welsh. One example given was of a school offering nine different streams: two Welsh medium classes, plus one Welsh as a first language stream but with only one subject studied through the medium of Welsh; in addition there was also one Welsh as a second language class which also studied one subject through Welsh, together with three Welsh as a second language classes streamed for fluency in Welsh, as well as one 'remedial' Welsh class and one 'remedial' English class. Thus many schools may offer a variety of different types of provision. The Welsh Office report noted that there was little movement of pupils between classes once streamed.

In more anglicized areas of Wales, mixed ability groupings for Welsh were more common, despite the fact that pupils from different feeder primary schools had often achieved considerably different levels of Welsh. However, rather than encouraging the development of mixed ability teaching strategies, the 1983 HMI report claimed that 'pupil attainment is generally higher when they are placed in teaching groups according to their ability in their second language' (p. 8).

This presents a rather different picture from developments in language teaching for bilinguals in England, which have stressed integration of first and second language learners, although it should be noted that some 'community languages' teachers themselves have expressed concern over whether classes should be seen as first language or modern languages classes; and whether language classes open to all comers can meet the linguistic needs both of fluent users of that language and of second language learners. The Welsh experience has so far appeared to have been based on fairly firm grouping arrangements, at least after initial parental choice of placement in the early years.

Provision for speakers of languages other than English and Welsh

The 1987 NFER survey of provision for bilingual pupils received responses from five out of the eight Welsh LEAs. Welsh LEAs were asked to indicate clearly what provision was for Welsh and what for any other languages. One LEA objected to the assumption the questionnaire contained that Welsh was a 'community language'. A senior officer explained:

> The fundamental difficulty lies in your implied definition of 'ethnic' or 'community language' which can be interpreted as that relating to a minority 'ethnic' group and which is different from the predominating language in society at large. In the context of large tracts of this authority it is English which has the minority 'ethnic' status since in-migrants, in order to assimilate into the indigenous culture, need to acquire the Welsh language which is the everyday life of the local community.

This response underlines the importance of the power of linguistic groups to define their own status and the place of their languages in their local communities. Speakers of the 'community languages' of England and speakers of Welsh in Wales currently tend to start from different structural positions within the society. It is likely that the fact that the senior officer belonged to a Welsh speaking community which had gained political and administrative power in the LEA, influenced the attitude of the LEA to Welsh, rather more than the actual number of speakers. According to Welsh Office statistics (1988), just 21 per cent of primary pupils spoke Welsh at home in this LEA. This figure would enable one to present a rather different view of the dominance of Welsh within the community.

The desire for pupils to be able to develop literacy in their own language and for the local society to develop at least a minimal communicative ability in the everyday use of languages shared by so many residents does not on the face of it necessarily appear so different for Welsh compared to many of the so-called community languages in certain areas of England. However, no speakers of one of those widely spoken local languages in England were able to respond to the survey as director of education, as in the example above.

Turning to details of provision, one Welsh LEA had established three Welsh language centres for 'in-migrants' to facilitate the learning of Welsh. In addition to schools mainly teaching through the medium of Welsh in Welsh speaking areas, a number of designated bilingual primary and secondary schools had been set up in English speaking areas. The 'vast majority' of LEA teachers were claimed to be bilingual themselves. LEA language policy was for all pupils to have the opportunity of acquiring a knowledge both of Welsh and English by age 11. However, in the more English speaking areas not all schools were yet offering such provision.

In stark contrast to this LEA, another responding Welsh LEA claimed to have just 120 Welsh/English bilingual teachers altogether in its schools, with five special teachers of Welsh funded under a Welsh Office grant working across primary schools in the authority. Despite comparatively low provision for Welsh, 1981 Census figures indicated that the authority had a Welsh speaking population of 13 per cent, so linguistic demography alone seems insufficient to account for the great difference in approach to provision between the LEAs.

As has already been noted above, it appeared not uncommon for Welsh LEAs to have policies on Welsh for all pupils which were not yet fully met in practice. In the struggle to develop Welsh provision, it was clear that some LEAs felt that questions about provision for other languages were irrelevant to their situation. However, the 1987 NFER survey found that four out of the five Welsh LEAs responding were making some English as a second language provision available for speakers of languages other than English or Welsh.

One LEA provided a total of three 'ESL' teachers, working peripatetically as a team, providing in-class support to speakers of other languages in both primary and secondary schools. Another LEA had a total of seven English support staff (five primary, two secondary), both team and school based, providing part-time language classes and in-class support across the LEA to approximately 97 'EFL children', thought to be mainly Japanese and Chinese speakers. A third LEA made special provision in just one school by one English support teacher, for 'a significant number of pupils whose parents are attending the local university, drawn primarily from Middle Eastern, Asian and Commonwealth countries.' None of these three LEAs claimed any Section 11 funding for this provision.

A fourth LEA, however, claimed Section 11 funding for 15 of its 15.5 English language support posts, and also provided two bilingual classroom support teachers (languages unspecified). These posts were fairly evenly divided across the primary and secondary sectors.

One LEA adviser commented that he was aware of the presence of a number of Italian and Cantonese speakers in the LEA. The authority had decided to re-introduce the attachment of Italian language assistants to some schools for Italian GCSE work, to support the learning of these 'third generation' Italian speakers. However, there had been 'no request' for any Cantonese provision and none was planned.

No provision for voluntary community language classes appeared to have been made by any of the respondents, the only grants made being for Welsh medium nursery schools and playgroups.

The responses to the NFER survey indicated the existence of languages other than Welsh and English in Welsh schools. However, none of the LEAs responding had conducted language surveys of their schools, and awareness of linguistic diversity appeared low. One adviser listed the 'five languages most widely spoken in the LEA' as 'Pakistan, India, Bangladesh, African (various), European (various)'. This listing is similar to some of the categorizations of languages found in the very earliest ILEA language surveys, and indicates a need to raise linguistic awareness.

Tovey (1988) suggested:

> To the newly enfranchised Canadian Francophone, 'multi-culturalism' may be as bitter a pill to swallow as is the suggestion that there are many varieties of Welsh culture, some of them created through English, to the Welsh language nationalist.

It would seem that Wales also has to take account of a wider linguistic diversity within official bilingualism in planning its educational provision. Although minority linguistic groups are likely to be small in number in Wales (although perhaps larger than currently expected), there appears to have been little thought given to the place of these other languages within the curriculum, or to wider strategies for developing linguistic awareness among teachers. *None of the Welsh LEAs responding to the NFER survey claimed to have provided any in-service post-Swann either on linguistic diversity in schools and society, nor on supporting bilingual pupils' learning in the mainstream where their stronger languages were other than Welsh or English.*

The in-depth study

As part of the NFER project, a more detailed study was made of one primary school with an attached Welsh medium unit in a Welsh LEA.

The Welsh LEA visited had a Welsh speaking population of just 8.4 per cent (OPCS, 1981). No area within the LEA had a greater number of Welsh speakers than 29 per cent, most areas having between 0–9 per cent of Welsh speakers (Baker, 1985). Political differences aside, this linguistic profile made this Welsh LEA interesting to compare to a number of English LEA areas which have one numerically dominant linguistic minority population of over 8 per cent of the total population.

The LEA had a clear language policy, aiming to provide Welsh medium education to all who wished it for their children; as well as the intention of teaching Welsh as a second language as a compulsory curriculum subject for all other pupils until the second year of secondary school.

According to the Welsh Office (1988) report, there were 28 primary and three secondary schools in which there were classes receiving their education solely or mainly through the medium of Welsh in the LEA. As many as 12 per cent of primary pupils received an education solely or mainly through the medium of Welsh. In addition, five more primary schools taught some lessons through the medium of Welsh, although mainly for those pupils learning Welsh as a second language.

In the secondary school, 7 per cent of all secondary pupils were taught Welsh as a first language. Only two secondary schools in the LEA still did not teach Welsh as a second language. Apart from the three designated bilingual secondary schools, two further secondary schools taught Welsh both as a first and as a second language to pupils, according to their language backgrounds. All the other secondary schools in the LEA taught Welsh as a second language. However, 34 per cent of all primary pupils and 46 per cent of all secondary pupils in the LEA's schools did not receive Welsh second language lessons, despite the LEA's stated policy.

The Welsh medium unit in the primary school visited was opened in 1977.The school was open plan and purpose built, in a small village within easy commuting distance of a nearby city. The school had strong parental support and a generous PTA.

At the time of the NFER visit, the school had 327 pupils on roll, with 87 pupils in the 'Welsh Section'. There were 11 classes, eight English medium and three Welsh medium, covered by 13 teachers including the head. Because of the low numbers, the Welsh medium classes were vertically grouped, with class one covering reception and middle infants; Class 2 for 28 upper/middle infants and first year juniors; and Class 3 with second, third and fourth year juniors (33 children). In addition, there was a nursery attached which took children part-time, either in a Welsh medium session or in an English medium session, according to parental choice and available places. Currently the English medium 'shift' in the nursery was full, with 18 children; the Welsh 'shift' had 11 children, but not all of these would enter the Welsh medium section of the school.

Pupils in the Welsh medium section had the opportunity to transfer to a nearby Welsh medium secondary school, which maintained close links with its feeder primaries.

No language survey had been carried out by the school. Parents could choose either the Welsh or English section for their children in the early years. Later entry of English speaking children into the Welsh section was discouraged. Most new nursery entrants came from English speaking backgrounds. Only a small proportion of pupils in the Welsh section came from a totally Welsh speaking home background, but many of the English speaking children's parents had learnt or were learning Welsh themselves to support their children. A number of pupils in the Welsh section were said still to speak Welsh only at school or with school friends.

Apart from all the teachers in the Welsh section, three teachers in the English medium section were Welsh–English bilinguals, as was the Head and the 'remedial reading' teacher, who worked across both sections. Welsh was heard as frequently as English in the staffroom. Out of 13 school governors, eight were bilingual. However, the elected parent representatives all had children in the English medium section, a result the head thought 'inevitable' where the English section parent body was larger.

When the school was opened, it had been intended to have Welsh and English medium classes operating side-by-side, both using the open plan areas together. However, after two years this arrangement had been changed and a separate 'Welsh section' had been set up in one area of the school. The reason for this lay in the fact that most children in the Welsh medium section had English speaking home backgrounds. In this context it was found hard for the Welsh medium teachers to establish the use of Welsh and a Welsh ethos in close contact with the English medium activities.

The separation of Welsh and English medium peers, however, was a cause of concern both to the school and to the LEA. The LEA had issued a policy statement in which it made clear

> The Authority does not believe in segregation and would not support any arrangements which would be divisive in nature.
> Parents and staff of children being taught through the medium of Welsh and of children being taught through the medium of English must appreciate and acknowledge the existence of both the Welsh Unit and the English Medium Section of the school.

The policy document went on to lay down guidelines for integrating activities, school functions, and associations.

The school had mixed sports teams, integrated playtimes and regular joint bilingual assemblies. Nevertheless, within the separate section pupils had developed a separate identity, and pupils tended to make friends within their own sections, not to mix in the playgrounds, and to bandy names at each other ('Welsh cakes'; 'English mustard'), albeit in a reasonably amicable fashion.

The appointment of a bilingual head clearly helped to break down separation of the two 'sections' and to introduce a regular bilingual element across the school. Pupils were encouraged to deliver messages across the school bilingually as appropriate. English medium pupils were encouraged to join the weekly after-school Welsh activities in the 'Urdd', a youth group for Welsh cultural activities. As well as more formal Welsh as a second language lessons for all pupils in the English medium section, teachers were encouraged to find contexts for these pupils to use Welsh actively.

As allocation to the Welsh or English medium sections depended on parental choice, there were also a small number of pupils with Welsh speaking backgrounds in the English medium section of the school.

To help bridge the two sections, school postholders were appointed across the school. Unfortunately, schemes of work were developed by the postholders themselves, rather than involving curriculum working groups; however, these were also shared across the sections.

In the Welsh Section, the medium of the full curriculum was Welsh. English was not introduced until the first year of Junior school, in order to allow Welsh to be fully established as the language of all communication in the classroom. Despite the fact that many children were from English speaking homes, by Class 2 all peer talk both in the classroom and in the playground was observed to take place in Welsh. Even in the English lesson in Class 3, Welsh was dominant, although there was rather more code-switching among peers as pupils discussed their written work: e.g. 'Na, four across yw hwnna' ('No, that's four across') in doing an English crossword. However the majority of talk was in Welsh, as in other lessons. Even asking for a spelling: 'Sut mae sillafu "going"?' ('How do you spell "going"?') or looking in the dictionary: 'Dyma "holiday"' ('Here's "holiday"'), peer talk was mainly in Welsh.

It was only in Class 1 that some English was used among the infant children. Some of these younger children spoke in English to the class teacher, who accepted English from the children without comment, but rephrased and answered in Welsh. She also repeated instructions in different ways in Welsh, rather than translating them into English. The first-year teacher commented: 'It's very daunting at the beginning of the year – there's so much English. But by now (October) there's already a lot of Welsh.' By the time children had reached the first year juniors, their class teacher commented that at the start of English lessons: 'I'm the only one speaking English – they all answer me in Welsh.' (This example of the difficulty of changing the language used in school for a small part of the day may sound familiar to minority languages teachers attempting to introduce 'home' language lessons into English classrooms.)

The dominance of Welsh in the classroom was considered essential to maintain and develop the language in a context in which English was otherwise dominant in the society. *There was an emphasis throughout the Welsh section on 'modelling' Welsh for the children, through teacher talk formally and informally around the classroom, storytelling, and assemblies. Oral work was encouraged through drama, reciting poems, singing and discussion sessions. The Welsh 'Scheme of Work' suggested that 'introducing or correcting a sentence pattern in the form of a song gives variety and is easier to remember'.*

With the emphasis on the development of Welsh, there was no concern expressed by teachers that pupils would not be able to develop literacy in English. The Welsh 'Scheme of Work' stated that the Welsh teacher's aim was to 'ensure that his pupils reach the same standard in the two languages as fellow pupils in an English school reach in one language'.Welsh medium schooling was not seen as causing any problems in developing reading in English.

By Class 3 (vertically grouped, 8–11 years) children were expected to read a library book either in Welsh or English alternately every week. The Welsh medium library contained recently published attractive reading material in Welsh and English.

Writing was a rather different matter. An infant teacher said: 'Once they can read in one language, they have no trouble reading in the second. But they do have trouble with spelling.' For example, it was said to be common to find pupils writing 'thrw' for 'through' in the junior years. However, the teachers took a long-term view of writing development, and encouraged parents to do the same, not to be continually comparing children's English writing to that done by pupils in English medium classes, on the assurance that there would be continued support for the development of children's writing skills in the early years of secondary schools, and that at this age confidence was more important that complete correctness.

However, compared to much English primary pedagogy, the Welsh medium education had a strong focus on correctness of expression and the development of a standard language. The Welsh 'Scheme of Work' stated: 'A language has its own uses and rules and we must honour and keep it or the oral and written language will cease to be a meaningful communicating medium.'

This insistence on the 'purity' and public ownership of language, rather than seeing language as the personal possession and medium of self-expression of the child is sometimes also met within linguistic minority communities in England, and needs more discussion among teachers in England. *It suggests that some of the basic premises of 'child-centred' language pedagogy need reappraising in a multilingual society as culturally relative assumptions.* It was interesting to note, however, that Welsh usage also remained open to negotiation between teacher and class. At one point the teacher used the South Wales word for 'liver' ('afu'), this was queried by pupils with parents from North Wales, who asked whether it meant the same as 'iau' ('liver').

This was not the only example of underlying linguistic diversity in the school. Apart from one French speaking child in the nursery, there was one pupil in the English medium junior school who was of Asian origin. When asked by his teacher whether his parents spoke a language other than English at home, this child answered that they spoke 'some strange language'. This answer appears to indicate a need for the school to reappraise its approach to linguistic diversity if it is to make all pupils feel secure that their home or parents' languages and cultures are valid in the school system.

The basis of the curriculum in the Welsh medium section were two language teaching schemes, 'Cynllun y Ddraig' and 'Cynllun y Porth'. According to the 'Scheme of Work', these materials were the core from which the other areas of the curriculum were drawn. In developing syllabus materials such as these, the place of Welsh and Welsh culture within an increasingly multilingual rather than simply bilingual context needs to be considered. Currently, the study of topics such as 'Red Indians' and 'Tribes through the Ages' seemed less than helpful in developing such issues. The current topic 'Important Visitors', covering the Viking, Roman and Norman invasions did not seem to develop useful themes in this area. However, one teacher from a nearby mining area described a project carried out in his school which researched the growth of the mining population, and the contribution to Wales of 'in-comers' as the mines attracted workers from India, Scotland, London, etc., in the last century.

Although there were few curriculum development initiatives under-way in the school, at least one teacher was involved in national curriculum development in Welsh. A further resource available to the school was a peripatetic Welsh language teacher, who visited regularly. There were no extra allowances made by the LEA for schools with two different language sections.

The need for designated language sections in schools if Welsh medium education was to be maintained and developed in Wales was stressed by the Head, who pointed out that many former 'natural' Welsh schools were having to switch to English medium provision because of the influx of older monolingual English speaking pupils.

The Welsh experience clearly implies that continuity and consistency in provision are necessary if pupils are to receive an education in two languages and achieve high standards in both. However, the benefits of bilingual education have to be set against the fact of at least some degree of separation from peers receiving monolingual education.

Perhaps only minority linguistic communities themselves are able to decide whether the balance makes bilingual education preferable in each particular context. The last word in this section is left to a Welsh–English bilingual researcher:

> The protagonists of Welsh-medium education – providers and
> consumers – have historically made their case on the basis of
> a mixture of pragmatic, common-sense and emotional reasons.
> Here it is fair to say that the pioneers of the movement
> which led to the setting up of designated Welsh schools have
> led the way. These were Welsh-speaking parents, marooned
> in anglicised towns, wishing to procure for their children a
> Welsh-medium education such as was 50 years ago available
> only in the Welsh rural heartland. The demands they made
> were about language maintenance, and arose out of a fierce
> language loyalty. They were not concerned with pedagogic
> principles or research results, or whether bilingualism was

linked to cognitive advantage or disadvantage. They held out for what they wanted, and they got it (Price, 1987).

Contrary to Swann (GB. DES, 1985), which dismissed the relevance of the Welsh context to provision for bilingual pupils in England, analysis of bilingual education in Wales appears to offer interesting contrasts and parallels, and raises a number of potentially fruitful questions. The issues of community participation in decision making and the availability of bilingual teachers will be taken up briefly in the next section. But more general questions also remain open for wider discussion. These include political and practical questions about the possibility of developing bilingual provision in England parallel to monolingual English education, as in Wales; about the desirability of teaching local community languages to monoglot pupils and teachers, as in Wales, if a multilingual society is to be created; and, if attempting to provide for other languages within a common curriculum and integrated classroom, how to ensure continuity and progression in the bilingual programmes on offer, so that the introduction of other languages (whether first or second languages) can be of real educational value to pupils.

8 Conclusion

Bilingualism can offer positive advantages in education and life. It can offer the individual two windows through which to view the world... Each area must examine its conscience and make a start, however small and insignificant this at first may appear to be. Such small beginnings can grow into a major movement which, as it gathers momentum, can bring a new awareness to thousands of children who are not now receiving their rightful heritage ('Primary Education in Wales', GB. DES, 1967: p. 213).

Implicit policy on bilingualism

This book has shown how in England in the mid-1980s a substantial number of LEAs were beginning to develop provision for the first languages of pupils in their schools, and for developing a shared awareness within schools of languages use in the local community for all pupils. Even more widespread was an expression of interest in and a wish to be seen to be involved in supporting pupils' languages other than English on the part of LEA respondents. This suggested a general readiness post-Swann to develop provision, provided that a central policy lead and support for its implementation was forthcoming.

However, in the absence of any clear policy statement on supporting bilingualism and on the place of locally spoken languages other than English in the curriculum, there appeared to be a large number of constraints on the development of provision for bilingual pupils in LEAs in England. Some constraints which we have already identified were:

(a) The absence of clear structures for consultation with minority linguistic groups on appropriate provision.

(b) The absence of funding to support and encourage LEAs to provide training for bilingual teachers.

(c) Unclear rules for the administration of regulations for obtaining qualified teacher status from the DES, which did not encourage LEAs to employ and support the applications of overseas qualified teachers.

(d)   Unclear regulations for the administration of Home Office Section 11 funding which had led some to wrongly believing that funding was not available for any community languages posts under the new criteria.

(e)   The absence of clearly marked national in-service priority funding (under GRIST) for helping schools to respond to bilingualism.

(f)   The absence of any central curriculum and materials development body for bilingualism.

It was clear that, despite expressions of good will, most LEAs expected any future development of provision for bilinguals to be supported by extra, special funding. However, in examining Home Office Section 11 funding in Chapter 2, we saw that there had been an apparent policy decision taken within the Home Office not to fund new posts for community languages as modern languages options in the future, presumably on the grounds that, since the courses are open to all pupils, they were not targeted at meeting the special needs of pupils of Commonwealth origin. In contrast, to date there has been no opposition to funding posts for English language support within the mainstream classroom, even where, as we have seen, these posts increasingly involve full class cooperative 'team teaching', to meet the linguistic needs and support the learning of the whole class alongside the class or subject teacher. Indeed, the Secretary of State had accepted the CRE's (1986) recommendations that Section 11 funding should be withdrawn from teaching posts located in separate language centres, that form of provision having been found to be discriminatory. The withdrawal of funding for community languages options posts, then, appears to be an implicit statements of policy on community languages.

Section 11 as a source of education funding itself appears to present an even greater anomaly than before in the context of the new Education Bill (1988). First, the emphasis in the 1966 Local Government Act on LEAs determining their own specific needs will seem somewhat anachronistic in the new system in which power is simultaneously centralized and in some measure devolved directly to schools. Secondly, since Section 11 is only payable directly to LEAs, no extra provision for minority group pupils would be available to schools 'opting out' of local authority control. This would be serious, since schools may have the power to refuse admission to pupils for whom appropriate provision could not be made by existing staffing.

It is understood that the future of Section 11 funding in education is already under review by a joint Home Office/DES team, with a report to ministers due in December 1988. Changes in legislation may be likely in the near future. It seems imperative for all those involved in education to be fully aware of the *extent* of current reliance on this form of funding, as revealed in Chapter 2, in order that the effects of changes in funding on provision for pupils can be monitored carefully. It seems ironic that just as the system has begun to offer some power to minority ethnic groups to define and monitor provision at the local level, the future of Section 11 should be brought under review. The participation which the system had begun to initiate for minority groups in determining appropriate provision would need to be replaced in any new system.

There have been few direct policy statements formulated on educational provision for minority groups by central government. However, central government does shape provision for bilingual pupils in crucial ways through the control of funding arrangements. It is interesting to note that provision for bilinguals in Wales as in England has been distanced from the DES, with funding allocated in Wales through the Welsh Office and in England through the Home Office. In both cases, provision has been left very much to voluntary claims for funding based on local authorities' perceptions of their own priorities.

This approach has been criticized by Rawkins (1979) as leading to an unco-ordinated and wasteful use of resources. A similar criticism is made of Gaelic education by Mackinnon (1988), who claims that some areas of Scotland offer both primary and tertiary education in Gaelic medium, but not even a form of bilingual education at secondary level. Earlier chapters of this book have indicated the *ad hoc* and patchy nature of bilingual provision in England within LEAs. Continuity and progression have rarely seemed to be a feature of provision for bilingual pupils in the British Isles.

On the other hand, the advantage of a decentralized system is that it does allow local authorities flexibility in provision, giving opportunities for local community pressure in setting priorities.

Rawkins (1987) suggests that indirect funding arrangements are part of a government strategy for avoiding explicit policy making on controversial issues:

> On language related questions, as on race relations, the British state has, where possible, avoided basic policy commitments. Conflict between Welsh speakers and monolingual English speakers, as between whites and nonwhites, is focused on struggles around access to scarce material and symbolic resources (p. 27).

The lack of explicit policy makes it harder for politically active members of minority groups to demand rights. It leads to variation in provision across the country, confining radical applications of funding to local areas with very strong minority groups. It may also lead to conflicts at local level over the allocation of resources to minority groups, encouraging some to prefer to adopt a low profile.

One clear effect of decentralized policy, whether a deliberate strategy or not, is that the inevitable conflicts between local groups over resources or differing priorities are left to be contained and managed at the local level, allowing central government to operate at a general level of apparent consensus. Thus struggles over community languages provision in schools in England have tended to take place within local Section 11 or minority consultative group bodies, rather than in central policy making committees, such as the National Curriculum working groups. In Wales, again, conflicts are locally contained.

National policy or politics of neglect?

In completing a large-scale review of research into the education of pupils of South Asian origin for the Swann Committee, Taylor with Hegarty (1985) commented that the absence of a clear central policy direction on educational provision for linguistic minorities in the past decade 'may have been necessary in order for both ethnic communities and society at large to come to terms with the existence of a multicultural society'. However, the result was that by the 1980s pupils within different LEAs and schools were experiencing very different forms of provision, depending on where they went to school.

We have seen in this book the sometimes contradictory influences of the Swann Report on LEA policy and of Home Office Section 11 funding policy in moulding LEA provision. Both these sources gave direction to LEAs during the time of the study, in the absence of central policy on supporting the education of bilingual pupils.

Since then, legislation has been proposed to institute a new national curriculum in which 'pupils should be entitled to the same opportunities wherever they go to school' (GB. DES/Welsh Office, 1987). The entitlements proposed, however, were not couched in terms of general principles of rights, but rather as specific programmes of study, with attainment targets set for achievement in different curricular areas at 7, 11, 14 and 16 years. At the time the Bilingual Pupils' Project was completed, this national curriculum was still in the process of being drawn up within subject working groups.

The National Curriculum was to be available to pupils 'regardless of sex, ethnic origin or geographical location' (GB. DES/Welsh Office, 1987). In the original documentation, there was no mention of any restrictions on the medium through which the programmes of study might be delivered. In 1988, however, the Secretary of State's terms of reference to the English Working Group asked them to bear in mind 'the cardinal point that English should be the first language and medium of instruction for all pupils in England'. This statement was a strong indication of intended policy on the development of bilingual education in England.

Despite the recent increase in involvement of large numbers of LEAs in the teaching of community languages and bilingual support, as revealed in this book, there was little sign of central support and encouragement for these approaches to curriculum development in the terms of reference presented to the curriculum working parties. It may be that there was a general lack of awareness about how widespread these initiatives were.

Certainly it seemed surprising that the Kingman Committee (GB. DES, 1988a) saw their brief as 'primarily concerned with children who speak English as a mother tongue'. This exclusive position was very different from that of many LEAs as reported in the survey, and in contradiction to the basic position taken up by Swann.

There did appear to be some clear moves to re-establish the priority of English in England in opposition to attempts to establish a view of England as a multilingual as well as a multicultural society. But while confirming the importance of providing access to forms of standard English for all pupils within the mainstream classroom, the English Working Group's first report (GB. DES, 1988f) contested the establishment of English as the sole legitimate language of the classroom and medium of all instruction.

> It is not within our brief to make recommendations about the teaching of other languages. However, as the Bullock Report clearly stated in 1975: 'No child should be expected to cast off the language and culture of the home as he (or she) crosses the school threshold, and the curriculum should reflect this' (p. 10).

The publication of the English Working Group's primary report (GB. DES. 1988f) confirmed the need for LEAs to develop comprehensive language policies which were inclusive not exclusive of the language needs of bilingual pupils. The report stressed the need for whole school involvement in developing language policies and structures which encompassed English and the other languages spoken and taught in the school, and which met the needs of all pupils. However, paradoxically, the report itself was constrained by its terms of reference largely to treating English in isolation.

In contrast to the English Working Group's report, the DES policy statement on modern languages in the same year (GB. DES, 1988b) indicated that in other areas of the curriculum the pupil population in England was still being seen as a monolingual and homogeneous cultural group, except for certain exceptional localized 'pockets', rather than as part of a multilingual and multicultural society.

Thus although the modern languages policy statement (GB. DES, 1988b) referred to the 'climate of awareness of languages' created by 'the presence in a locality of significant numbers of people whose mother tongue is not English', the involvement of community languages in 'language awareness' courses, for example, was limited to just those areas 'where they are represented in the school' itself.

The place of languages widely spoken by communities within England in the languages curriculum was scarcely mentioned within the policy statement. In addition to the teaching of French, it was stated that:

> as a trading nation we need speakers of other European
> languages and of Arabic, Japanese, Chinese and other Asian
> languages. There is, however, very little teaching capacity in
> these languages, and it is unlikely to be a cost effective use
> of resources to provide them within schools for pupils of
> compulsory school age.

The earlier 1986 draft document continued: 'except perhaps where they are the languages of the home for a significant proportion of pupils'. However, this clause was omitted in the 1988 document, suggesting an increased opposition to the inclusion of community languages within the curriculum. There was no reference to community languages teaching provision already in existence in LEAs.

The 1987 NFER survey found that community languages already had a place on the curriculum in over 640 schools in more than a third of all LEAs, and that therefore their exclusion from discussion in national policy would ignore the basic reality of existing provision.

The 1986 DES draft policy document stated:

> The place such community languages should take in the school
> curriculum is an important and complex question which in our
> view merits more detailed consideration than was possible in
> the consultations which preceded this statement. We intend
> therefore to publish a consultative document on this issue
> in the near future (para. 8).

This document on community languages has never been published. Instead, two years later, the 1988 policy statement reported: 'We intend to consult separately on this issue in due course' (para. 8). It would appear that no explicit policy lead will be available for LEAs in the near future, despite the development of a national curriculum. A preliminary consultative document issued by the DES in March 1988 indicated that there may be space for schools to offer some listed local community languages within the national curriculum as modern languages options, on condition that all pupils are given the opportunity to choose one of the working languages of the EC instead. There appears to be little space for the study of more than one language other than English within the curriculum. Parental wishes are given high priority. There is no encouragement for schools to widen horizons by including a study of local community languages in the curriculum for all pupils.

Opportunities within the national curriculum for ethnic minority pupils to develop their full range of linguistic skills look limited; opportunities for all pupils to learn the languages of the community of which they are a part appear even more limited.

Unlike the other 'community languages', however, Welsh is to be included in the national curriculum alongside another modern language within the borders of Wales for both majority English speaking and minority Welsh speaking pupils (see Chapter 7), either as a first or second language, or in the form of full bilingual education.

It is interesting to note that the argument about including the languages of local communities in the curriculum for their cultural value, versus a more 'utilitarian'view in which the requirements of the 'job market' are judged to be paramount, was also raised in the debate about the place of Welsh in the primary curriculum in Wales in 1967 (The Gittins Reports, GB. DES, 1967). The different perspectives are essentially reflections of political arguments about the purpose of schooling in society. The Gittins Report came down firmly on the side of developing cultural richness in society through supporting bilingualism in the schools. Interestingly, however, the decision to support bilingualism also led to an increase in the instrumental value of learning Welsh, since there was an ensuing demand for Welsh speakers as, for example, teachers, broadcasters, and translators. Supporting bilingualism for its cultural value may well also enhance its instrumental value in society.

Since the national curriculum developments, Welsh bilingual provision is rapidly being compartmentalized, and placed on a very different footing from the other minority languages in the education system. For example, the primary English curriculum proposals (GB. DES, 1988f) make special allowances to exempt primary pupils in Welsh medium schools from the first stage of assessment at age 7. In contrast, in England, where the terms of reference state that all pupils should be educated through the medium of English, no special exemptions were recommended. This appears to ignore the reality of a small but growing number of infant classrooms identified in the NFER study which were beginning to operate bilingually.

Drawing on the Welsh experience

While the Swann Report (GB. DES, 1985) dismissed the Welsh experience of bilingual education as 'far from comparable' with the English situation, apparently because of the different legal status of Welsh, a closer study of provision in Wales suggests that there is much to be learnt from Wales about organizational arrangements, about different views of language and language teaching, and also about some of the political constraints on the development of provision for minority groups which may be central to the acceptance of bilingual education in England.

In fact, the legal status of Welsh has been used to argue not for bilingual education for Welsh speakers, which since the Gittins Report (GB. DES, 1967) has officially been an accepted form of provision, but for the need for *all* pupils in Wales to learn Welsh. It is only this debate over the place of Welsh in the education of *non-Welsh speakers* which has made the history of the development of Welsh language provision not directly comparable to the English situation, where minority languages have not gained equal official status with English.

Direct responsibility for education in Wales was handed over to the Welsh Office as recently as 1970, when bilingual education was already well established. So it seems that Welsh medium education was initiated and implemented in circumstances very little different from those now existing in England: the presence of high concentrations of certain linguistic groups in some areas; some *ad hoc* provision in schools; a growing demand in certain localities for the recognition of certain languages in the curriculum; a number of schools in which the linguistic minority group was in fact a majority; and a lack of any central policy on language, which enabled local initiatives to be taken, provided they could be met without extra resources. In later years, of course, increased recognition and resources from the Welsh Office have led to the rapid increase and spread in provision in Wales, as we saw in the last chapter.

It would not be wise to overstress the similarities between the Welsh bilingual context and the context of minority groups in England. However, it should be recognized that there are also significant differences in attitudes towards and provision for bilingual education between areas within Wales. The practicalities of provision in England will also vary from linguistic community to community, with each having different aspirations and needs. The situations in which different linguistic groups find themselves are diverse across England and Wales. In this book, then, we have attempted to move Wales into the mainstream of educational discussion, rather than to treat it as an isolated exception.

There is a need for further examination of the continuities and differences between the Welsh and English situations, in order to see how far it might be possible to develop a unified national policy towards languages in education which draws on the Welsh political and educational experience. This experience gives a central place to community consultation and participation in the direction of the education service, and to offering a variety of different forms of provision.

The direct involvement of linguistic minority groups in decision making related to educational provision has been rare in England as opposed to Wales. Linguistic minority group perspectives rarely inform debate on languages provision, except within special Section 11 structures. It seems important that minority language issues should be raised in mixed ethnic group forums, since it is necessary to raise the language awareness of the whole society if bilingual language provision is to be developed in a positive context. From the list of sources of evidence appended to the Report on the teaching of English (GB. DES, 1988) and the National Curriculum English Working Party Report (GB. DES, 1988f), it would appear that most consultation was with professional bodies, and that no consultation was made with linguistic minority community organizations, although the Scottish Education Department and Welsh Office presented evidence to Kingman.

On assessment, the Welsh experience again offers more subtle approaches to ascertaining language backgrounds and setting norms than is currently developed in England (for example Price, Powell and Whetton, 1987). It is to be hoped that this experience will be considered in formulating national systems of assessment.

The Welsh experience suggests that bilingual education in areas with large numbers of pupils sharing the same languages need not necessarily be more expensive than monolingual education, provided there is an adequate supply of bilingual class and subject teachers. Indeed, integrated English medium provision which requires large numbers of teachers extra to normal staffing numbers is likely to be far more expensive, especially where substantial in-service is required to enable teachers to work alongside one another, and to prepare schools to deploy extra staff effectively. Bilingual provision would, however, unlike English language support, require a reappraisal of staffing needs rather than a redeployment of existing teachers. This prioritizing of bilingual skills in teacher employment caused some conflicts in Wales (Rawkins, 1987). The existence of a large pool of monolingual Section 11 staff may explain why there has been more concern in LEAs to find new roles for English language support teachers than to develop training courses to increase the numbers of bilingual staff.

It was only the presence of large numbers of Welsh speaking teachers in Wales which permitted the development of Welsh medium education, at first informally in the 'natural' Welsh schools, and later in the planned Welsh medium provision. Because many of the staff in schools in Wales were already Welsh speaking, bilingual education has been possible without massive investment in extra staff, as we have seen in the last chapter. Similarly, the presence of Gaelic speaking primary teachers enabled a recent bilingual programme to be developed in the Western Isles of Scotland (Murray and Morrison, 1984).

Baker (1985) suggests that the presence of Welsh speakers in the education service was not accidental. The importance of bilingual primary school teachers, if the Welsh language was to survive, was recognized by the Welsh speaking community at the turn of the century. It requires an act of will for minority communities to retain and pass on their languages and cultures, and this commitment must be a crucial factor in encouraging young people to choose teaching as a profession.

However, again referring to the Welsh situation, Baker points out that the problem of bilingual teacher shortages does not lie in the lack of candidates with linguistics skills, but in the failure of teaching as a profession to attract them; and that some financial recognition should be offered for these special qualifications, in the same way as it is suggested that increments or training grants might be made for other 'shortage subjects'. Ultimately, however, such inducements would depend on the willingness of central government to prioritize the delivery of a bilingual education.

There are obvious reasons for wanting to link provision for bilinguals in England with provision in Wales. Within the Welsh system, central government through the Welsh Office has accepted that there are cognitive benefits to be gained through developing bilingualism (Welsh Office, 1980). Parental and pupil choice of the balance of languages used in education have been stressed as a central right where language provision has been extended beyond Welsh second language courses.

Within this framework of choice, 'good practice' in Wales has provided the option of separate Welsh and English medium provision, but has also offered the opportunity for Welsh speakers who choose to attend English medium schools to be able to extend their bilingualism through Welsh as a first language lessons in many schools.

The Welsh experience shows that policy and provision for bilingual communities cannot be monolithic, but is complex and many faceted. Welsh LEAs have needed to consider the place of 'natural' Welsh medium schools (schools in localities where the majority of pupils and teachers share common languages); the setting up of formal Welsh medium schools for those who choose Welsh medium education where 'natural' Welsh schools are not available; and the provision of both Welsh as a first language and Welsh as a second language courses, in English medium schools. Different combinations of provision have been made in different localities.

More specific analyses of provision

In the introduction to this book the term 'bilingual' was considered to be too vague to be helpful in assessing the educational provision needed in different schools in England. It was suggested that one needed to be far more specific about the particular language backgrounds, attitudes towards languages and linguistic needs of pupils in order to plan appropriate provision in each locality.

Similarly, in this conclusion, following the findings of the study and the experience of Welsh provision, I would like to suggest that the simple designation of posts as 'ESL', English language support, and bilingual support has outlived its usefulness. The increasing use of the title 'Section 11' teacher is even less helpful. Only when it becomes more usual to detail exactly the types of provision required in different schools, for different pupils, will we be able to be specific enough about the very different sorts of skills, qualifications and experience needed in postholders to meet the objectives entailed. The new Section 11 criteria, which require detailed analysis of the needs to be met by posts and specific job descriptions, support such an approach.

This book has stressed the importance of reappraising whole school language policies, and, indeed, national policies, for their ability to respond to complex multilingual situations. We have seen that bilingual pupils form a substantial proportion of the school population, and are not confined to exceptional localised areas, but go to school in most LEAs. It is likely that within flexible policies, some forms of extra provision for different language needs will sometimes be required. For example, a summary of some of the different types of extra provision which may be required from time to time in different English-medium schools in order for them to provide equal opportunities for bilingual pupils from different backgrounds and with different experiences includes:

(a) Procedures for the reception of pupils newly arrived in the country with little or no English, and their induction into the school.

(b) The teaching of basic literacy to older pupils who have not yet learnt to read and write.

(c) Supporting teachers in making the curriculum accessible to all pupils and supporting pupils in meeting the demands of the curriculum.

(d) Extra support in providing access to standard written forms of English for older pupils.

(e) Providing access to the spoken and written forms of the first language or standard written language of the pupil's community.

It is possible to see how more specific analysis of the extra provision needed in a particular school would constitute a more coherent approach to support for language needs in multilingual schools, developing procedures under the sort of headings presented above (reception, curriculum support, basic literacy, advanced literacy, communications skills and study skills). Instead of expecting one postholder to fulfil all the roles, schools could call on the most appropriate expertise throughout the school and community to staff the different areas.

Such an appraisal of provision also brings together those areas so unnaturally separated when dealing with bilingualism as 'community languages support' and 'ESL'. Provision could be made in pupils' languages other than English where that was more useful and where possible, or in English only where bilingual provision was not practicable. So, reception procedures could be conducted in pupils' first languages, perhaps drawing on peer, parental and community support. Support for pupils' learning across the curriculum might draw on their stronger languages, if bilingual staff were recruited within subject departments or as cross-curriculum support teachers. Early literacy provision might be approached first through pupils' stronger languages, since research has indicated that literacy skills are transferable. As in Wales, languages teaching courses might be more differentiated. More advanced language programmes might be offered as first language courses for pupils already fluent in that language; second language courses could be offered for pupils with less familiarity with the language, alongside pupils from different language backgrounds; or more general language awareness courses which included local languages might be offered in parallel courses.

Finally, advanced literacy courses for older pupils could draw on each of the languages used by bilingual pupils in focusing on texts, to develop an explicit knowledge about language systems.

All this provision would of course be in addition to curriculum courses in English and wherever possible in at least one local language, as well as a chosen foreign language, as in the Welsh National Curriculum model.

In-service and training programmes on provision for bilingual pupils would also need to be made more specific, with courses clearly indicating the sorts of issues they proposed to cover. More languages courses might also be included as course modules for teachers. Of course, all in-service courses would need to develop provision with the needs of pupils from a diversity of linguistic backgrounds in mind. This book has suggested that less expenditure on extra school based monolingual staffing and more on in-service development for schools may be required. There remains an urgent need for all teachers to know more about language in learning and about how to teach the languages necessary for pupils to achieve in the curriculum, drawing on the resources their pupils already possess.

In some cases, extra posts might not be needed by schools at all, but rather access to audio-visual and written materials in different languages, or in-service training for staff, or the temporary support of outside agencies to provide skills to meet less frequently encountered needs. The development of peer support systems and co-operative group learning styles would be part of a whole school approach.

This study has indicated the valuable role of advisory services in supporting change in schools. These services need to be protected if schools are to be enabled to continue to develop more complex strategies for meeting the needs of pupils from diverse linguistic backgrounds. However, the more effective services appeared to be those which integrated and shared a variety of cross-curricular skills, rather than isolated 'specialist' services for bilinguals, so that language needs and the role of pupils' languages other than English could be considered in all courses and projects.

We have seen how bilingual provision in England has consisted mainly in the provision of extra staff to schools. The provision of extra teachers, whether operating bilingually or only in English, has implications for the management of schools. In Chapters 4 and 6 it was suggested that schools need to be prepared for support teachers. Primary school structures have traditionally been based on a simple structure of one teacher per class under a head and deputy. Where a number of extra teachers are to be deployed in the mainstream, thought needs to be given to new line management and school

MOVING INTO THE MAINSTREAM

organization, with perhaps a formal team structure across the year groups. In secondary schools, the department or faculty structure can cause some difficulties for cross-curricular staff; there is a need either for regular departmental liaison systems with support departments, or the development of integral support structures within each department. More research is needed to develop and disseminate strategies of managing cross-curricular language support.

More research is also needed into ways of developing effective team teaching partnerships in-class. The pairing of student teachers on teaching practice and the development of teacher-tutor roles for supporting new teachers in their probationary year would be fruitful places to begin more systematic research into developing professional team teaching relationships. Unless more attention is paid to the questions of how to deploy extra staffing and how teachers can work together professionally, the massive expenditure on staffing English and bilingual language support posts can scarcely be justified by the effectiveness of provision.

In a number of schools the percentages of pupils sharing the same languages are such that the development of full bilingual education programmes would seem to be perfectly feasible, if desired by the local community. The Swann fear of 'segregation' cannot be a legitimate argument against bilingual provision in areas in which schools are already clearly divided on racial and linguistic lines. For example, in one town visited, out of four secondary schools, three were almost all White, while a third had over 70 per cent of Black and bilingual pupils. In another city, it was possible to find pupils streamed within a 'Language (meaning English) Development Class' for their entire secondary school career. When this is legally possible in the system, it seems hard to argue against optional streaming for bilingual education, where research indicates this may have positive cognitive and affective advantages for pupils without lowering standards of achievement in the second language by school leaving age.

However, the availability of sufficient bilingual staff to staff a full bilingual programme would be crucial before the option of bilingual schooling could become a reality. With less than 3 per cent of students in their final year of teacher training coming from minority ethnic group backgrounds, there would seem to be an urgent need to attract people from minority linguistic groups into teaching if any alternatives to monolingual English education are to be developed. While access courses might help recruitment, a CRE (1988) report pointed out the need for a reappraisal of the selection procedures for higher education in general. Unless more successful efforts are made to attract bilinguals into teacher training, future possibilities for bilingual provision would seem very limited.

In conclusion

From the 1960s to 1988, the major theme in English education in approaching the issue of ethnic diversity has been social cohesion and avoidance of conflict between racially defined groups in the society. However, within the Swann Report (GB. DES, 1985), it has been acknowledged that for such social cohesion to be more justly maintained, established mainstream structures would have to change; that rather than cultural and linguistic diversity being 'problems', the problem was the prevalence of a hostile and exclusive notion of culture, which needed reconstructing. The indications are that future policy will not be based on this premise, but will be based on the assumption that the new curriculum adopted will somehow be 'culturally neutral' and thus equally accessible to all. However, it has already been noted that there appears to have been no attention paid to minority ethnic group consultation to date on the content of the national curriculum.

A national curriculum which overlooks linguistic and cultural diversity and is unprepared to monitor and address discrimination from within the system itself is likely in the end to encourage a demand for separate bilingual schooling. In this context, there is a danger that the effect of any separate structures for bilingual education would be to leave the majority of English medium provision operating within an even more monolingual and ethnocentric system, with consequent negative effects on minorities.

There appears to be general consensus across the political spectrum that English language support within English medium schooling should be provided within the mainstream classroom. There must be some concern, however, that if priority is not given to reappraising whole school teaching strategies for language support in mixed groupings, responsibility for the language development of pupils learning English as a second language will be limited to individual 'remedial' work carried out by support teachers in the back of classrooms. This is unlikely to be effective. At current staffing levels English support teachers could not have enough contact with all the pupils learning English as a second language to support them adequately across the curriculum if an individual support role is adopted. Unless the national curriculum guidelines work from the baseline of teachers working within linguistically varied classrooms, it seems likely that English support teachers could become the 'buffers' between a mainstream system which is unresponsive to linguistic diversity and the demands of minority ethnic groups for equality of opportunity in English medium schools.

As part of the development of the national curriculum, there is an urgent need to monitor the ways in which bilingual pupils fit into assessment schedules and programmes of study for all. Yet, as well as the more specific monitoring of the outcomes of the system, it is to be hoped that one consequence of the 'move to the mainstream' in recent years would be the recognition and incorporation of a more clearly multilingual (as opposed to monolingual) perspective into all classroom research and curriculum development projects in future, whether on language assessment, home–school liaison, languages teaching, or maths and science education, for example. The beginnings of such a move are currently seen within the SCDC Writing and Oracy projects, and are to be welcomed. The perspective is also fundamental to the ILEA (1988) Primary Language Records system, for all pupils. However, in order to develop this broader perspective successfully, there is clearly a need to encourage the participation of more bilingual workers in the field of mainstream education research and curriculum development, and onto the steering panels which manage all such research.

In the apparent contradiction between 'mainstream' and 'specific' provision, special provision in this country has come to be seen as 'compensatory education', with the attendant dangers of low teacher expectations and low status. It has often defined minority needs from the majority perspective, and excluded or marginalized certain pupils from general educational debate and practice. However, the Welsh experience suggests that provision for minority groups can have positive outcomes for pupils, where minority groups participate in defining their own needs and appropriate provision.

In contrast to the concept of specific provision, it is useful in the current climate to stress that 'mainstream' educational provision need not always have positive effects for minority groups either. Indeed, one form of 'education for all', or 'education for one nation', can be a continuation of a long history of assimilation, with only superficial surface gestures towards diversity. The emphasis in that form of 'mainstreaming' is on giving all pupils the same 'diet', but a diet designed by and for one cultural group. It may be inclusive, but is indifferent to diversity, and has in the past appeared to lead to social stratification along socioeconomic class and ethnic group lines.

It is, then, not useful to set up a simple dichotomy between special provision and mainstream provision for bilinguals, assuming one to be progressive, the other regressive. A bland acceptance of 'education for all', with an unwillingness to face up to conflicts of interest between ethnic groups, and the assumption of a 'harmony' model which does not acknowledge underlying tensions, may lead to the uptake of mainstream approaches without a full understanding of the original objectives of bringing about whole school change. In other words, it may lead to cosmetic changes in schools rather than a move towards achieving equality for pupils.

Finally, whether national policy recognizes languages other than English in the curriculum or not, the languages are already in the classrooms of England and Wales. This book has focused on planned LEA provision for bilingual pupils. But even in classrooms where there was no official use of local community languages, as one moved around the tables it was impossible to miss hearing pupils talking to one another over their work in a variety of languages. In every classroom I visited, there were a number of pupils who were also learning to write languages other than English, either from their parents or in community run classes. From the infant school up, many children were able to discuss thoughtfully accent, dialect and the use of different languages in different places and with different people. From valuing the languages children bring with them into schools and celebrating diversity in classrooms, we need to move towards a more educational development of the knowledge about languages in society that children in multilingual schools already have and are willing to share. There is much to be learnt both about language and society from adopting a bilingual perspective.

Appendix

Table A: *The English LEAs studied in depth*

	Total pupils	Bilingual pupils %	Largest linguistic groups	CL teachers	English support teachers
Ayton (Metropolitan)	166,000	N/K	Panjabi Urdu Bengali	16	221*
Beedon (Metropolitan)	85,000	23%	Panjabi Urdu Gujarati	25	353*
Seabury (London)	33,982	41%	Gujarati Urdu Panjabi	4	78
Deeshire (Non-Metropolitan)	98,000	N/K 'Ethnic Minority' 5%	Panjabi Italian Urdu	3	37
Edham (London)	44,000	N/K 'Ethnic Minority' 25%	Gujarati Panjabi Urdu	1	74
Fordham (London)	29,000	27%	Panjabi Gujarati Urdu	20 (19 ESL/CL)	123*

* Including staff based at English Language centres.
This tables does not include bilingual classroom assistants and NNEBs.

Table B: *The English junior schools studied in depth*

	Total no. of pupils	Bilingual pupils %	Section 11 staff	All Bilingual staff	Bilingual Support/ CLT
Ayton	407	96	1.5	3	0
Beedon	364	44	1.8	0	0
Seebury	323	72	1	5	1 (asst.)
Deeshire	396	91	3	2 (assts.)	2 (assts.)
Edham	199	17	0.5	0	0
Fordham	271	69	2.1	0.5	0.5

References

ALLADINA, SAFDAR (1985a).'Multilingualism or Language Deprivation', in *Language and Power: Dynamics of Change and Control*. London: North London Community Group Conference Report, Wembley.

ALLADINA, SAFDAR (1985b).'Research Methodology for language use surveys in Britain'. In: NELDE, P. (ed.) *Methods in Contact Linguistic Research*. Bonn: Dummler.

BAKER, C. (1985). *Aspects of Bilingualism in Wales*. Clevedon: Multilingual Matters.

BAKER, C. (1988). *Key Issues in Bilingualism and Bilingual Education*. Clevedon: Multilingual Matters.

BOURNE, J. (1987). *Changing Perceptions, Changing Ways*. London: University of London Institute of Education.

BOURNE, J. (1988). 'Natural Acquisition' and a 'Masked Pedagogy', in *Applied Linguistics*, Vol. 9,1. Oxford: Oxford University Press.

BROADBENT, J. (1986). 'Missing Figures: Community Languages in Maintained Education'. In: PRINTON, V. (ed.) *Facts & Figures: Languages in Education*. London: CILT.

BROADBENT, J. (1987). *The Inclusion of Community Languages in the Normal Curricular Arrangements of LEA maintained schools in England and Wales*. London: University of London Institute of Education.

BRUMFIT, C., ELLIS, R. and LEVINE, J. (eds) (1985). *English as a second language in the U.K.* ELT Documents 121. Oxford: Pergamon/British Council.

COMMISSION FOR RACIAL EQUALITY (CRE) (1982). *Ethnic Minority Community Languages: A Statement*. London: CRE.

COMMISSION FOR RACIAL EQUALITY (CRE) (1986). *The Teaching of English as a Second Language*. London: CRE.

COMMISSION FOR RACIAL EQUALITY (CRE) (1988a). *Learning in Terror: A Survey of Racial Harassment in Schools and Colleges.* London: CRE.

COMMISSION FOR RACIAL EQUALITY (CRE) (1988b). *Ethnic Minority School Teachers: A Survey in 8 LEAs.* London: CRE.

COUNCIL FOR THE WELSH LANGUAGE (1978). *A Future for the Welsh Language.* Cardiff: HMSO.

CRAFT, M. and ATKINS, M. (1983). *Training Teachers of Ethnic Minority Community Languages.* Nottingham: University of Nottingham School of Education.

CUMMINS, J. and SWAIN, M. (1986). *Bilingualism in Education.* Harlow: Longman.

DALPHINIS, M. (1985). *Caribbean and African Languages.* London: Karia Press.

DELAMONTE, S. and GALTON, M. (1986). *Inside the Secondary Classroom.* London: Routledge and Kegan Paul.

DODSON, C. (1985). 'Second Language Acquisition and Bilingual Development: A Theoretical Framework', *Journal of Multicultural and Multilingual Development,* 6,5. Avon: Multilingual Matters.

EGGLESTON, S., DUNN, D., ANJALI, M. with WRIGHT, C. (1986). *Education for Some.* Trentham: Trentham Books.

ELLIS, R. (1985). 'Policy and Provision for ESL in Schools', in Brumfit, C., Ellis, R. and Levine, J (eds).

EUROPEAN COMMUNITIES. (EC) (1977). *Council Directive on the Education of Children of Migrant Workers:* 77,486. Brussels, EC.

EUROPEAN COMMUNITIES. (EC) (1984). *Report on the Implementation of Directive 77/486/EEC on the Education of the Children of Migrant Workers'* COM(84) 54 Final, Brussels, 10 February.

FISHMAN, J. and LOVAS, J. (1972). 'Bilingual Education in a Sociolinguistic Perspective'. In: SPOLSKY, B. (ed.) *The Language Education of Minority Children.* Rowley, Massachusetts: Newbury House.

GALTON, M., SIMON, B. and CROLL, P. (1980). *Inside the Primary Classroom.* London: Routledge and Kegan Paul.

GILES, H. and BYRNE, J. (1982). 'An Intergroup Approach to Second Language Acquisition', *Journal of Multilingual and Multicultural Development,* 3,1. Clevedon: Multilingual Matters.

GOLDMAN, R. (1967). *Research and the Teaching of Immigrant Children.* London: National Committee for Commonwealth Immigrants.

GORMAN, T. (1974). 'The development of language policy in Kenya with particular reference to the educational system'. In WHITELEY, W. (ed.) *Language in Kenya.* Nairobi: Oxford University Press.

GREAT BRITAIN. DEPARTMENT OF EDUCATION AND SCIENCE (GB. DES) (1967). *Primary Education in Wales* (The Gittins Report). London: HMSO.

GREAT BRITAIN. DEPARTMENT OF EDUCATION AND SCIENCE (GB. DES) (1975). *A Language for Life* (The Bullock Report). London: HMSO.

GREAT BRITAIN. DEPARTMENT OF EDUCATION AND SCIENCE (GB. DES) (1981). Circular 5/81 'Directive of the Council of the European Community on the Education of the Children of Migrant Workers'. London/Cardiff: DES.

GREAT BRITAIN. DEPARTMENT OF EDUCATION AND SCIENCE (GB. DES) (1982). 'Education (Teachers) Regulations' Schedule 5. London: DES.

GREAT BRITAIN. DEPARTMENT OF EDUCATION AND SCIENCE (GB. DES) (1984). *Mother Tongue Teaching in School and Community: An HMI Enquiry in Four LEAs.* London: HMSO.

GREAT BRITAIN. DEPARTMENT OF EDUCATION AND SCIENCE (GB. DES) (1985). *Education for All* (The Swann Report). London: HMSO.

GREAT BRITAIN. DEPARTMENT OF EDUCATION AND SCIENCE (GB. DES) (1986). *Foreign Languages in the School Curriculum.* London: HMSO.

GREAT BRITAIN. DEPARTMENT OF EDUCATION AND SCIENCE (GB. DES) (1987). Draft Circular on 'Ethnically-based statistics on School Teachers'. London: DES.

GREAT BRITAIN. DEPARTMENT OF EDUCATION AND SCIENCE (GB. DES) (1987b). Circular 9/87 'LEA Training Grants Scheme: Financial Year 1988/9'. London: DES.

GREAT BRITAIN. DEPARTMENT OF EDUCATION AND SCIENCE (GB. DES) (1988a). *Report on the Committee of Inquiry into the Teaching of English Language* (The Kingman Report). London: HMSO.

GREAT BRITAIN. DEPARTMENT OF EDUCATION AND SCIENCE (GB. DES) (1988b). *Modern Languages in the School Curriculum.* London: HMSO.

GREAT BRITAIN. DEPARTMENT OF EDUCATION AND SCIENCE (GB. DES) (1988c). *Notes of Guidance for the Chair of the National Curriculum Working Group.* London: DES.

GREAT BRITAIN. DEPARTMENT OF EDUCATION AND SCIENCE (GB. DES) (1988d). *Statistics of Education: Schools 1987.* London: HMSO.

GREAT BRITAIN. DEPARTMENT OF EDUCATION AND SCIENCE (GB. DES) (HMI) (1988e). *A Survey of the Teaching of English as a Second Language in Six LEAs.* London: DES.

GREAT BRITAIN. DEPARTMENT OF EDUCATION AND SCIENCE (GB. DES) (1988f). *English for ages 5–11* 'National Curriculum English Working Party Report'. London: DES.

GREAT BRITAIN. DEPARTMENT OF EDUCATION AND SCIENCE (GB. DES)/Welsh Office (1985). *The Educational System of England and Wales.* Cardiff: Welsh Office.

GREAT BRITAIN. DEPARTMENT OF EDUCATION AND SCIENCE (GB. DES)/Welsh Office (1987). *The National Curriculum 5–16: A Consultation Document.* London: DES.

GREAT BRITAIN. Parliament (1985). 'Better Schools' (Cmnd. 9469). London: HMSO.

GREAT BRITAIN. Statutes (1966). 'Local Government Act: 1966'. London: HMSO.

HALL, S. (1983). 'Education in Crisis' in Wolpe, A-M. and Donald, J. (eds) *Is There Anybody Here from Education?* London: Pluto.

HARPER, F. (1987). 'Support or Development?', in *What Next? Report of a Conference by the London and S.E. Course Tutors' Group.* RSA Dip.TESL in Multicultural Schools, Enfield, mimeo.

HART, S. (1986). 'Evaluating Support Teaching', *Gnosis*, 9, 26–31.

HOME AFFAIRS COMMITTEE (HAC), Parliament, House of Commons (1985). 'The Chinese Community in Britain'. London: HMSO.

HOME OFFICE (1986). Circular 72/86. London: Home Office.

HOULTON, D. and WILLEY, R. (1983). *Supporting Children's Bilingualism.* York: Longman for Schools Council.

INDIAN WORKERS' ASSOCIATION (IWA) (1987). *The Regeneration of Racism.* Southall: IWA.

INNER LONDON EDUCATION AUTHORITY (ILEA) (1984). *Improving Secondary Schools* (The Hargreaves Report). London: ILEA.

INNER LONDON EDUCATION AUTHORITY (ILEA) (1985). *Improving Primary Schools* (The Thomas Report). London: ILEA.

INNER LONDON EDUCATION AUTHORITY (ILEA) (1986). *1985 Language Census.* London: ILEA.

INNER LONDON EDUCATION AUTHORITY (ILEA) (1986). *Review of Languages Provision.* London: ILEA.

INNER LONDON EDUCATION AUTHORITY (ILEA) (1988). *The Primary Language Record.* London: ILEA.

KIRP, D. (1979). *Doing Good by Doing Little.* London: University of California Press.

LEVINE, J. (1981). 'Developing Pedagogies for Multilingual Classes', *English in Education*, 15/3.

LINGUISTIC MINORITIES PROJECT (LMP) (1983). 'The Schools Language Survey'. LMP/LINC Working Paper 3. London, Institute of Education.

LINGUISTIC MINORITIES PROJECT (LMP) (1984). *Schools Language Survey: Manual of Use*. London: Institute of Education.

LINGUISTIC MINORITIES PROJECT (LMP) (1985). *The Other Languages of England*. London: Routledge and Kegan Paul.

LITTLE, A. and WILLEY, R. (1981). *Multi-Ethnic Education: The Way Forward*. London: Schools Council.

MACKINNON, K. (1988). 'Ane End of Ane Auld Sang – or New Dawn?', a paper presented at the British Sociological Association conference, Edinburgh, mimeo.

MITCHELL, R., MCINTYRE, D., MACDONALD, M. and MCLENNAN, S. (1987). 'Report of an Independent Evaluation of the Western Isles' Bilingual Education Project', 1984–86. University of Stirling.

MORTIMORE, P., SAMMONS, P., STOLL, L., LEWIS, D. and ECOB, R. *The Junior School Project*. London: ILEA.

MUKHERJEE, TUKU (1985). 'ESL: An Imported New Empire', in *Language and Power: Dynamics of Change and Control*. London: North London Community Group Conference Report, Wembley.

MURRAY, J. and MORRISON, C. (1984). *Bilingual Primary Education in the Western Isles Scotland*. Stornoway: Acair.

NICHOLAS, J. (1988). 'British Language Diversity Surveys (1977–87): A critical examination', *Journal of Multilingual and Multicultural Development*, 2/1. 15–33.

OFFICE OF POPULATION CENSUSES AND SURVEYS (OPCS) (1983). 'Census 1981'. London: HMSO.

PATTANAYAK, D. P. (1981). *Multilingualism and Mother Tongue Education*. Delhi: Oxford University Press.

PRICE, E. (1987). 'Welsh Mother Tongue Teaching to Minorities in Wales', Paper to the Organisation Mondiale pour l'Education Prescolaire (OMEP) Conference. Bangor, Gwynedd.

PRICE, E. and DODSON, C. (1978). *Bilingual Education in Wales 5–11*. London: Evans/Methuen Educational for the Schools Council.

PRICE, E., POWELL, R. and WHETTON, C. (1987). *Prawf Darllen Cymraeg/Welsh Reading Test* (Animals). Windsor: NFER-NELSON.

RAMPTON, M. (1987). 'A Non-Educational View of ESL in Britain', *Adolescence and Language Use* Working Paper 1. London: Sociological Research Unit, Institute of Education.

RAWKINS, P. (1979). *The Implementation of Language Policy in the Schools of Wales*. Centre for the Study of Public Policy, University of Strathclyde.

RAWKINS, P. (1987). 'The Politics of Benign Neglect', *International Journal of the Sociology of Language*, 66, 27–48.

REES, F. (1989). *Languages for a Change*. Windsor: NFER-NELSON.

REEVES, F. (1983). *British Racial Discourse*. Cambridge: Cambridge University Press.

REID, E. (ed.) (1984). *Minority Community Languages in School*. London: Centre for Information on Language Teaching.

REID, E. (1988). 'Linguistic Minorities and Language Education – The English Experience', *Journal of Multilingual and Multicultural Development*, 9/1 and 2. Clevedon: Multilingual Matters.

RICHARDSON,R. (1985). 'Each and Every School: Responding, Reviewing, Planning and Doing', *Multicultural Teaching*, 3/2.

ROSEN, H. and BURGESS, T. (1980). *Languages and Dialects of London School Children*. London: Ward Lock Educational.

SAIFULLAH KHAN, V. (1976). 'Provision by Minorities for Language Maintenance', *Bilingualism and British Education: The Dimensions of Diversity*, CILT Reports and Papers 14. London: CILT.

SKUTNABB-KANGAS, T. (1981). *Bilingualism or Not: The Education of Minorities*. Clevedon: Multilingual Matters.

STERN, H. (1983). *Fundamental Concepts of Language Teaching*. Oxford: Oxford University Press.

STUBBS, M. (1980). *Language and Literacy: The Sociolinguistics of Reading and Writing*. London: Routlege and Kegan Paul.

TANSLEY, P. (1986). *Community Languages in Primary Education: Report from the SCDC Mother Tongue Project*. Windsor: NFER-NELSON.

TANSLEY, P. and CRAFT, A. (1984). 'Mother Tongue Teaching and Support: A Schools Council Enquiry', *Journal of Multilingual and Multicultural Development*, 5/5. 366–84.

TAYLOR, M. with HEGARTY, S. (1985). *The Best of Both Worlds*. Windsor: NFER-NELSON.

TAYLOR, M. (1987). *Chinese Pupils in Britain*. Windsor: NFER-NELSON.

TAYLOR, M. (1988). *Worlds Apart?* Windsor: NFER-NELSON.

TAYLOR, P. (1986). *Expertise and the Primary School Teacher*. Windsor: NFER-NELSON.

TOVEY, H. (1988). 'Book Review', in *Language, Culture and Curriculum*, 1/1. Clevedon: Multilingual Matters for the Linguistics Institute of Ireland.

TOWNSEND, H. (1971). *Immigrant Pupils in England: The LEA Response*. Windsor: NFER-NELSON.

TOWNSEND, H. and BRITTAN, E. (1972). *Organization in Multiracial Schools*. Windsor: NFER-NELSON.

TSOW, M. (1983). 'Analysis of responses to a national survey on mother-tongue teaching in LEAs 1980–82', *Education Research*, 25/3. 202–8.

WELSH OFFICE (1965). 'Legal Status of the Welsh Language' (The Hughes Parry Report). London: HMSO.

WELSH OFFICE (1980). 'Welsh in the School Curriculum: Proposals for Consultation by the Secretary of State for Wales'. Cardiff: Welsh Office.

WELSH OFFICE (HMI WALES) (1983). *Welsh in the Secondary Schools of Wales.* London: HMSO.

WELSH OFFICE (1988). 'Statistics of Education in Wales: Schools, No. 1, 1987'. Cardiff: Welsh Office.

WILLIAMS, C. (1981). 'The Territorial Dimension in Language Planning', *Language Problems and Language Planning*, 5/1. 57–73.

YOUNG, K. and CONNELLY, N. (1981). *Policy and Practice in the Multi-racial City.* London: Policy Studies Institute.

THE NFER RESEARCH LIBRARY

Titles available in the NFER Research Library

	HARDBACK	SOFTBACK
TITLE	*ISBN*	*ISBN*
Joining Forces: a study of links between special and ordinary schools (Jowett, Hegarty, Moses)	0 7005 1179 2	0 7005 1162 8
Supporting Ordinary Schools: LEA initiatives (Moses, Hegarty, Jowett)	0 7005 1177 6	0 7005 1163 6
Developing Expertise: INSET for special educational needs (Moses and Hegarty (Eds))	0 7005 1178 4	0 7005 1164 4
Graduated Tests in Mathematics: a study of lower attaining pupils in secondary schools (Foxman, Ruddock, Thorpe)	0 7005 0867 8	0 7005 0868 6
Mathematics Coordination: a study of practice in primary and middle schools (Stow with Foxman)	0 7005 0873 2	0 7005 0874 0
A Sound Start: the schools' instrumental music service (Cleave and Dust)	0 7005 0871 6	0 7005 0872 4
Course Teams–the Way Forward in FE? (Tansley)	0 7005 0869 4	0 7005 0870 8
The LEA Adviser – a Changing Role (Stillman, Grant)	0 7005 0875 9	0 7005 0876 7
Languages for a Change: diversifying foreign language provision in schools (Rees)	0 7005 1202 0	0 7005 1203 9
The Time to Manage? department and faculty heads at work (Earley and Fletcher-Campbell)	0 7005 1233 0	0 7005 1234 9

	HARDBACK	SOFTBACK
GCSE in Practice: Managing assessment innovation (Grant)	0 7005 1239 X	0 7005 1240 3
Moving into the Mainstream: LEA provision for bilingual pupils (Bourne)	0 7005 1235 7	0 7005 1236 5

For further information contact the Customer Support Department, NFER-NELSON, Darville House, 2 Oxford Road East, Windsor, Berks SL4 1DF, England. Tel: (0753) 858961   Telex 937400 ONECOM G Ref. 24966001